Twentieth-Century Science | # Weather and Climate

Decade by Decade

Twentieth-Century Science

Weather and Climate

Decade by Decade

Kristine C. Harper, Ph.D.

Set Editor: William J. Cannon

Facts On File
An imprint of Infobase Publishing

WEATHER AND CLIMATE: Decade by Decade

Facts On File, Inc.
An imprint of Infobase Publishing
132 West 31st Street
New York NY 10001

ISBN-10: 0-8160-5535-1
ISBN-13: 978-0-8160-5535-7

Library of Congress Cataloging-in-Publication Data
Harper, Kristine.
Weather and climate : decade by decade / Kristine C. Harper.
p. cm. — (Twentieth-century science)
Includes bibliographical references and index.
ISBN 0-8160-5535-1 (acid-free paper)
1. Meteorology—History—20th century. 2. Climatology—History—20th century. 3. Physical sciences—History—20th century. I. Title. II. Series.
QC855.H37 2007
551.509'04—dc22 2006012549

Facts On File books are available at special discounts when purchased in bulk quantities for businesses, associations, institutions, or sales promotions. Please call our Special Sales Department in New York at (212) 967-8800 or (800) 322-8755.

You can find Facts On File on the World Wide Web at
http://www.factsonfile.com

Text design by Dorothy M. Preston and Kerry Casey
Cover design by Dorothy M. Preston and Salvatore Luongo
Illustrations by Bobbi McCutcheon
Photo research by Elizabeth H. Oakes

Printed in the United States of America

VB FOF 10 9 8 7 6 5 4 3 2 1

This book is printed on acid-free paper.

In memory of my father,
Terrell Grover Harper,
who taught me how to tap a barometer

Contents

Preface

The 20th century witnessed an explosive growth in science and technology—more scientists are alive today than have lived during the entire course of earlier human history. New inventions including space-ships, computer chips, lasers, and recombinant deoxyribonucleic acid (DNA) have opened pathways to new fields such as space science, bio-technology, and nanotechnology. Modern seismographs and submarines have given earth and ocean scientists insights into the planet's deep-est and darkest secrets. Decades of weather science, aided by satellite observations and computer modeling, now produce long-term, global forecasts with high probabilities (not certainties) of being correct. At the start of the century, science and technology had little impact on the daily lives of most people. This had changed radically by the year 2000.

The purpose of Twentieth-Century Science, a new seven-volume book set, is to provide students, teachers, and the general public with an accessible and highly readable source for understanding how science developed, decade by decade, during the century and hints about where it will go during the early decades of the 21st century. Just as an edu-cated and well-informed person should have exposure to great literature, art, and music and an appreciation for history, business, and economics, so too should that person appreciate how science works and how it has become so much a part of our daily lives.

Students are usually taught science from the perspective of what is cur-rently known. In one sense, this is quite understandable—there is a great deal of information to master. However, very often a student (or teacher) may ask questions such as "How did they know that?" or "Why didn't they know that?" This is where some historical perspective makes for fas-cinating reading. It gives a feeling for the dynamic aspect of science. Some of what students are taught today will change in 20 years. It also provides a sense of humility as one sees how brilliantly scientists coped earlier with less funding, cruder tools, and less sophisticated theories.

Science is distinguished from other equally worthy and challenging human endeavors by its means of investigation—the scientific method—typically described as

a) observations

b) hypothesis

c) experimentation with controls

d) results, and

e) conclusions concerning whether or not the results and data from the experiments invalidate or support the hypothesis.

In practice, the scientific process is not quite so "linear." Many related experiments may also be explored to test the hypothesis. Once a body of scientific evidence has been collected and checked, the scientist submits a paper reporting the new work to a peer-reviewed journal. An impartial editor will send the work to at least two reviewers ("referees") who are experts in that particular field, and they will recommend to the editor whether the paper should be accepted, modified, or rejected. Since expert reviewers are sometimes the author's competitors, high ethical standards and confidentiality must be the rule during the review process.

If a hypothesis cannot be tested and potentially disproved by experiment or mathematical equations it is not scientific. While, in principle, one experiment can invalidate a hypothesis, no number of validating experiments can absolutely prove a hypothesis to be "the truth." However, if repeated testing, using varied and challenging experiments by diverse scientists, continues to validate a hypothesis, it starts to assume the status of a widely accepted theory. The best friend a theory can have is an outstanding scientist who doubts it and subjects it to rigorous and honest testing. If it survives these challenges and makes a convert of the skeptical scientist, then the theory is strengthened significantly. Such testing also weeds out hypotheses and theories that are weak. Continued validation of an important theory may give it the stature of a law, even though it is still called a theory. Some theories when developed can revolutionize a field's entire framework—these are considered "paradigms" (pronounced "paradimes"). Atomic theory is a paradigm. Advanced about 200 years ago, it is fundamental to understanding the nature of matter. Other such paradigms include evolution; the "big bang" theory; the modern theory of plate tectonics, which explains the origin of mountains, volcanoes, and earthquakes; quantum theory; and relativity.

Science is a collective enterprise with the need for free exchange of information and cooperation. While it is true that scientists have strong competitive urges, the latter half of the 20th century witnessed science's becoming increasingly interdisciplinary. Ever more complex problems, with increasing uncertainty, were tackled and yet often eluded precise solution.

During the 20th century, science found cures for tuberculosis and polio, and yet fears of the "dark side" of science (e.g., atomic weapons) began to mount. Skepticism over the benefits of science and its applications started to emerge in the latter part of the 20th century even as its daily and positive impact upon our lives increased. Many scientists were sensitive to these issues as well. After atomic bombs devastated Hiroshima and Nagasaki, some distinguished physicists moved into the life sciences and others started a magazine, now nearly 60 years old, *The Bulletin of the Atomic Scientists*, dedicated to eliminating the nuclear threat and promoting peace. In 1975, shortly after molecular biologists developed recombinant deoxyribonucleic acid (DNA), they held a conference at Asilomar, California, and imposed voluntary limits on certain experiments. They encouraged adoption of regulations in this revolutionary new field. We are in an era when there are repeated and forceful attempts to blur the boundaries between religious faith and science. One argument is that fairness demands equal time for all "theories" (scientific or not). In all times, but especially in these times, scientists must strive to communicate to the public what science is and how it works, what is good science, what is bad science, and what is not science. Only then can we educate future generations of informed citizens and inspire the scientists of the future.

The seven volumes of Twentieth-Century Science deal with the following core areas of science: biology, chemistry, Earth science, marine science, physics, space and astronomy, and weather and climate. Each volume contains a glossary. Each chapter within each volume contains the following elements:

- background and perspective for the science it develops, decade by decade, as well as insights about many of the major scientists contributing during each decade
- black-and-white line drawings and photographs
- a chronological "time line" of notable events during each decade
- brief biographical sketches of pioneering individuals, including discussion of their impacts on science and the society at large
- a list of accessible sources for Additional Reading

While all of the scientists profiled are distinguished, we do *not* mean to imply that they are necessarily "the greatest scientists of the decade." They have been chosen to represent the science of the decade because of their outstanding accomplishments. Some of these scientists were born to wealthy and distinguished families, while others were born to middle- and working-class families or into poor families. In a century marked by two world wars, the cold war, countless other wars large and small, and unimaginable genocide, many scientists were forced to flee their countries of birth. Fortunately, the century has also witnessed greater access to the scientific and engineering professions for women and people of color, and ideally all barriers will disappear during the 21st century.

The authors of this set hope that readers appreciate the development of the sciences during the last century and the advancements occurring rapidly now in the 21st century. The history teaches new explorers of the world the benefits of making careful observations, of pursuing paths and ideas that others have neglected or have not ventured to tread, and of always questioning the world around them. Curiosity is one of our most fundamental human instincts. Science, whether done as a career or as a hobby, is after all, an intensely human endeavor.

Acknowledgments

As a former applied meteorologist, I constantly find weather and climate fascinating. As a historian of science specializing in 20th-century atmospheric science, I find the history of scientific development in these fields to be endlessly compelling. Writing this book allowed me to indulge my interests in both the science and the history of meteorology and climatology, and for that opportunity, I am extremely grateful.

Many thanks to Greg Good for connecting me to the project editor Bill Cannon, and to Bill for asking me to write about weather and climate in the 20th century. My appreciation also to the editor Frank Darmstadt, who has steered me along and kept me on the path of careful writing; the artist Bobbi McCutcheon, who managed to decipher my primitive sketches and turn them into wonderful illustrations; and Beth Oakes for tracking down all the great photographs.

I also thank the Dibner Institute for the History of Science and Technology at the Massachusetts Institute of Technology, which provided me a quiet space to work in and access to all the materials I needed to write while I was in residence as a postdoctoral fellow. The American Meteorological Society's Graduate Fellowship in the History of Science also funded research for parts of this book.

A huge thank you goes to my husband, Ron Doel, for his love, support, and steady encouragement.

Introduction

Weather and climate—two subjects that many people think they know a lot about. Humans have been wondering and complaining about the weather, bad weather in particular, since they first walked on the face of the Earth. Perhaps it was this very familiarity with weather and climate that prevented these areas of study from being considered part of mainstream science until the middle of the 20th century. This book traces the fascinating and often frustrating history of the transformation of the study of weather phenomena and climatic conditions into the scientific disciplines of meteorology and climatology.

First emerging as a bona fide science in the mid-19th century, meteorology rose—from weather-guessing art to barely reputable science to a computer-driven science bearing on some of the most important issues of the 20th century—as a result of a number of factors. They include the improvement of old instruments and the development of new ones; the creation of research and educational institutes for gathering data, exchanging ideas, and educating young scientists about the atmosphere; and the rise of the aviation industry, which demanded better information about atmospheric processes. In many ways, meteorology and climatology became increasingly scientific disciplines because of the needs of military forces during 20th-century wars.

In a science based on physics and mathematics, meteorologists experienced many more difficulties studying the atmosphere than did their physics colleagues who were studying electricity, magnetism, motion, and atomic properties. The physicists' research took place in the tightly controlled confines of a laboratory. Meteorologists did not have that luxury. With the vast, constantly changing atmosphere as laboratory, atmospheric scientists first had to develop instruments that would accurately measure temperature, air pressure, humidity, wind direction and speed, and the amount of fallen precipitation—and then figure out a method of lifting them into the air to measure these properties many thousands of feet above Earth's surface. Starting with kites and balloons, meteorologists of the early 20th century perfected ingenious methods for capturing these critical data.

Science, however, does not equal data collection. Science requires the analysis of data to determine what they might mean and how they fit together to describe observed phenomena in terms of formalized rules often expressed as mathematical equations. Sometimes scientists can use these data to determine why these phenomena occur. Other times they cannot. To gain scientific knowledge, people first need to learn the knowledge gained by their predecessors. They do so by receiving advanced education in colleges and universities. People also need to share and test new ideas. The establishment of research institutes and observatories, such as the Leipzig Geophysical Institute in Germany and the Bergen School of Meteorology in Norway, were important to data gathering, the development of theories about atmospheric processes, and the training of a cadre of young, gifted scientists who were drawn to the mysteries of weather and climate.

Scientific advancement also depends on patrons: individuals, philanthropic foundations, businesses, or government agencies that provide funding for equipment and training. Governments had long been consumers of weather and climate information because the safety of their citizens and adequate food supplies depended on good weather information. But a new consumer appeared in the early 20th century that would provide a tremendous boost to meteorology's prospects for disciplinary advancement: the aeronautics community. Pilots, in their flimsy canvas and wood flying machines, needed information about the atmosphere to take off, fly, and land safely. A special relationship developed between meteorologists and aviators: Meteorologists provided forecasts and the aviators provided information about the atmosphere that helped to improve the forecasts.

Although aviation needs alone might have been sufficient to launch meteorology into a respected scientific position, wars created special circumstances that moved meteorology from forecasting art to physical science, and climatology from being a branch of geography to a science in its own right. During wars, combatant countries need food for soldiers and citizens left in what are often difficult circumstances. Meteorologists were called upon to examine atmospheric conditions that could aid the harvest. Increasingly mechanized war-fighting techniques demanded specialized knowledge of weather and climate. These demands drew new people into these fields—people who looked at the atmosphere more mathematically and physically than people had in previous centuries. These new meteorologists and climatologists used tools that had developed from wartime technologies such as radar, computers, rockets, and later satellites to advance their knowledge of atmospheric processes and of their relationship to the Earth. The use of these calculating and remote sensing tools expanded rapidly in the last half of the 20th century as human impact on climate became more apparent.

By the end of the 20th century, weather had moved from the back page of the newspaper, where one could find the daily forecast, to the front page, as news of catastrophic storms such as Hurricane Andrew, widespread drought in Africa and South Asia, and flooding in major river valleys caused death and destruction. Melting glaciers, rising sea levels, water shortages, and temperature extremes added compelling evidence that Earth's temperature was rising. No longer just a topic of casual conversation, by the end of the century changes in weather and climate conditions had become issues of international importance. Scientists, diplomats, and others involved in science policy were engaged in United Nations–sponsored gatherings whose mission it was to analyze the current state of the Earth-atmosphere system and determine its future.

This book discusses how scientists radically changed their ideas about weather and climate during the course of the 20th century. No longer content with determining tomorrow's weather, atmospheric scientists seek answers about current and future climate conditions by peering into the past to uncover information about Earth's atmosphere tens of thousands of years ago. Issues of weather and climate have never been more important to the world's population than they are today, because they have the potential to affect the way people live significantly. The middle and high school students of today will inherit an Earth-atmosphere system that behaves differently than the one experienced by their parents and grandparents. A few of those students may wish to take up the challenge of solving scientific problems related to weather and climate or help to set governmental policies related to fossil fuel emissions, water distribution, posthurricane disaster planning, or air quality standards. Everyone has a stake in Earth's atmosphere. It is important for all citizens to understand what scientists know and how they know it. The way this knowledge is used will affect everyone in the 21st century and beyond.

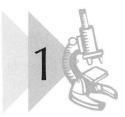

1

1901–1910: **From Forecasting Art to Physical Science**

Until the end of the 19th century, meteorology's practitioners were primarily concerned with forecasting the weather, not understanding its origins. *Climatology* was similarly devoid of scientific content. Both were descriptive instead of explanatory. Meteorologists and climatologists were often considered not to be scientists, and the work they did was not really considered science. That started to change as the 20th century dawned. These two disciplines would see radical changes as men from a variety of academic backgrounds applied their talents to atmospheric problems. Meteorology was poised to make the transition from forecasting art to physical science.

Meteorology as Forecasting Art

In 1900, most people equated meteorology with weather forecasting. Meteorologists did not explore how air circulated through the *atmosphere*,

Station chief (at desk) and a colleague at a U.S. Weather Bureau local forecast office, about 1900 (NOAA Photo Library)

or why some winter storms produced heavy rain. They predicted the next day's weather. This was a difficult task without satellites, *radar*, and high-speed computers. Meteorology was not a science. It was an art.

Modern meteorology depends on assembling massive amounts of surface and upper-air data from around the world at least four times per day. Data collection depends on high-speed communication lines that carry weather observations to supercomputers within minutes. At the turn of the 19th century, forecasters faced the challenging task of predicting the next day's weather on the basis of a relatively small number of surface observations that arrived via telegraph twice daily.

Most forecasters spent their entire lives in one location. Starting out as teenage trainees, they learned how to make sense of the "signs of the sky"—the different cloud types and the order in which they marched across the sky. After many years, the best forecasters had an innate feel for the atmosphere. They recognized the sky conditions preceding stormy weather. They also realized that the weather rarely changed radically from one day to the next. Forecasters often made a *persistence forecast* because weather tended to persist from one day to the next. They also used climatological records of average temperature and precipitation to make

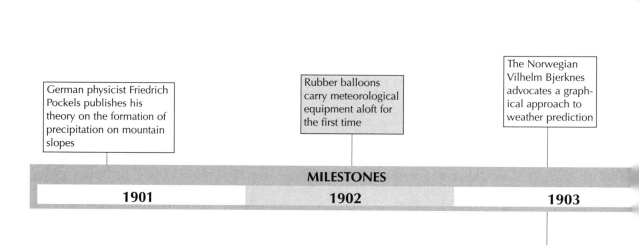

German physicist Friedrich Pockels publishes his theory on the formation of precipitation on mountain slopes

Rubber balloons carry meteorological equipment aloft for the first time

The Norwegian Vilhelm Bjerknes advocates a graphical approach to weather prediction

MILESTONES

1901   **1902**   **1903**

The Wright brothers successfully complete the first manned airplane flight at Kitty Hawk, North Carolina

forecasts. For example, northern Maine winters are bitterly cold and snowy. Without any other information, a forecaster would expect below-freezing temperatures. The forecaster's job did not include explaining the weather. His only job was to give people in the local area enough knowledge of upcoming weather so they could go about their daily routines.

Official forecasts were typically for 24 hours, but people plan their time more than one day ahead. Farmers with crops and livestock susceptible to weather damage were particularly interested in long-range

The U.S. meteorologist Cleveland Abbe was an early supporter of a scientifically rigorous meteorology. (AIP Emilio Segrè Visual Archives)

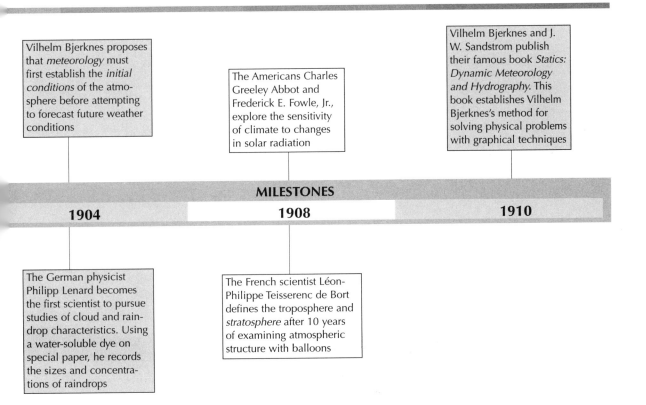

Vilhelm Bjerknes proposes that *meteorology* must first establish the *initial conditions* of the atmosphere before attempting to forecast future weather conditions

The Americans Charles Greeley Abbot and Frederick E. Fowle, Jr., explore the sensitivity of climate to changes in solar radiation

Vilhelm Bjerknes and J. W. Sandstrom publish their famous book *Statics: Dynamic Meteorology and Hydrography.* This book establishes Vilhelm Bjerknes's method for solving physical problems with graphical techniques

MILESTONES

1904   **1908**   **1910**

The German physicist Philipp Lenard becomes the first scientist to pursue studies of cloud and raindrop characteristics. Using a water-soluble dye on special paper, he records the sizes and concentrations of raindrops

The French scientist Léon-Philippe Teisserenc de Bort defines the troposphere and *stratosphere* after 10 years of examining atmospheric structure with balloons

"Weather Prophets"

Prior to the end of World War II, only government weather offices provided national forecasts. Before radio and television, forecasts were often posted in public places such as post offices and train stations, and occasionally printed in some big city newspapers. As a government service, weather forecasts were free. Free or not, most people were dissatisfied with them.

Forecasts were most effective when they were tailored to a specific customer, for example, a farmer, construction firm, or road crew. Government forecasts were not tailored. By trying to meet everyone's needs, often they met no one's needs. People who needed long-range forecasts were willing to pay for them and they looked to whoever was willing to provide them.

Entrepreneurs who saw an opportunity to make money from long-range weather forecasting were referred to as weather prophets. Weather prophets shared some common characteristics:

- They were not part of a scientific community.
- Most had absolutely no training in meteorology.
- They dismissed government forecasters as "failures" because they declined to give long-range forecasts.
- Weather prophets claimed that unlike government forecasters, they could produce an accurate forecast well in advance—and they could do so without even making a meteorological observation.

Weather prophets did not analyze weather data to make predictions. Some made forecasts based on the behavior or appearance of animals. For example, heavily furred animals in the fall indicated a very cold winter. Others forecasted the weather by the motion of the Moon across the night sky, or by the position of planets and stars. Some weather prophets depended upon *periodicities:* recurring cycles of hot or cold, dry or wet weather. A few just used climatological records, basing their forecasts on long-term averages of temperature and precipitation—free information available from the U.S. Weather Bureau.

Weather prophets had a variety of backgrounds: Clergymen, naturalists, farmers, and woodsmen were equally likely to be weather prophets. They were accepted by the general public because most people thought meteorology was about guessing the weather, and one person's guess was as good as another's. Weather prophets had successful careers because so little was known about the atmosphere. For meteorologists, tired of taking time from their busy days to answer the nonscientific claims of weather prophets, the time had come to put their work on a more scientific footing.

weather forecasts. The U.S. Weather Bureau refused to provide such predictions because there was no science to support them. Others who made weather predictions were not worried about atmospheric science. They were very pleased to provide farmers with long-range forecasts—for a price.

A Layered Atmosphere

Since the invention of the *barometer* by the Italian scholar Evangelista Torricelli (1608–47) in 1644, early scientists had been trying to determine the thickness of the atmosphere. By the end of the 17th century, scientists knew that air *pressure* decreased with height. It seemed logical that at some altitude there would be no pressure at all and they would have reached the top of the atmosphere. Of course, people could not actually get to the top because they would run out of air first. An equation to calculate the atmospheric thickness was not easily created either. Air temperature cools with height as the molecules move farther away from each other, and so air temperature affects air pressure. In order to determine atmospheric thickness, scientists would need to get instruments to a much higher altitude than they could safely reach by climbing mountains.

Using balloons to carry instruments aloft, the French scientist Léon-Philippe Teisserenc de Bort (1855–1913), founding director of the Observatoire de Météorologies Dynamique de Trappes (Dynamic Meteorology Observatory of Trappes), discovered in 1898 that the atmospheric temperature steadily decreased up to 6.8 miles (11 km) above Earth's surface. As the altitude continued to increase, the temperature remained constant (*isothermal*). Teisserenc de Bort was stunned by the results. He performed the experiment repeatedly, always getting the same measurement. After four more years of investigations, Teisserenc de Bort presented his discovery of the "upper inversion" to the Academy of Sciences in Paris. (Today an *inversion* is defined as a layer of the atmosphere that is warmer than the one below it.) The German scientist Richard Assman (1845–1919) confirmed the result. On the basis of these experimental data, in 1908 Teisserenc de Bort defined two atmospheric layers: the troposphere and the stratosphere.

The term *troposphere* is from the Greek root *tropein*, which means "to turn or to change." The troposphere is the region of the atmosphere closest to Earth where the air is constantly stirred or "turned" by the rising of warm air and falling of cold air. Teisserenc de Bort thought the troposphere was 6.8 miles (11 km) thick, but its thickness is not uniform and it varies with latitude and season. Warm air is thicker, so the troposphere is 9.3–12.4 miles (15–20 km) thick at the equator, but only 6.2 miles (10 km) thick at the colder poles. For the same reason, the troposphere is thicker in the summer than in the winter.

Teisserenc de Bort chose the term *stratosphere*, or "even space," for the layer above the troposphere because the gases within it are undisturbed. The stratosphere includes the isothermal region (now called the *tropopause*) and extends to a height of 31 miles (50 km). Unlike in the troposphere, where temperature decreases with height, in the stratosphere the temperature either remains isothermal or increases with height. This discovery confused early investigators because it ran counter to the commonly held view that temperature always decreased with height. The French physicist Charles Fabry (1867–1945) proved in 1913 that the heating was due to large amounts of ozone gas (O_3) in the upper stratosphere. Stratospheric ozone absorbs the energy from solar ultraviolet radiation, preventing it from reaching Earth. The temperature at 31 miles (50 km) above Earth's surface is approximately 32°F (0°C) (freezing), while the temperature at 6.8 miles (11 km) is approximately -121°F (-85°C). With little air movement, the stratosphere provides a smooth ride for jets.

Having determined that weather only took place in the lower 6.8 miles (11 km) of the atmosphere, scholars could most profitably spend their time focused on the movement of air within the troposphere. Discoveries of stratospheric characteristics would await improved instrumentation.

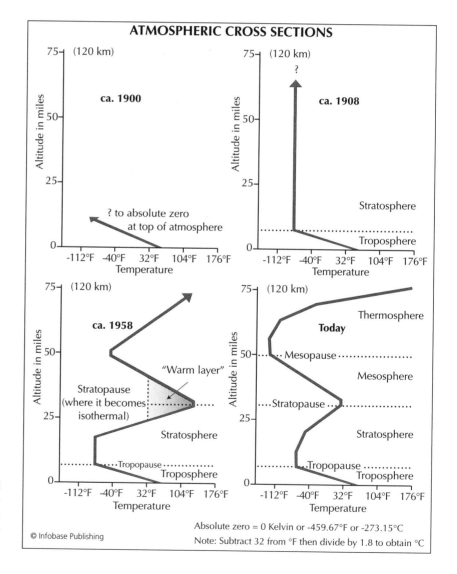

As new techniques increased knowledge of the upper atmosphere, scientists discovered how temperature changed with height.

Physics Meets Meteorology

While meteorologists had been forecasting the weather, a very small number of scientists, mostly physicists, had been developing theories to explain the formation of *cyclones*—areas of counterclockwise turning air associated with low air pressure and stormy conditions. (Cyclones turn clockwise in the Southern Hemisphere.) By 1900, theories of cyclonic development, life, and death depended on the principle of energy conservation. The first law of thermodynamics, in particular, relates the conversion between thermal and mechanical energy. (For example, the result of shaking up lead shot in a closed tube [mechanical energy] is that the lead shot becomes warmer [thermal energy]). Acting on this law, the thermal theory of cyclone formation stated that the initial drop in air pressure in the center of a cyclone (more commonly referred to as a storm) was caused by *latent heat* released when the water vapor carried by upward moving currents of warm air cooled and condensed. The air pressure then increased in this locally heated area, causing the air to flow out the top of the cyclone. As air moved up within the cyclone, the pressure at the surface dropped. Air flowed into the cyclone from all sides, causing the entire cyclone to spin in a counterclockwise direction. The thermal theory of cyclones required that warm air rise up in cyclones and cold air sink in *anticyclones* (air columns that rotate clockwise). As long as there were no high-elevation observations, there was no reason to doubt the theory's validity. By 1900, balloons and kites started carrying thermometers aloft and the returning data did not support the theory. Meteorologists would need a new theory to describe how cyclones, and anticyclones, behaved. They needed to apply additional physical principles.

The Ukrainian-born Max Margules (1856–1920) trained in theoretical physics at Vienna University in Austria, and later at Berlin University in Germany. He left theoretical physics to take a position with the Zentralanstalt für Meteorologie (Meteorological Institute) in Vienna in 1882. Although his work focused on the physics and chemistry of air, Margules became increasingly intrigued by meteorology. By the 1890s, he had become convinced that the most profitable way to make progress in meteorology was to combine theoretical work with observational data. Acting on his ideas, Margules set up a small network of observational stations around Vienna in 1895 and studied the resulting data. He examined the temperature and pressure changes that occurred during the passages of "waves"—or stormy weather. On the basis of years of analysis, Margules began to formulate new ideas about the characteristics and behavior of *air masses*—continent-sized, relatively homogeneous parcels of air—and their relationship to cyclone formation.

It was well known from physics that fluids under high pressure seek to reach equilibrium with fluids under lower pressure as long as an outflow path exists. Since air is a fluid, it flows from areas of high pressure to areas of low pressure. In other words, wind is produced by the difference in pressure, or the *pressure gradient*, between two locations. Margules was skeptical that the energy released by the pressure gradient alone was sufficient to provide energy to a cyclone. What was missing, he thought, was the energy *source* that kept the pressure gradient in place so the wind continued to blow. After several more years of analysis and computation, Margules developed a *model*—a simplified way of looking at the atmosphere—that explained the energy source. Kinetic energy was released, he wrote in his 1903 paper "Die Energie der Stürme" (The energy of storms), when two adjacent air masses have markedly different temperatures and an unstable relationship. This occurs when cold air lies over warmer air. Since warm air rises, it punches up through the colder air, which then sinks down into the warmer air. The combination of a large mass of air and a velocity induced by the air movement leads to very large amounts of kinetic

The movement of air from high to low pressure combined with the effects of a spinning Earth causes air to move counterclockwise and into low-pressure centers, and clockwise and out of high-pressure centers.

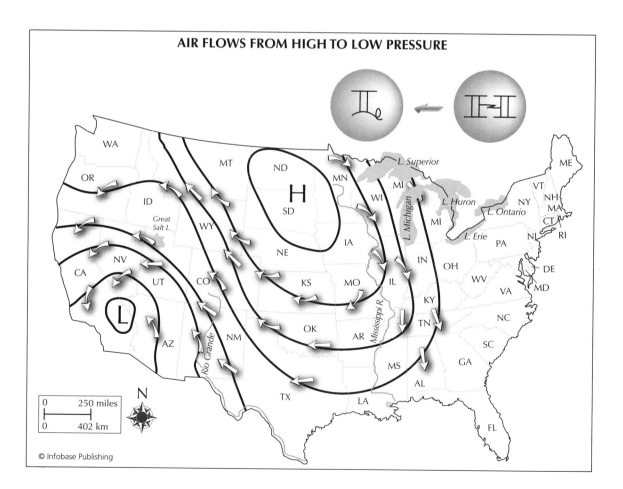

AIR FLOWS FROM HIGH TO LOW PRESSURE

© Infobase Publishing

energy. Although some of this kinetic energy would be dissipated in the real world because of friction and some heat would be lost because air is not confined in a box, it would still be more than sufficient to maintain a pressure gradient, and hence horizontal wind, within the cyclone.

Three years later, in 1906, Margules published another paper, "Zur Sturmtheorie" (On the theory of storms), which clarified his earlier ideas. In addition to the development of cyclones, due to displacement of warm air by cold air, he acknowledged that the release of latent heat due to the *condensation* of rising (and cooling) water vapor would contribute to the kinetic energy in the system. Margules's 1906 paper was not translated into English and very few scholars were aware of it until the 1920s and 1930s, when his theoretical work became widely accepted. Despite, or perhaps because of, his work in theoretical meteorology, Margules was opposed to weather forecasting. He did not think meteorology was sophisticated enough to support prediction. According to the historian of science Gisela Kutzbach, Margules believed that forecasting was "immoral and damaging to the character of the meteorologist."

One contemporary scholar who was aware of Margules's work but disagreed with his assessment of the place of weather forecasting in meteorology was the Norwegian Vilhelm Friman Bjerknes (1862–1951). A theoretical physicist working on problems of fluid dynamics in the late 1890s, Bjerknes had been encouraged by a colleague to turn his attention to meteorological and oceanographic problems after he published his famous circulation theorem in 1898. The fluid-filled atmosphere and oceans were the ideal place to apply equations defining fluid circulation. Discussing the matter with colleagues, Bjerknes was concerned that theoretical physicists were not addressing this scientific problem. He was stunned to find out that most meteorologists did not adhere to any kind of scientific rigor: That is, they did not use mathematics to describe their work. Bjerknes was not sure he wanted to associate with such people.

Meteorology was ripe for change in the early 1900s. Balloons were carrying men to new heights, where they collected data that would make possible studies of atmospheric circulation. The potential for a new age in meteorology appeared to Bjerknes. He would apply mathematical rigor and physical laws to forecasting the weather.

In his 1904 paper, "Das Problem der Wettervorhersage, betrachtet vom Stundpunkte der Mechanik und der Physik" (The problem of weather prediction, considered from the point of view of mechanics and physics), Bjerknes proposed a fundamentally new path for meteorology that attracted the attention of European meteorologists and led to much discussion in the scientific community. The first step would be to determine the *initial conditions* of the atmosphere. He would need a closely spaced network of surface and upper air stations to collect data for calculating future weather. At the time, there were few surface stations and no upper air stations. A few aeronautical observatories launched balloons irregularly but had no good way to retrieve the data. Processing weather data from thousands of stations would be a huge task. Nations would need to share their observations, necessitating better communication and data handling systems. If those problems could be solved, meteorologists would be able to use the equations of motion from physics to predict the future state of the atmosphere. In other words, the time had come to use physics and mathematics to *calculate the weather*. Bjerknes made clear that it was possible for meteorology to be a rigorous science. The days of meteorology as an art, he thought, were over.

Measuring Initial Conditions

Margules's and Bjerknes's ideas depended very heavily on one thing: timely, accurate data collected from all atmospheric levels. This was a very complicated problem for a number of reasons.

Scholars had observed the atmosphere in a systematic way since at least the time of Aristotle, but these observations were *qualitative* until the time of the Scientific Revolution (ca. 1550 to 1700). Qualitative observations gave relative information about temperature (hot or cold), wind (very windy or calm), clouds (overcast or clear), and precipitation (rain, hail, or drizzle). During the Scientific Revolution, craftsmen and scholars working together had developed thermometers, barometers, and *hygrometers*. *Anemometers* and wind vanes were perfected later. Once these instruments were standardized and affordable and produced consistently reliable information, weather observers could collect *quantitative data* that attached numerical values to the weather element. For example, instead of recording *cool,* the observer would note 39.2°F (4°C).

What Margules, Bjerknes, and a new generation of meteorologists needed for theory development and accurate forecasts were quantitative observations taken with accurate instruments using standard methodologies. In the early 20th century, mercurial barometers were extremely accurate. Those used by weather stations could measure the pressure to 0.001 inch (0.025 mm) of mercury. Rooftop thermometers usually gave higher values in winter than those closer to the ground. Anemometers were reasonably accurate at low speeds, but not at high speeds. Hair hygrometers reacted too slowly to changing moisture content. Meteorologists needed to address instrumentation problems. They would need time and money to do so.

Setting aside the problem of equipment accuracy, there was also a problem with the timing and reporting of observations. Both Margules and Bjerknes needed observations taken simultaneously everywhere. If

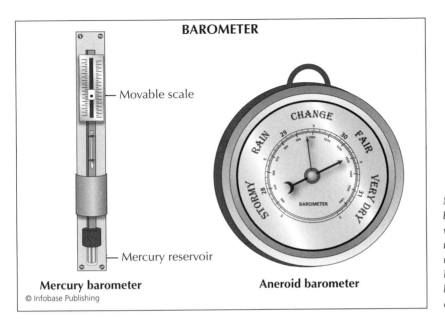

BAROMETER

— Movable scale

— Mercury reservoir

Mercury barometer
© Infobase Publishing

Aneroid barometer

Mass-marketed aneroid barometers, complete with weather descriptions to accompany pressure measurements, were much less accurate than mercury barometers used by weather observatories.

stations took observations on a schedule of their own devising, it would be impossible to analyze the atmospheric situation at a specific time. Bjerknes needed to convince scientists across Europe and in England to coordinate their observations.

In addition, not everyone used the same *units* to report his findings. Some stations reported air pressure in inches of mercury and some reported in millimeters of mercury (the height of the mercury in the tube). Similarly, wind speeds were reported in miles per hour, nautical miles per hour (knots), and kilometers per hour. Some stations reported temperatures using the Fahrenheit scale (freezing at 32°) and some used the Celsius scale (freezing at 0°). In order to solve the physical equations defining atmospheric processes, Bjerknes argued, all stations would need to report in *absolute units*. An absolute unit is based on fundamental units of length (meter or foot), mass (kilogram or slug), and time (seconds). Air pressure reported as "millimeters of mercury" did not equate to the units used for pressure (pounds/square inch or newtons/square meter). A conversion would need to be made. In addition, all stations would need to report their pressure readings as if they were at sea level. If they did not do so, higher-altitude stations would always show a lower pressure reading than lower-altitude stations even when they were experiencing exactly the same weather. If all stations reported as if they were at sea level, then it would be possible for Bjerknes and his colleagues to draw a map of the atmospheric conditions at Earth's surface—a necessary condition for making a forecast for the next day.

Surface observations were just part of the story. Bjerknes realized that in order to solve the equations, he needed upper air data. Most upper air observations were taken with instruments carried aloft by balloons and kites at aerological observatories, which supported manned-balloon flights. Because the observations were taken just in advance of the flights—not at regularly scheduled times—they were of limited use to meteorologists, who needed to consider observations that were taken at the same time. They also tended to be qualitative. The balloon pilots were not concerned with exact measurements. They often wanted to know the height of the cloud *ceiling* and the direction of winds aloft. Bjerknes was terribly frustrated. As the historian of science Robert Marc Friedman noted in his 1993 book *Appropriating the Weather*, Bjerknes wrote a letter of complaint to the president of the Carnegie Institution in Washington, D.C., which was providing funds for his project. Bjerknes grumbled, "In as much as my work is dependent upon such observations it cannot bring more out of them than their quality admits."

To overcome data problems, Bjerknes turned to the International Commission for Scientific Aeronautics during its 1909 meeting. He pointed out that the study of weather conditions in the upper atmosphere could make a tremendous contribution to aeronautics. As flight became more common, such studies could provide accurate predictions to pilots and keep them safe during takeoff, flight, and landing. To be useful, Bjerknes told those attending, upper air data had to be collected at the same time and in the same way each day. The audience finally started to accept his message. Within a short period, other prominent scientists joined Bjerknes in his quest for absolute units and simultaneous observation times. The German climatologist Wladimir Köppen (1846–1940) of the Deutsche Seewarte (German Naval Observatory) in Hamburg and William Napier Shaw (1854–1945), head of the British Meteorological Office, both supported Bjerknes. Despite their efforts, absolute units were not widely accepted until the next decade, and they were not universally adopted until 1929. It would take even longer for meteorological stations to agree on standard observation times.

Global Warming—a Good Thing

Climatology was a subdiscipline of physical geography in the early 20th century. Climatologists spent most of their time creating classification schemes used by government and industry to identify appropriate places to settle and the best kinds of crops to plant. By mid-20th century, climatology would become a physical science as scientists examined the changing global *climate*. The first investigations into "global warming" took place at the end of the 19th century and carried over into the early 20th century. As in meteorology, some of the most important people entering the debate were Scandinavians.

Balloons and Kites

Upper air observations depended on balloons and kites. The pioneering Montgolfier brothers of French ballooning, Jacques-Étienne (1745–99) and Joseph-Michel (1740–1810), had made their first manned flight on June 4, 1783, and manned balloons had been much improved by the early 20th century. Because of lack of oxygen, balloon-borne observers could not climb as high as the stratosphere and survive. Better unmanned balloons and kites capable of carrying meteorological equipment needed to be created.

The first unmanned observation balloon, introduced in 1892, carried a balloonsonde—a container of meteorological equipment that registered data and then dropped to the ground when the balloon burst at high altitude. Unfortunately, meteorologists could not get the data unless they could find the container. That meant searching in the direction that the balloon was last seen flying or hoping that someone would find the container and return it to the observatory that launched it.

Until 1901, constant-volume balloons were made of expensive varnished silk. The introduction of inexpensive, sturdy rubber balloons was a major improvement. They could reach 12.4 miles (20 km) before bursting and the equipment boxes were equipped with little parachutes that allowed them to float gently to Earth. Of course, there was still the problem of finding the box after it landed. The instrument boxes carried relatively inexpensive thermometers, barometers, and hygrometers. Ink pens moving across graph paper recorded the temperature, pressure, and humidity. Although the balloons were able to reach great heights, the ink froze in the recording pens when the temperature dropped below freezing. Once that technical difficulty was resolved, amateur meteorologists and professional scientists launched hundreds of balloons. They also used balloonsondes to retrieve air samples. Scientists examined the samples and determined that the relative percentages of gases that compose air remain constant with height.

Observers also used *pilot balloons,* which carried no instruments, to determine upper-level wind velocity. They tracked the balloons with a surveying device called a *theodolite,* an instrument that indicated the direction of flight and angle of ascent. Since the balloons rose at a constant rate, using a timepiece and basic trigonometry the observer computed the balloon's height, distance, and velocity. This only worked if there was no cloud cover or the cloud ceiling was high. Even though pilot balloons were red, they were still difficult to see in the fog and were quickly hidden by low-lying clouds. Relatively inexpensive, pilot balloon use spread rapidly after 1906. By sending a pilot balloon off just in advance of a takeoff, observers could tell pilots what kinds of winds to expect—a vital piece of information for flyers in manned balloons.

Large box kites also carried instruments to great heights. Because the observer reeled the instrument box back in with the kite, no one had to go out and find it to obtain the data. The kites needed strong winds to stay aloft and were ineffective on calm or low-wind days. When kites crashed, the long metal wires holding them often fell down onto high-voltage electrical lines, endangering the observer and short-circuiting the entire power grid. For these reasons, kites were gradually phased out.

Kites, tethered balloons, and free-floating balloons were important additions to the meteorologist's toolbox in the early 20th century. The use of the data for improved predictions, however, would have to wait until the next decade and the continued work of Vilhelm Bjerknes.

Weather observers launch a large box kite from an early 20th-century aerological observatory. (NOAA Photo Library)

The Nobel Prize–winning Swedish chemist Svante August Arrhenius (E. F. Smith Collection, Rare Book & Manuscript Library, University of Pennsylvania)

In his 1896 article "On the Influence of Carbonic Acid in the Air upon the Temperature of the Ground," the Swedish physical chemist Svante August Arrhenius (1859–1927) claimed that pollution from burning fossil fuels (coal, oil, gas, peat) to provide energy to heavy industry and to heat homes might warm the atmosphere. (This possible change in climate was called *anthropogenic* because it was caused by the actions of people.) Carbonic acid (also called carbon dioxide, CO_2, gas) in the atmosphere would absorb long-wave radiation leaving Earth and reradiate it back to the surface. Since the Little Ice Age had just ended in 1850, a warmer atmosphere would be good. "Global warming" would postpone another ice age, might produce a period of enormous plant growth, and would contribute to a better climate. A warming atmosphere was not considered bad in 1896—particularly by northern Europeans who endured harsh winters. For most people, warmer was better.

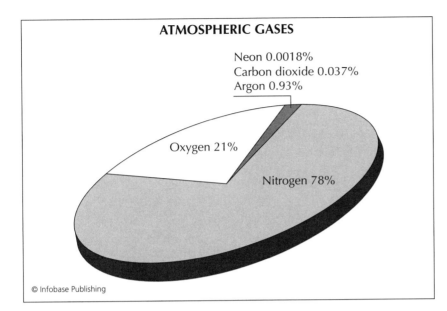

ATMOSPHERIC GASES

Neon 0.0018%
Carbon dioxide 0.037%
Argon 0.93%

Oxygen 21%

Nitrogen 78%

© Infobase Publishing

When the extremely small percentage of atmospheric carbon dioxide increases, the atmospheric temperature increases too.

Just a few years later, in 1899, Arrhenius's colleague Nils Ekholm (1848–1923) computed a doubling of CO_2 level and increasing global temperatures if coal-burning rates remained unchanged. As did Arrhenius, Ekholm thought warmer was better. Indeed, if it were possible to control the amount of CO_2 being pumped into the atmosphere by industrial smokestacks, people could prevent the arrival of a new ice age.

A dissenting voice entered the debate in 1900. The Swedish physicist Knut Ångström (1857–1910) argued that CO_2 was not the cause of atmospheric warming—water vapor was. Both CO_2 and water vapor absorbed long-wave radiation, and since the percentage of water vapor in the atmosphere could be as much as 100 times greater than that of CO_2, additional CO_2 would make little difference. One scientist who agreed with Ångström's conclusion was the Smithsonian Institution's director, Charles Greeley Abbot (1872–1973), an astronomer who was a solar radiation expert.

The American geologist Thomas Chrowder Chamberlin (1843–1928) agreed with Arrhenius. Chamberlin was looking for a mechanism to explain the periodic occurrences of ice ages. His question: What caused Earth to become so cold that glaciers advanced toward the equator, and then what caused it to warm up again so that the glaciers retreated back toward the poles?

In the early 20th century, there were three prominent theories that addressed this question. The first maintained that the ice ages came and went because the amount of incoming solar radiation changed with time. The second held that glacier development was influenced

Scientist of the Decade: Vilhelm Bjerknes (1862–1951)

As did most theoretical meteorologists of the early 20th century, the Norwegian Vilhelm Friman Koren Bjerknes began to study the atmosphere after receiving his doctorate in physics. His father, Carl Anton Bjerknes (1825–1903), was a physicist, and young Vilhelm was immersed in physics from an early age.

Because Carl Bjerknes found it difficult to build and operate experimental apparatus, he called upon Vilhelm to design and create what he needed. At age 19, Bjerknes accompanied his father and their equipment to the 1881 Paris International Electric Exhibition and demonstrated their experiments. The impressed judges awarded Carl Bjerknes a *diplômes d'honneur* alongside such prominent scientists and inventors of the day as Thomas Edison and Alexander Graham Bell. Upon returning home to summarize the results, Carl Bjerknes suffered such terrible writer's block that he turned to Vilhelm for assistance in completing the project. The young Bjerknes, trying to finish his master's degree in mathematics and physics (awarded in 1888 from the University of Kristiania), found himself torn between helping his clearly distressed father and protecting his future career. Although he endeavored to concentrate his studies in areas that could ultimately be helpful to his father, Bjerknes decided that he must leave Norway and study on the European continent to have a chance at a research career.

Having won a fellowship to study abroad, Bjerknes left for Paris in 1889 and traveled to Germany to join the laboratory of the physicist Heinrich Hertz (1857–94) in 1890. Convinced that a German lab, particularly one belonging to a scientist as esteemed as Hertz, would be much better outfitted than those in relatively poor Norway, Bjerknes was shocked when he discovered a rundown, neglected lab. As the only worker, he did not enjoy the expected camaraderie of fellow physics graduate students. Bjerknes found himself working exceedingly long hours in isolation as he designed and built equipment that would allow the study of *resonance* phenomena in electric waves. Pleased with the efforts of his young protégé, Hertz encouraged Bjerknes to pursue his doctorate in Germany. Because his father needed him at home, Bjerknes returned to Norway and continued his doctoral studies there. Although Bjerknes's research on the ways metals affect the propagation of electric waves attracted considerable attention among academics, Carl Anton's requests for assistance turned him back toward hydrodynamics. To ensure that his son remained in Scandinavia and did not return to Germany, Carl Anton arranged for a teaching position for him at the Stockholm Högskola.

Bjerknes had originally planned to continue his work on electric waves in Stockholm, but the lack of facilities as well as his father's insistence that their work required his full attention finally led him to abandon the work he had started with Hertz and turn to hydrodynamics in 1895. Within two years, his efforts to make a connection between hydrodynamics and electromagnetic force fields resulted in Bjerknes's famous circulation theorem. In his initial research presentation, he only discussed the potential application to electromagnetic phenomena. Then in February 1898, Bjerknes made another presentation to the Stockholm Physics Society. He had decided to include some applications to the oceans

by changes in atmospheric and oceanic circulations, the building and destruction of mountain ranges, and volcanic activity, which threw large amounts of debris into the atmosphere. The third theory was that degrees of glaciation depended upon the chemical composition of the

and the atmosphere because some of those in attendance—including Svante Arrhenius and Nils Ekholm—were particularly interested in those areas. Their enthusiasm for his ideas spurred him to action.

Bjerknes explained that with upper-air data his theorem could help test Ekholm's theory that air currents appearing in cyclones resulted from unevenly distributed pressure and density. As Ekholm brought him up-to-date on meteorological thought, Bjerknes found out that Arrhenius intended to use the circulation theorem in a book he was writing on the atmosphere and oceans. He also discovered that Ekholm was convinced that the circulation theorem could help to unravel the nature of low-pressure systems that track across the middle latitudes (30°–60° latitude). To investigate these cyclones, the Physics Society raised money for a series of kite experiments in Bjerknes's honor. Although most of his time was devoted to helping his father, Bjerknes could hardly ignore the efforts of his colleagues. As he wrote in a letter to his wife in June 1899, he could not help "getting sucked into the meteorological vortex."

The pressure to devote more time to meteorology intensified as news of his accomplishments spread. American and German scientific journals asked him to contribute articles. As the 20th century began, Bjerknes became more heavily involved in meteorological studies. Whereas he had had difficulty attracting attention for his ideas from the physics community, the international *geophysics* community not only noticed what he did, but encouraged his work and sought out his ideas for publication. He was having an easier time obtaining funding for his research, and he could finally see a viable future in atmo-

spheric research that had been woefully missing in his earlier electromagnetic resonance studies. Bjerknes became convinced that he might even be able to establish a research school—an institution where he could both influence the research agenda and direct the work of handpicked assistants. Although physicists rarely associated with their less scientifically rigorous meteorological colleagues, Bjerknes saw an opportunity to use physics to understand the atmosphere.

Spending increasing amounts of time discussing the atmosphere with colleagues, by 1903 Bjerknes had developed the rather far-fetched idea that weather could be forecast mathematically if it could be defined by physics. Writing to an oceanographer in 1904, he proclaimed, "I want to solve the problem of predicting the future states of the atmosphere and ocean. I had previously closed my eyes to the fact that this actually was my goal, I must confess, partially for fear of the problem's enormity and of wanting too much." That the problem was enormous was an understatement—100 years later it is still not solved.

Bjerknes plunged into his new work. In 1906, he traveled to the United States, where he presented his new ideas on weather forecasting at Columbia University in New York, and then later at the Carnegie Institution in Washington, D.C. The Carnegie was especially interested and funded his project. Bjerknes returned to Norway, ready to confront the European meteorological establishment—and create a new meteorology based on a rigorous application of physics and mathematics to extensive and accurate surface and upper air data. As the decade closed, he was laying the groundwork, in the words of the historian Robert Marc Friedman, to "construct a modern meteorology."

atmosphere, including the percentages of CO_2 and water vapor. Most scientists settled on just one of these solutions. Chamberlin combined them to formulate his own theory about the onset and departure of ice ages.

Chamberlin focused on the changes in CO_2 based on geological events. Mountain building, through volcanic eruption, adds CO_2 to the air. As the mountains changed the landscape, they also changed the paths of air and water currents. Newly built mountains would be attacked by precipitation that would erode rock. Increased periods of erosion would correspond with a reduction of atmospheric CO_2, which would lead to lower temperatures and, because there would be less space between the air molecules, less water vapor. Changes in ocean circulation would result in increased absorption of CO_2 as Earth moved into an ice age, and a release of CO_2 as Earth emerged from an ice age.

Although theories abounded, those studying climate change did not have sufficient tools or data to investigate their speculations. Many more theories would be proposed before the end of the century. Scientific investigation of these theories would be aided by the increased number of weather observation stations being established in mountains and deserts, and in the Tropics and polar regions. Additional observations and studies would be used to describe climatic characteristics over larger portions of the world—particularly those that were tied to the economic and political interests of the British and Austro-Hungarian Empires, and later, the United States. The shift to increased scientific applications of climatology was yet to come.

Further Reading

Arrenhius, Svante. "On the Influence of Carbonic Acid in the Air upon the Temperature of the Ground." *Philosophical Magazine* ser. 5, 41 (1896): 237–276. In this paper, Arrhenius proposes that burning fossil fuels for heating and factories will add carbon dioxide to the atmosphere and cause the temperature to rise.

Conover, John H. *The Blue Hill Meteorological Observatory: The First 100 Years—1885–1985*. Boston: American Meteorological Society, 1990. In this nicely illustrated volume, Conover traces the development and testing of meteorological instruments—including kites and balloons—at Harvard's Blue Hill Observatory.

Fleming, James Rodger. *Historical Perspectives on Climate Change*. New York and Oxford: Oxford University Press, 1998. Fleming looks at how climate change was perceived from the end of the 19th century through the late 1950s. He also analyzes proposed causes for climate change and their acceptance or rejection by the scientific community.

Friedman, Robert Marc. *Appropriating the Weather: Vilhelm Bjerknes and the Construction of Modern Meteorology*. Ithaca, N.Y.: Cornell University Press, 1989. Friedman analyzes the development of the Bergen School, the research school created and promoted by Vilhelm Bjerknes, and its influence on 20th-century meteorology.

Kutzbach, Gisela. *The Thermal Theory of Cyclones: A History of Meteorological Thought in the Nineteenth Century.* Boston: American Meteorological Society, 1979. Kutzbach explains how meteorological ideas on the structure of cyclonic circulations and their associated weather systems evolved during the 19th century and influenced meteorological thought in the 20th century.

Larsen, Erik. *Isaac's Storm: A Man, a Time, and the Deadliest Hurricane in History.* New York: Vantage, 2000. The story of the 1900 hurricane that killed unknown thousands of people in Galveston, Texas. This book provides insight into weather forecasting at the turn of the 20th century.

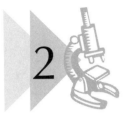

2

1911–1920:
Calculating the Weather

Meteorologists focused on the whys behind the weather at the same time they worked to improve weather forecasts. Advances in aeronautics provided opportunities to gather data at higher altitudes and put pressure on meteorologists to develop upper-level forecasts critical for flight safety. Mid-decade, as war spread across Europe, accurate weather data and forecasts became vitally important to soldiers on the ground and in the air as new war fighting techniques required carefully tailored forecasts. Scientific investigations on climate change continued also, with the emphasis shifting from anthropogenic carbon dioxide to solar variations. These new efforts encouraged the adoption of mathematically rigorous scientific tools as proposed and promoted by Vilhelm Bjerknes.

Why Frost?

The German meteorologist Alfred Lothar Wegener (1880–1930), best known for his theory of continental drift, had a wide variety of geophysical interests. Fascinated by Greenland, he made several expeditions to this frozen wasteland before his tragic death during a blizzard. Capitalizing on Greenland's ample opportunities to observe meteorological phenomena under freezing conditions, Wegener studied the formation of *hoarfrost*—the interlocking crystals formed by direct deposition of water vapor onto objects of small diameter or on snow surfaces (*surface hoar*). As his colleagues were, he was looking for physical mechanisms behind observable meteorological events.

In his 1911 book *Thermodynamik der Atmosphäre* (Thermodynamics of the atmosphere), Wegener explained his hoarfrost formation theory, which depended upon an observation that ran counter to contemporary thought on water behavior. In the early 20th century, scientists thought that water existed in three phases: solid (ice), liquid (water), and gas (water vapor). During the phase change from water to ice, the temperature of a container of water had to be lowered to 32°F (0°C) before it would begin to freeze. As ice formed, the water remained

The German meteorologist and geophysicist Alfred Wegener conducted extensive studies in Greenland. (Alfred Wegener Institute for Polar and Marine Research)

at the freezing temperature. Only after the entire container of water was frozen did the temperature drop below freezing.

Wegener discovered that water could be a liquid at a temperature *below* 32°F (0°C)—that is, when it was *supercooled*. Supercooling may take place in very small, pure water droplets without dust or other contaminants. Supercooled clouds, which may have temperatures as low as -40°F (-40°C), are actually quite common, but their presence was unknown until specially outfitted aircraft were able to take upper-air observations.

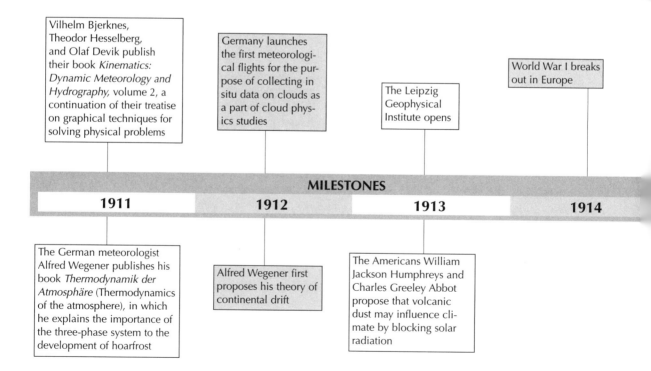

Vilhelm Bjerknes, Theodor Hesselberg, and Olaf Devik publish their book *Kinematics: Dynamic Meteorology and Hydrography,* volume 2, a continuation of their treatise on graphical techniques for solving physical problems

Germany launches the first meteorological flights for the purpose of collecting in situ data on clouds as a part of cloud physics studies

The Leipzig Geophysical Institute opens

World War I breaks out in Europe

MILESTONES

1911   **1912**   **1913**   **1914**

The German meteorologist Alfred Wegener publishes his book *Thermodynamik der Atmosphäre* (Thermodynamics of the atmosphere), in which he explains the importance of the three-phase system to the development of hoarfrost

Alfred Wegener first proposes his theory of continental drift

The Americans William Jackson Humphreys and Charles Greeley Abbot propose that volcanic dust may influence climate by blocking solar radiation

On the basis of the presence of supercooled droplets, Wegener developed a theory explaining the growth of ice crystals. Atmospheric water vapor, as all gases do, exerts a pressure on the objects it surrounds. When all water vapor is at the same temperature, it exerts a vapor pressure proportional to its quantity in the air. Wegener discovered that vapor pressure near a frozen surface is less than the vapor pressure just a very small distance away. Since all substances move from areas of high pressure to areas of low pressure, the water vapor is drawn toward the frozen surface, where it condenses and then freezes. If the water vapor surrounding the frozen surface is supercooled, as soon as the water vapor is drawn toward the frozen surface it immediately becomes an ice crystal. When the process continues repeatedly, the ice crystals grow and hoarfrost results.

Although Wegener's discovery might not seem important, it was extremely valuable to airplane pilots. A light coating of frost on an airplane does not affect flight safety, but a large sheet of ice may cause the pilot to lose control. If a pilot continues to fly through supercooled clouds after the first crystals form, they will continue to grow. If the droplet size is very small and the temperature of the supercooled clouds is very low, *rime* ice results. If the droplet size is larger and the temperature of the supercooled clouds is "warm" (close to freezing), *glaze ice* forms.

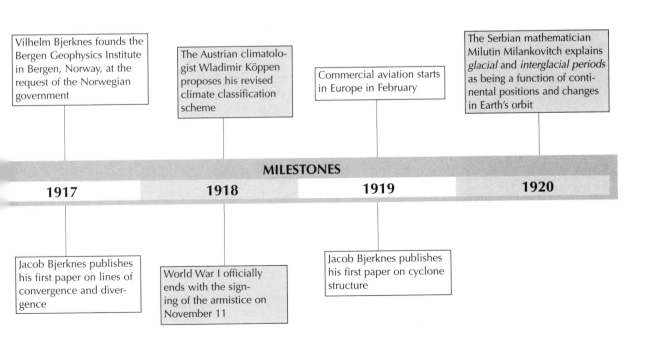

Vilhelm Bjerknes founds the Bergen Geophysics Institute in Bergen, Norway, at the request of the Norwegian government

The Austrian climatologist Wladimir Köppen proposes his revised climate classification scheme

Commercial aviation starts in Europe in February

The Serbian mathematician Milutin Milankovitch explains *glacial* and *interglacial periods* as being a function of continental positions and changes in Earth's orbit

MILESTONES

1917 | **1918** | **1919** | **1920**

Jacob Bjerknes publishes his first paper on lines of convergence and divergence

World War I officially ends with the signing of the armistice on November 11

Jacob Bjerknes publishes his first paper on cyclone structure

Wegener's work on hoarfrost crystals like these led to later work on precipitation processes. (NOAA)

Early 20th-century aircraft were very fragile and could not withstand ice accumulations. Once Wegener published his theory, meteorologists briefed pilots on areas to avoid during flight. By the 1930s, meteorologists struggling to understand the physical mechanism behind the formation of raindrops would use Wegener's study of frost formation as a starting point in the new research field called cloud physics.

Weather on the Front Lines

War erupted in Europe in August 1914, as the German army raced across the plains of France and stopped a few miles short of Paris. In past conflicts, field commanders had not considered the tactical or strategic use of weather information. As the Nobel Prize–winning physicist and U.S. military meteorology coordinator Robert A. Millikan (1868–1953) wrote in his 1919 article "Some Scientific Aspects of the Meteorological Work of the United States Army," "Prior to 1914 a meteorological section was not considered a necessary part of the military services." The weather would do what it would do—and the armies on the ground and the navies at sea would continue their missions regardless of the conditions. Part of this thinking can be traced to the state of meteorology at the time. With little in the way of a physical theory, and without the capability to tie information from *empirical* observations to existing physical theory, weather forecasters on the front lines would have been minimally effective. Unlike earlier wars, this war was heavily mechanized. The effective use of aviation, poison gas, and longer-range artillery depended upon weather conditions. Weather forecasts had to be detailed—"partly cloudy, cooler, with light wind" at the airstrip was of absolutely no use to a pilot flying more than 100 miles (160.9 km) to reach his target.

German military strategists had recognized the importance of weather for future aerial operations. The countries being drawn into this conflict had not. British and French forces very quickly realized that the use of poison gas demanded a knowledge of atmospheric conditions. When lobbing gas canisters at the enemy while taking shelter in the myriad trenches snaking throughout the French countryside, combatants wanted assurance that their attack would be successful. If the wind shifted over their positions, they could be poisoned. If the wind were blowing too hard, the gas would disperse before reaching the enemy. Knowledge of low-level wind behavior became extremely important.

Upper-level winds also affected the prosecution of the war. German airships loaded with bombs and heading for London were blown off course to the north and east by unexpected winds aloft. Once the allies started to use increased numbers of airplanes and balloons for reconnaissance, it was clear they would lose pilots and aircraft unless they had adequate meteorological support. By 1917 tremendous improvements in aircraft construction allowed pilots to fly bombing runs day and night. These aircraft operated significantly lower and more slowly than today's high-performance aircraft, but winds still affected fuel loading and bomb release. Pilots also needed to know whether clouds would obscure their targets.

Winds also affected long-range artillery. Wind has virtually no effect over short distances, but over long distances high winds can force ordnance well off target. Since shells went high into the atmosphere and then arced down, cloud cover and turbulence within the clouds had to be considered. Flamethrowers were another new weapon for which wind speed and direction made a difference. Sending a flame into the wind could be deadly to the person handling the weapon.

The war demanded extensive surface and upper air observations. Everyone involved in the conflict quickly established dense networks of observation stations connected by radio sets. Forecasters, operating in unfamiliar areas for which they possessed no forecasting rules, quickly created a variety of ad hoc predictive techniques that did not take into account the physical mechanisms producing the observed phenomena.

Vilhelm Bjerknes, in Leipzig, Germany, during the early war years, realized the value of Germany's upper-air network. Knowledge of incoming weather allowed German military leaders to make better decisions about troop movements and attacks. Bjerknes was convinced that aviation would continue to expand in postwar Europe. He would seek a way to coordinate an international effort to tie empirical data with physical

*Military meteorologists provided wind forecasts that were important to trench-bound soldiers launching or trying to escape from poison gas attacks during World War I. (*The Nations at War, *by Willis John Abbot [1917])*

reasoning for a stronger meteorology. His opportunity occurred when Norway called him home.

The Bergen School

In 1917, after three years of war, living conditions were deteriorating throughout Europe. Vilhelm Bjerknes, director of the Leipzig Geophysical Institute since 1913, had lost most of his assistants to the German military and many of them had died. He had imported several Norwegians to help, including Jacob, his 19-year-old son, but he was struggling to keep up with his research tying upper-air data and aeronautical activities with a more rational, scientific basis for meteorology. Bjerknes needed to leave Leipzig.

The opportunity to pursue his work in a more conducive location arose on March 17, 1917. The Norwegian oceanographer Bjørn Helland-Hansen (1877–1957), the first professor of the Bergen (Norway) Museum, had been leading a research team and providing training in oceanography and marine biology for more than a decade. Helland-Hansen and his colleagues had gained significant international recognition by the middle of the decade. He saw an opportunity to create a site where oceanographers, meteorologists, and those geophysicists studying terrestrial magnetism and *auroras* could work together and enhance their individual research projects. In 1916, Helland-Hansen had proposed establishing a geophysical institute at the museum. The museum council's acceptance of the plan inspired many private donations, and the Bergen Geophysics Institute was born. Initially, there would only be two professorships: one in oceanography, filled by Helland-Hansen, and the second in meteorology. Vilhelm Bjerknes was the choice for the second post.

Accepting the offer, Bjerknes returned to Bergen as soon as the semester ended in Leipzig. Upon his arrival, Bjerknes discovered that working space was at a premium. Setting up his temporary research area within a small corner of the museum's oceanographic laboratory, he started seeking a more suitable location that would lend itself to the fulfillment of his ultimate plan: the creation of a Norwegian meteorology school.

Bjerknes knew that he would need the support of geophysicists throughout Scandinavia. His chance to make a fruitful alliance with the Bergen Meteorological Observatory appeared in spring 1918. Norway was experiencing a severe food shortage and the government was supporting a special weather forecasting unit to provide detailed weather information to farmers during the summer growing season. Bjerknes supported the government's goal of increasing crop yields through better weather forecasts. He also intended to use this opportunity to increase forecast precision. Bjerknes and his assistants (his son, Jacob, and the Swedish meteorologist Halvor Solberg [1895–1974]) became a combination theoretical research team and forecasting unit. Their work would lead to advances in both theoretical meteorology and weather forecasting.

Solberg took over forecasting for east Norway, while Jacob assumed responsibility for the west. Their task was hampered by the lack of established weather observation stations and the overall lack of observational data due to the war. During wartime, particularly when the conflict engulfs an entire continent, combatant nations do not share meteorological data that could be used by enemy forces in planning military operations. Before the war, Norway had depended upon weather observations received via telegram from Great Britain, Iceland, and the Faroe Islands. Now the observations were secret and Norway, a long, narrow country whose weather sweeps in off the North Sea, could not create a surface pressure map and plot the track of low-pressure storm systems into the country. If Bjerknes and his assistants were going to aid Norway's farmers, they had to find a way of providing accurate rain forecasts based on local information. To be effective, their new method had to be grounded on a physical understanding of the atmosphere.

Bjerknes increased the number of observation stations from three to 60 by recruiting sailors and fishermen manning the war-related U-boat watch stations scattered throughout the islands composing Norway's extensive North Sea archipelago. These islands were the first to experience stormy weather before it swept over the country, and the sailors and fisherman were already outstanding weather observers because their lives and livelihoods depended upon reading the sky. Bjerknes also recruited lighthouse keepers, farmers, and fishermen living along the coastline.

The West Norway Observation Network was critical for both forecasting and theoretical investigation. (Based on figure 3, Robert Marc Friedman, *Appropriating the Weather*)

The island-based stations provided extremely accurate wind reports. Weather observation stations typically reported wind direction by quadrant, for example, north-northwest or east. To meet defense needs, the U-boat lookouts had to provide more precise directions. They reported the wind direction in 5°, not 45°, increments. Wind measurements on exposed islands were also much more accurate than those on

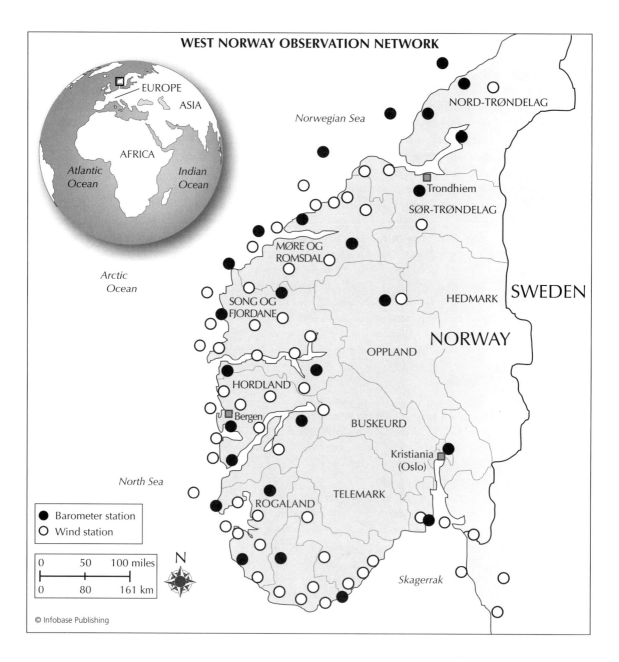

WEST NORWAY OBSERVATION NETWORK

EUROPE
ASIA
AFRICA
Atlantic Ocean
Indian Ocean
Arctic Ocean

Norwegian Sea

NORD-TRØNDELAG

Trondhiem

SØR-TRØNDELAG

MØRE OG ROMSDAL

SONG OG FJORDANE

HEDMARK

SWEDEN

NORWAY

OPPLAND

HORDLAND

Bergen

BUSKEURD

Kristiania (Oslo)

North Sea

TELEMARK

ROGALAND

Skagerrak

● Barometer station
○ Wind station

| 0 | 50 | 100 miles |
| 0 | 80 | 161 km |

N

© Infobase Publishing

the mainland because they were subject to less topographic interference. Bjerknes hoped that the analysis of these accurate wind reports would lead to a new method of rain prediction by identifying *lines of convergence*, that is, locations where air was rushing into a long, narrow area of the atmosphere.

While he was analyzing incoming data and discovering the presence of convergence lines, Jacob also analyzed data collected by Scandinavian climatology stations. He found that lines of convergence were invariably associated with cyclones. Furthermore, Jacob noticed air currents from two different air masses—one warm and one cold—met at the *line of convergence* running through the cyclone. He began looking for other instances of this phenomenon during the summer of 1918. By summer's end, he suspected that there might actually be two lines of convergence associated with a cyclone. Warm air flowed into the back of one line associated with a broad swath of moderate rain. Cold air flowed into the back of the second associated with a narrow band of intense rain. The "warm" convergence line always seemed to point in the direction that the cyclone was moving. If true, Jacob could use this feature to predict the cyclone's movement and the areas of rain accurately. As he used this new method, Jacob's forecast errors dropped significantly.

Jacob Bjerknes's work on cyclone structure produced this cross section, which shows the movement of air in relation to a low-pressure center. (Based on figure 6, Robert Marc Friedman, *Appropriating the Weather*)

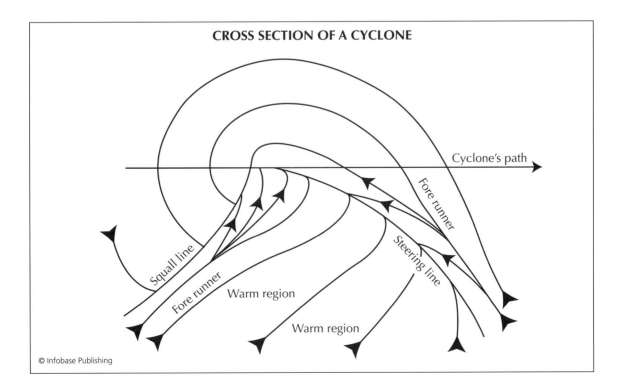

CROSS SECTION OF A CYCLONE

Cyclone's path

Fore runner

Steering line

Squall line

Fore runner

Warm region

Warm region

© Infobase Publishing

Jacob Bjerknes's interpretation of data from the closely knit network of observation stations yielded an important breakthrough on both the structure and movement of cyclones. In fall 1919, at age 21, he published his often-cited article "On the Structure of Moving Cyclones" in the Norwegian scientific journal *Geofysiske publikasjoner* (Geophysics publications); later the article in the U.S. Weather Bureau's publication *Monthly Weather Review*. Jacob described the structure of the cyclone's surface features and then inferred its three-dimensional structure on the basis of surface evidence and upper-air data—a result that is still found in almost every basic meteorological textbook.

Research Meets Practice

The Bergen School, with its emphasis on using practical weather forecasting as a way to advance both meteorological theory and weather prediction, was an oddity in the early 20th century. Research schools—academic entities focused on one scientific discipline and featuring a charismatic leader surrounded by numerous "disciples"—were not usually known for pursuing practical applications. On the other hand, institutions that focused on practical applications were not generally associated with theoretical development.

Vilhelm Bjerknes did not intend to become involved in practical weather forecasting—it was actually the furthest thing from his mind. Desiring to set up an institution equivalent to the Leipzig Geophysical Institute, Bjerknes had the primary goal of placing meteorology on a firm physical and mathematical footing to allow calculation of future atmospheric conditions. Although he envisioned improved weather forecasts in the distant future, he did not think he would be starting his new research program in Norway with weather forecasting.

Bjerknes discovered that by directly addressing the problems of weather prediction for farmers and aviators he and his assistants quickly learned what aspects of the atmosphere—temperature, pressure, wind velocity, humidity—were critical to understanding physical processes. The necessity of providing these weather services presented Bjerknes with the resources to further his atmospheric studies. Had Norway not been experiencing food shortages, and had it not been preparing to expand its aviation capabilities, Bjerknes might not have received the funding and government cooperation needed to carry out his research plan.

The purpose of theoretical meteorology has always been to define atmospheric motions and phenomena with the rigorous techniques of mathematics and physics. It is possible for meteorologists to develop a wonderful theory that explains current conditions and is unable to predict atmospheric conditions in the next day or two. Most theorists were not concerned with matching their physical understanding to future weather. Jacob Bjerknes was not just developing theory: He wanted to ensure that his theory was predictive. When his agricultural forecasts were not accurate, he examined where his theory might have failed. Jacob's methods moved theory closer to atmospheric behavior, and in turn increased meteorologists' ability to predict weather more accurately.

The Bergen School was the first that fully melded theoretical research with the practice of weather forecasting. In the next decade, the methods they developed spread rapidly through the international meteorological community.

By the end of the decade, the work of Jacob and his father, Vilhelm, attracted the attention of some of the brightest young meteorologists of the century, including the Swedes Carl-Gustav Rossby (1898–1957) and Tor Bergeron (1891–1977), both of whom would make discipline-changing discoveries by midcentury. Students from Denmark, Norway, and Sweden visited Bergen to take courses and return home with the Bjerkneses' methods. Vilhelm Bjerknes's dream of a Norwegian meteorology school was coming to life. The Bergen School of Meteorology, that rare combination of theoretical and practical meteorology, was taking shape.

A Perfect Couple: Aviation and Meteorology

Hot-air balloons, airships ("blimps"), and fixed-wing aircraft all operate in the atmosphere. From the time these first flying machines lifted off, the futures of aeronautics and meteorology became inextricably entwined. Observers in 19th-century hot-air balloons collected atmospheric data, but these were not systematic efforts. Once pilots determined that sharing atmospheric data with meteorologists directly enhanced flight safety, a symbiotic relationship developed between aviators and meteorologists.

On the morning of December 17, 1903, Wilbur (1867–1912) and Orville (1871–1948) Wright took their wood and canvas biplane to Kitty Hawk, North Carolina, for a test flight. Kitty Hawk had not become the launch site by chance. The Wrights had gathered climatological information about a number of potential takeoff sites before deciding that Kitty Hawk would provide the best conditions. With high pressure just to the east, the fragile little plane with Orville at the controls faced nose-first into a 20-mile- (32-km)-per-hour wind—providing just enough lift to get the Wright Flyer off the ground for 12 seconds of controlled, manned flight. By the fourth flight of the day, Orville was able to keep the plane airborne for 59 seconds and cover a total distance of 852 feet (260 m). The winds that enabled the Wrights to become airborne became gusty later in the day, flipped the plane over, and ended flights for the day. The connection between weather conditions and successful flight had been made.

The first Wright Flyer did not have a practical future. The Wrights continued to perfect their airplane and within three years were marketing a biplane. The U.S. Army purchased its first Wright airplane in 1909 for $25,000—the advent of military aeronautics. By the time World War I ended, the United States military had 14,000 airplanes. Most had been flown to France—a long, dangerous flight across the Atlantic with little weather information—for use by the American Expeditionary Force. The thousands of daredevil pilots released from active duty at war's end provided the manpower to get commercial avia-

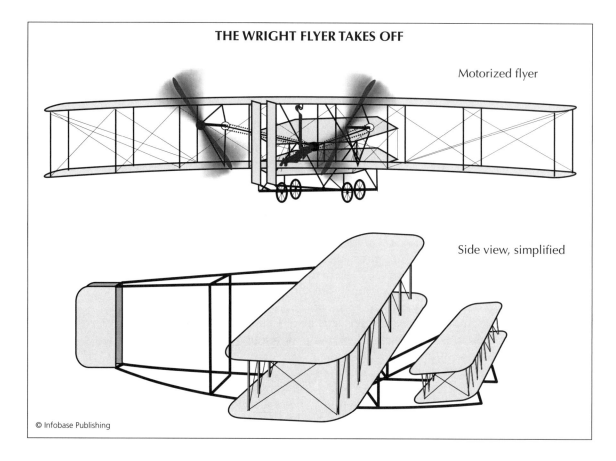

THE WRIGHT FLYER TAKES OFF

Motorized flyer

Side view, simplified

© Infobase Publishing

Aviation advances, including the launch of the Wright Flyer in 1903, required additional scientific studies of the upper atmosphere.

tion off the ground at the end of the century's second decade. The few remaining on active duty flew Army Signal Corps aircraft delivering U.S. mail between major cities.

Planes and pilots were in the air, but they received little viable weather support. Pilot balloon observations were becoming routine, but not every landing strip had an upper-air station. Some pilots contacted U.S. Weather Bureau city offices for takeoff and landing conditions. Others developed their own network of communications, with arriving pilots advising departing pilots about recently encountered flying conditions.

Commercial aviation started in Europe in February 1919, just three months after the signing of the armistice. Germany inaugurated commercial airplane service that linked Berlin, Leipzig, and Weimar. By the end of the summer, the rigid airships of the German Zeppelin firm DELAG resumed carrying passengers between Berlin and Friedrichshafen. Two British firms began flying between London and Paris, and French airlines started carrying passengers between Paris and Brussels. Aviation companies anticipated that aircraft would become the mode of transportation and cargo delivery in the future, and they were eager to be a part of it.

Flight forecasting did not immediately connect with airlines. Pilots were not always sure what weather information they wanted or needed. Some pilots knew exactly what they wanted: detailed, accurate forecasts for the entire continent days in advance—a completely impossible goal. Other pilots, still in the military daredevil mode, did not think they needed weather services. They were absolutely sure their planes could withstand any weather event, including thunderstorms, severe hail, icing, and high winds. Aircraft owners were eager for good meteorological support. If their planes crashed in bad weather, it would be difficult to attract paying passengers or contracts to carry the U.S. mail.

For their part, meteorologists needed the opportunities to explore the atmosphere that aviation could provide. Aircraft could carry meteorological instruments and take back data to weather stations. If the new airline transportation companies wanted better forecasts, they needed to provide funds for additional research and thus help to advance meteorological theory.

Some countries, including Great Britain and France, placed their weather services under the control of military authorities. In France, even academic meteorology posts were "militarized," much to the disappointment of meteorologists, who saw the discipline as being international and therefore not tied to the armed forces.

Aviation also changed international agreements on just what constituted a weather observation and how it would be transmitted via telegram. The same code number could indicate drizzle or a heavy downpour. Clouds were reported by the percentage of cloud cover—not by the kinds of clouds that were in the area. It made a tremendous difference to pilots whether there was a low, thin stratus layer that they could fly through to clear skies or numerous cumulonimbus clouds ("thunderclouds"), whose violent internal winds could knock their planes right out of the sky. Pilots also needed to know the expected visibility at the landing site. If fog was dense and horizontal visibility extremely limited, they would be forced to find another landing strip. Pilots had few options if they did not have enough fuel to reach the closest landing strip.

Taking observations once or twice a day had never been sufficient for analyzing atmospheric conditions, but until aviation requirements became clear, meteorologists could not argue for additional money to pay for those observations. Flight meteorologists needed many more observations per day to ensure safe takeoff and landing conditions. They needed to make forecasts for the next few hours, not for the next day. Aircraft could not fly across the United States or Europe on one tank of gas. They needed to land, refuel, and take off again. Pilots would get a weather prediction for the next stop, several hours away, and then take off. Meteorologists provided information on cloud cover, precipitation, surface winds, and visibility at the station, as well as information on winds aloft at flight levels between 3,000 and 6,000 feet (914 and 1,829 m).

As the decade closed, meteorologists all agreed that aviation support meant changes in observational techniques, reporting, and transmission. They did not agree on how to make the forecasts. Would they rely on their feel for the atmosphere—or would they move toward scientific techniques that offered the promise of calculating the weather?

Climates Classified

A location's *climate* is generally described by the long-term average of temperature and precipitation. The word itself is derived from the Greek *klima*, which means "slope." The well-traveled Greeks were aware that the countries lining the northern Mediterranean coast were warm and relatively moist compared to the dry desert regions east and south of the Mediterranean, and that countries in what we now call northern Europe were much colder. Trying to make sense out of these differences, they concluded that the angle (or slope) of the Sun's rays, which depend on latitude, made the difference.

Climate is influenced by more than latitude. As some scientists had hypothesized at the turn of the century, the amount of carbon dioxide and water vapor in the air might make a difference. Alfred Wegener considered how the positions of continents could make a difference in observed climate while developing his theory of continental drift, first posed in 1912. The U.S. Weather Bureau cloud physicist William Jackson Humphreys (1862–1945) and the Smithsonian Astrophysical Observatory director Charles Greeley Abbot both proposed in 1913 that volcanic dust could influence climate by blocking solar radiation. Despite these efforts to determine causal mechanisms for climate, most climatologists were content to classify climates. The task of climate classification would also face its own difficulties.

The main problem facing climatologists was to decide which weather elements (temperature, precipitation, humidity, cloud cover, prevailing wind) would be adopted to separate one climate from another. Even if just one weather element, temperature, for example, were selected, what attribute of temperature would one use? Would one use the average temperature? Two regions might have the same average temperature, and yet one might experience a daily temperature range of only 20°F (11°C) while another experiences a daily range of 60°F (28°C). The climates would be very different. The first would be relatively mild if the average turned out to be 60°F (15.6°C) with a high of 70°F (21°C) and a low of 50°F (10°C)—typical for a coastal location. On the other hand, the second example would provide a region with a high afternoon temperature of 90°F (32°C) and an overnight low of 30°F (-1°C)—typical for a desert. Clearly those two locations do *not* have the same climate.

To be useful, a climate classification scheme had to make use of years of old data that had been stacking up in boxes, as well as data that continued to flood in every month. There were three basic climate schemes.

The first was just a simple, descriptive scheme. It might describe a region by using some combination of vague references to temperature and humidity: hot and dry, warm and moist, cold and dry, or cold and moist. The second type compared climate with vegetation and emerged from the close relationship between naturalists and weather observers. Climate types were based upon the predominant form of plant life. An area covered in fir trees, for instance, would have a different climate from one covered with sagebrush. The third type of climate scheme tried to relate climate with the people who lived there and their way of life. For example, a region where people lived in igloos and donned sealskin garments had a different climate than a region where people lived in grass huts and wore few clothes. None of these schemes was very specific, and none was sufficient for climatologists looking for a more scientific climate scheme.

The Austrian climatologist Wladimir Köppen (1846–1940) started working on his climate classification scheme in the 1880s and continued to refine it until 1931. Because summer is the growing season, he first used summer temperatures and focused on the 50°F (10°C) *isotherm* (line drawn on a map such that the temperature everywhere along the line is 50°C [10°C]). Areas equatorward of the line were forested and areas poleward were tundra. If the average temperature was above 68°F (20°C), then it was tropical. Not satisfied with just using temperature, Köppen changed his focus to connecting climate with vegetation—a decision that

Wladimir Köppen's first attempt at climate classification focused on the location of the 50°F (10°C) and 68°F (20°C) lines of average summer temperature.

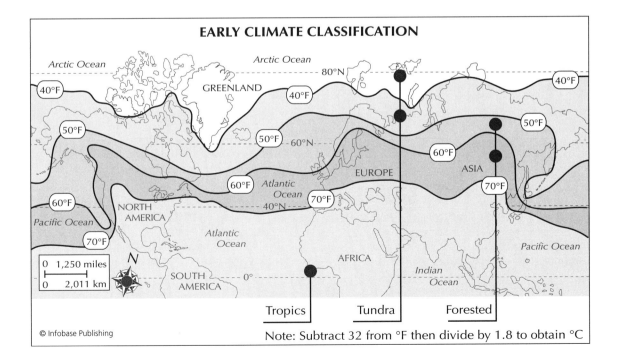

EARLY CLIMATE CLASSIFICATION

Arctic Ocean

Arctic Ocean

80°N

GREENLAND

40°F

40°F

40°F

50°F

50°F

60°N

50°F

60°F

60°N

EUROPE

ASIA

60°F

Atlantic Ocean

70°F

60°F

NORTH AMERICA

40°N

70°F

Pacific Ocean

Atlantic Ocean

70°F

Pacific Ocean

0 1,250 miles

0 2,011 km

N

SOUTH AMERICA

0°

AFRICA

Indian Ocean

Tropics   Tundra   Forested

© Infobase Publishing

Note: Subtract 32 from °F then divide by 1.8 to obtain °C

Earth Wobbles and the Ice Comes

The Serbian mathematician Milutin Milankovitch (1879–1958) was more interested in the mechanisms behind climate change than in regional climate classifications. Beginning in 1911, he spent 30 years researching the causes of long-term climate change. Milankovitch focused on changes in Earth's orbital characteristics and their influence on the amount of incoming solar radiation received on Earth's surface.

Planets follow elliptical paths around the Sun, but those orbital paths change slightly each year. Three characteristics of Earth's orbit slowly change over tens of thousands of years: the tilt of Earth's axis, the *eccentricity* (or degree of circularity) of Earth's orbital path, and the orientation of the axis of rotation (known as the wobble). These characteristics exhibit different cycles of change that affect the amount of *insolation*.

Earth rotates on an axis that forms an angle of 23.5° with the vertical. This is not a constant angle. It varies from 21.5° to 24.5° over a period of 41,000 years. When the angle is smallest (21.5°), there is a smaller difference between summer and winter temperatures than when the angle is greatest (24.5°). With a larger angle, winters are colder and summers are hotter because the insolation enters less directly in winter and more directly in summer.

The orbital eccentricity changes over 100,000 years, from being more circular (as it is now) to being more elliptical and then back to circular. When it is more circular, then the distance from Earth to the Sun changes little between seasons. When the orbit is at its most elliptical, there is a significant difference between the distance to the Sun in winter and in summer. The effect of eccentricity on Earth's climate also depends on the last orbital characteristic: the wobble.

Much as a spinning top wobbles on its axis, so too does Earth wobble on its axis. Over a period of 19,000 to 23,000 years, the axis wobble traces out a circle. The wobble determines the season during which Earth will be closest to the Sun. Earth is now closest to the Sun during the Northern Hemisphere winter, and farthest away during the Northern Hemisphere summer (reversed for the Southern

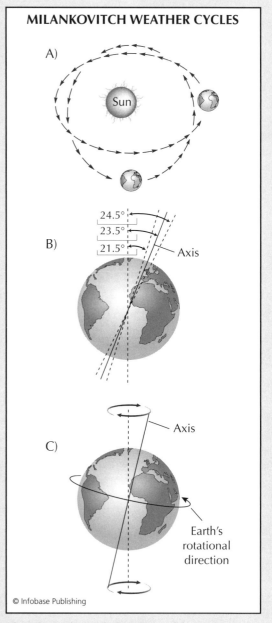

MILANKOVITCH WEATHER CYCLES

A)

B)

24.5°
23.5°
21.5°
Axis

C)

Axis

Earth's rotational direction

© Infobase Publishing

The Serbian Milutin Milankovitch argued that incoming solar energy increases or decreases with changes in (A) orbital eccentricity, (B) axis tilt, and (C) axis orientation (wobble).

Hemisphere). About 10,000 years ago, Earth was closest to the Sun during the Northern Hemisphere summer. That means it would have been hotter in the summer and colder in the winter in the Northern Hemisphere than it is today. In another 10,000 years or so, Earth will return to that situation.

The effect of these three orbital characteristics becomes clear when the extremes all match up. If the orbit is at its most eccentric and the wobble puts Earth much farther away from the Sun during the Northern Hemisphere winter, and if the angle of the axis is such that it is tipped away from the Sun during winter at 24.5°, then winters will be much colder and summers will be much warmer. None of these orbital variations changes the total amount of sunlight that strikes Earth's surface. They change the distribution of that sunlight that Milankovitch thought influenced the occurrence of ice ages.

Milankovitch looked at astronomical data for the 600,000 years prior to 1800 and hand-calculated the amount of insolation at different latitudes for each year. He then predicted that these cyclic changes would induce ice ages when the amount of solar radiation was the least during the summer months, thus reducing the summer snowmelt in high latitudes. Snow that fell during the winter would survive through the summer, to be added to that of the next year. Over thousands of years, the ice would build up and form glaciers, and those glaciers would advance toward the equator and produce an ice age.

Milankovitch continued to perfect his calculations and compare the results against *paleoclimate* data through the 1950s. Although new evidence of ice ages seems to match Milankovitch's periodicities, this remains a controversial theory for climate scientists.

struck some climatologists as a step backward because it seemed less "scientific" than just using weather elements.

By 1900, Köppen had revised his scheme to include the distribution of precipitation and concluded that there were six basic climate zones and 24 varieties of climate. Most climate varieties were associated with the plants and animals that lived in the region. The dividing lines between climates were dependent upon maximum and minimum temperatures and the amount of precipitation. He had a difficult time determining just what constituted an "arid" climate, since regions as different as the Sahara and Antarctica are both arid.

Continuing to revise and expand his ideas through the second decade, Köppen unveiled his improved scheme in 1918. Abandoning the connection with vegetation, he attached geographical names to the regions, for example, *tropical forests* or *deserts* or *savannas*. Köppen used letter codes so users could instantly identify a region's climate on a climate map.

Köppen's climatological studies and those of national weather bureaus were especially critical to agricultural interests. In the United States, most states had their own climatologist, whose job it was to determine the state's climate types and to advise farm bureau extension agents on crop selection. By the third decade of the century, Köppen's increasingly complex climate scheme was adopted around the world. The development and use of the ultimate Köppen climate classification scheme are discussed in chapter 4.

Scientist of the Decade: Vilhelm Bjerknes (1862–1951)—His Later Years

Vilhelm Bjerknes spent most of the first half of his life attempting to establish a career in physics, only to see it effectively derailed by his father's incessant demands for his assistance. After he decided to apply his circulation theorem to the oceans and atmosphere, his career opportunities improved dramatically.

Because of the reputation he had built in Norway, Bjerknes was asked to direct the new Leipzig Geophysical Institute in 1912. Creating a dynamic research program seeking to establish a physical and mathematical basis for describing the future states of the atmosphere, Bjerknes attracted not only some of his colleagues from Norway, but many of the top minds in Germany. When World War I began in 1914, many of his German assistants were called away to support the war effort and Bjerknes found his research program understaffed. After three more difficult yet productive years, Bjerknes returned to Norway to fill a post with the new Bergen Geophysical Institute and the Bergen Museum (now part of the University of Bergen).

At 55, Bjerknes had firmly established his reputation as one of the great men of meteorology. He combined research into theoretical meteorology with improvements in practical forecasting techniques to create a unique research school that attracted scholars and graduate students from all over the world. Bergen School scientists worked together to create a theory of cyclonic development that came to be known as the *polar front* theory and a method of weather data analysis known as air mass analysis.

Vilhelm Bjerknes's desire was to make the Bergen School the dominant training and research organization in international meteorology. To achieve that goal, he scoured Sweden to recruit graduate students and published his results in English language scientific journals such as *Nature* and *Monthly Weather Review*. Bjerknes also taught courses in his new analysis techniques and encouraged students from throughout Scandinavia and Germany to attend. These young converts to Bjerknes's theories returned home to teach others and spread the news about these new physics-based methods that showed so much promise for weather forecasting.

Impressing those who attended the International Meteorological Committee meeting in 1919, Bjerknes was selected to head the Commission for the Exploration of the Upper Atmosphere—a position that lent him enormous authority and influence within the discipline. He used his position to seek information on the connections between meteorology and aviation in European nations as well as to "sell" the Bergen School program.

Bjerknes remained at the Bergen Geophysical Institute until 1926, when he accepted a post as the chair of the Department of Applied Mechanics and Mathematical Physics at the University of Oslo. In addition to continuing his meteorological studies, Bjerknes carried on the hydrodynamical research started by his father, Carl Anton, in the 19th century. Bjerknes also planned to write a textbook on theoretical physics but completed only the first part of the project—a book on vector analysis.

Bjerknes retired in 1932 but remained active in meteorology and geophysics organizations and issues. That same year he became president of the Association of Meteorology of the International Union of Geodesy and Geophysics. During the worldwide depression of the 1930s, he wrote numerous articles on science policy that argued for increased governmental support for basic research at Norway's universities as a way of overcoming unemployment and economic depression.

Bjerknes received many awards and honors during his long life. He was elected to a number of national academies—organizations that include only the most respected scientific minds—including those of Norway, the Netherlands, Prussia (now part of Germany), the United Kingdom, and the United States. He also received the Agassiz Medal for Oceanography (1926), the Symons Medal for Meteorology (1932), and the Buys Ballot Medal for Meteorology (1933). Vilhelm Bjerknes died in Oslo on April 9, 1951, at the age of 89.

In the early 20th century, scientists conducting research on phenomena associated with weather and climate were just as likely to come from mathematics, physics, or astronomy backgrounds as from meteorology. One reason was that there were very few institutions of higher learning that focused on what we now call geophysics—the physics of the Earth. Consequently, individuals who had trained in other scientific and mathematical disciplines and became intrigued by atmospheric problems often attacked those problems from the distinct viewpoints they had gained while in graduate school. Although it might seem that meteorology and climatology would have advanced more quickly if this specialized training had been available sooner, that might not have been the case. Sometimes there is an advantage when people see problems in a different way. That was true for the mathematically educated Milankovitch—and it was also true for the meteorologist-scientist of this second decade: physics-trained Vilhelm Bjerknes.

Further Reading

Bates, Charles F., and John F. Fuller. *America's Weather Warriors: 1814–1985*. College Station: Texas A&M University Press, 1986. This readable account discusses military meteorologists and how they supported evolving styles of warfare from the early 19th century through the late 20th century.

Bjerknes, J. "On the Structure of Moving Cyclones." *Monthly Weather Review* 47 (1919): 95–99. Available online. URL: http://docs.lib.noaa.gov/rescue/mwr/047/mwr-047-02-0095.pdf. Accessed March 15, 2006. Jacob Bjerknes's often-cited paper describes the three-dimensional structure of low-pressure systems.

Haber, Ludwig Fritz. *The Poisonous Cloud: Chemical Warfare in the First World War*. New York: Oxford University Press, 1986. Haber discusses the devastating uses of chemical weapons during World War I.

Hallion, Richard P. *Legacy of Flight: The Guggenheim Contribution to American Aviation*. Seattle and London: University of Washington Press, 1977. This volume details how the Guggenheim family used its great wealth to advance commercial aviation, and the weather support that it needed, in the United States.

Martin, Geoffrey J. *Ellsworth Huntington: His Life and Thought*. Hamden, Conn.: Archon Books, 1973. This book about the geographer Huntington describes his influence on climatology in the early 20th century.

Millikan, Robert A. "Some Scientific Aspects of the Meteorological Work of the United States Army." *Monthly Weather Review* 47 (1919): 210–215. Available online. URL: http://docs.lib.noaa.gov/rescue/mwr/047/mwr-047-04-0210.pdf. Accessed March 15, 2006. The military's use of meteorology during World War I is reviewed.

Nebeker, Frederik. *Calculating the Weather: Meteorology in the 20th Century.* San Diego, Calif.: Academic Press, 1995. Nebeker presents the development of calculating devices and methods introduced to advance meteorology to a full-fledged science.

Shaw, Sir Napier. "The Outlook of Meteorological Science." *Monthly Weather Review* 48 (1920): 34–37. Available online. URL: http://docs.lib.noaa.gov/rescue/mwr/048/mwr-048-01-0034.pdf. Accessed March 15, 2006. The article contains excerpts from a speech made by Shaw on the future of the meteorological discipline.

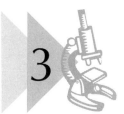

3

1921–1930: **Theory Development and Application**

In the immediate postwar years, European nations recognized the importance of strong military and civilian aviation programs and devoted financial resources to supporting meteorological services. As Bergen School techniques continued to evolve, European weather services adopted their air mass analysis and frontal theories. Not confined to forecasting the weather, these university-trained meteorologists also conducted extensive atmospheric research.

The United States was not so forward-looking. Demobilization at the close of the Great War left the nation with only a skeleton crew of trained meteorologists—most of whom had no college education at all—to provide general and aviation weather services to the entire country. The budget for the U.S. Weather Bureau was so small (two cents per capita) that the department struggled to keep up with competing demands from agriculture, industry, and aviation. With no dedicated meteorology programs in U.S. colleges and universities, the Weather Bureau was forced to train everyone on the job. Weak in mathematics and physics—the very subjects required for understanding Bergen School methods—and demoralized by being the lowest-paid scientists on the government payroll, bureau forecasters were extremely reluctant to adopt Bjerknes's methods.

The advances in mathematical meteorology did not eliminate work on statistical methods of forecasting based on "cycles"—many of which had absolutely no relation to factors related to the weather. Claims for these methods put meteorologists on the defensive as they attempted to dissuade the general population from listening to people they considered to be cranks and quacks. While some people still promoted cycles, the British meteorologist Lewis Fry Richardson was proposing that future weather could be forecast by finding a mathematical solution to the so-called primitive equations—the equations of motion, the hydrodynamic equation, and the thermodynamic equation. Although this first-ever attempt at numerical weather prediction was a huge failure, it did lead meteorologists to consider alternate ways of calculating the weather.

In the 1920s the rapid advances in meteorological theory that had been under development since the first decade of the century continued. Climatology remained a descriptive science but was increasingly used in the service of weather forecasting.

Cyclic Weather

Despite the Bergen School's influence on meteorological practice, some scholars persisted in their pursuit of elusive *weather cycles*. Weather cycles—recurring patterns of temperature, rainfall, or pressure—have been sought since ancient times, primarily as a way of predicting the weather months, if not years, in advance. The peak in studies of these *periodicities* occurred in the 1920s; research rapidly dropped off in the 1930s as new calculation techniques cast doubt on cycles. Most work on weather cycles was carried out by astronomers, economists, sociologists, and geologists—not by meteorologists.

In his four-volume *Manual of Meteorology* first published in 1925, the distinguished British meteorologist Sir Napier Shaw (1854–1945) summarized the state of meteorological knowledge in the first quarter of the 20th century. He listed more than 200 weather cycles ranging

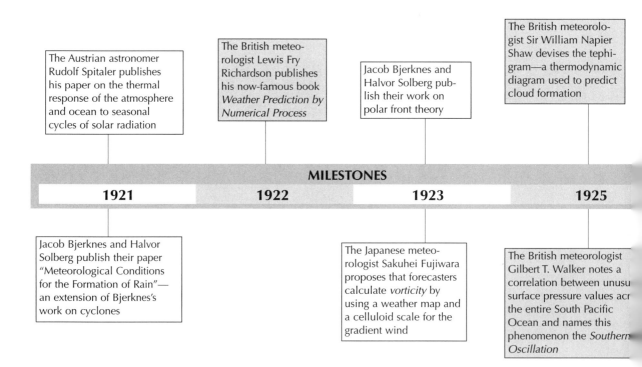

The Austrian astronomer Rudolf Spitaler publishes his paper on the thermal response of the atmosphere and ocean to seasonal cycles of solar radiation

The British meteorologist Lewis Fry Richardson publishes his now-famous book *Weather Prediction by Numerical Process*

Jacob Bjerknes and Halvor Solberg publish their work on polar front theory

The British meteorologist Sir William Napier Shaw devises the tephigram—a thermodynamic diagram used to predict cloud formation

MILESTONES

1921   **1922**   **1923**   **1925**

Jacob Bjerknes and Halvor Solberg publish their paper "Meteorological Conditions for the Formation of Rain"—an extension of Bjerknes's work on cyclones

The Japanese meteorologist Sakuhei Fujiwara proposes that forecasters calculate *vorticity* by using a weather map and a celluloid scale for the gradient wind

The British meteorologist Gilbert T. Walker notes a correlation between unusu surface pressure values acr the entire South Pacific Ocean and names this phenomenon the *Southern Oscillation*

from one to 260 years that had been discovered by analyzing observational data. At the time, weather cycles were considered legitimate forecasting tools because of two prevailing views of the atmosphere. One held that the atmosphere was "plastic" and the other that it was "resilient."

An external force could deform a plastic atmosphere—much as pressing clay deforms it. The atmosphere would remain in its new "deformed" state until influenced by another external force. In contrast, removing the external force from the resilient atmosphere restored it to its original state. Periodicities represented external forces that occurred repeatedly. Regular external influences included planetary and solar orbits and solar radiation. Volcanic eruptions spewing tons of debris into the air were an irregular influence. By determining a pattern in these events, scientists could predict corresponding weather patterns months or years in advance—an important advantage for those potentially affected by drought or flooding.

Until the end of the 19th century, scientists determined periodicities by graphing the relevant variables against time. The analyst looked for peaks and valleys in the data—extremes in weather conditions—and calculated the time between them. The graphical method was not very

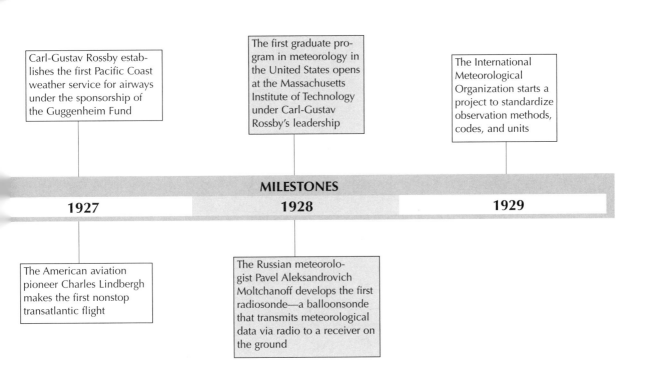

Carl-Gustav Rossby establishes the first Pacific Coast weather service for airways under the sponsorship of the Guggenheim Fund

The first graduate program in meteorology in the United States opens at the Massachusetts Institute of Technology under Carl-Gustav Rossby's leadership

The International Meteorological Organization starts a project to standardize observation methods, codes, and units

MILESTONES

1927   **1928**   **1929**

The American aviation pioneer Charles Lindbergh makes the first nonstop transatlantic flight

The Russian meteorologist Pavel Aleksandrovich Moltchanoff develops the first radiosonde—a balloonsonde that transmits meteorological data via radio to a receiver on the ground

accurate. If the analyst wanted to find a periodicity, he could usually modify the criteria just enough to create a pattern. As meteorology became more mathematical, some scientists used probability and statistics to analyze data more rigorously.

One of these men was the English physicist and applied mathematician Arthur Schuster (1851–1934), who introduced his mathematical theory of periodicity in 1897. He assigned a number indicating the correlation between a weather phenomenon and its occurrence. This calculation was extremely time consuming. To speed up the process, mathematicians created graphs and tables for meteorologists to use.

Some periodicities, for example, *diurnal* and seasonal changes, were trivial. Others were not. Two of the most prominent periodicities were the "11-year period" and the Brückner cycle. The "11-year period" was related to the length of time between successive *sunspot* minima or maxima. This period also corresponded to the frequency of South Indian Ocean cyclones, maxima and minima in rainfall and air pressure, famines in India, auroras, and "depression in trade"—a business event. Typically in what was called the sunspot period, when the number of sunspots was high, Earth experienced higher temperatures; when the sunspot number was low, temperatures were lower.

The cyclic nature of the number of sunspots has been linked to weather cycles, but the subject is still very controversial.

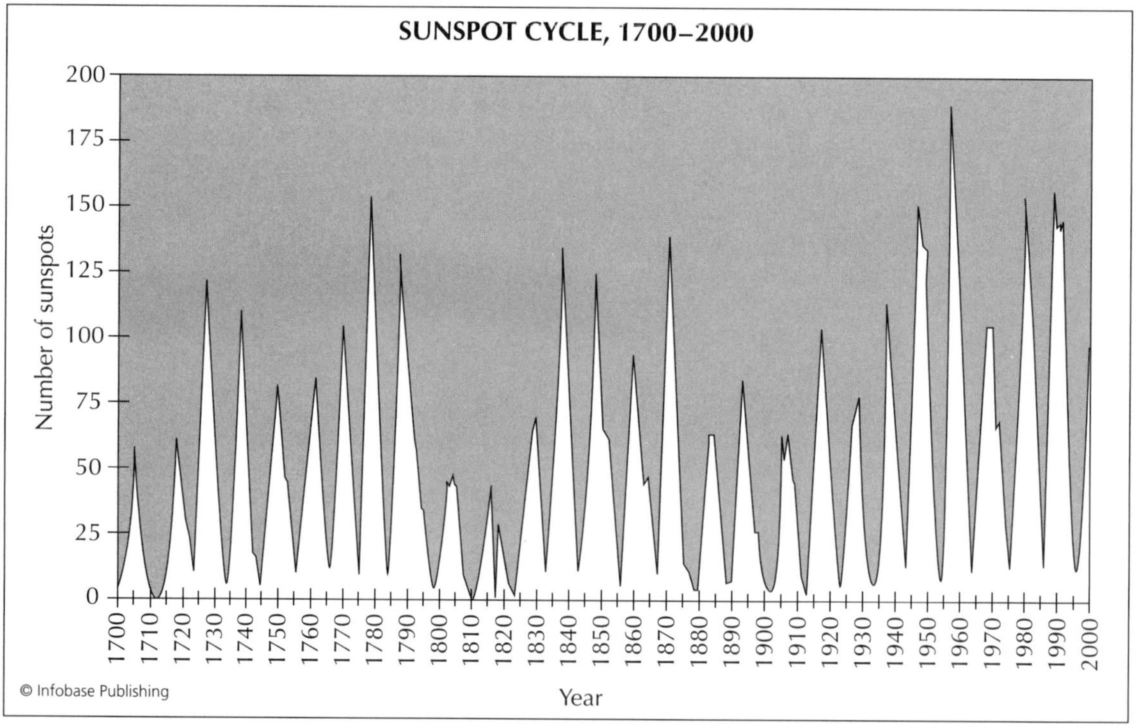

SUNSPOT CYCLE, 1700–2000

© Infobase Publishing

The Brückner cycle was 35 years long. The German geographer and meteorologist Eduard Brückner (1862–1927) discovered this cycle while trying to correlate the changes in water level for the Caspian, Black, and Baltic Seas with variations in alpine glaciers due to alternating warm/dry and cool/wet periods. This same periodicity appeared throughout the Northern Hemisphere and sometimes in the Southern Hemisphere. The Brückner cycle appeared to be solidly predictive years in advance. It was not. The cycle failed under rigorous mathematical scrutiny.

Despite "feeling" that weather periodicities were "real," meteorologists abandoned them. Their predictive abilities were virtually zero and they all lacked a physical mechanism that could explain the weather event. That did not stop others from continuing to tie weather events to unrelated, nonmeteorological occurrences. The prominent American economist Henry Ludwell Moore (1869–1958) published a 29-page article in *The Quarterly Journal of Economics* titled "The Origin of the Eight-Year Generating Cycle" that argued that eight-year crop cycles in England, France, and the United States and eight-year meteorological cycles could all be tied back to Venus's motion with respect to Earth and the Sun. Into the 1930s, statisticians claimed that Moon and star positions influenced Earth's weather. Meteorologists had already moved on to newer ideas. The lure of equations to define atmospheric motion was much stronger and attracting the best meteorological minds.

Richardson's Weather Factory

English meteorologist Lewis Fry Richardson (1881–1953) was determined to find a mathematical solution for weather forecasting. The son of prosperous Quaker (Society of Friends) parents, Richardson was the superintendent of Scotland's Eskdalemuir Observatory when World War I erupted. A pacifist, Richardson sought a leave of absence to provide noncombat assistance to the war effort. Denied leave, he resigned in 1916, volunteered to be a driver with the Friends' Ambulance Unit, and was assigned to a French infantry unit on the western front. Between ambulance runs, he decided to calculate temperature, pressure, and winds six hours into the future by using the basic equations of physics.

With paper and pencil, and an "office" of hay piled in a drafty barn-like building, Richardson spent every spare moment making his calculations with a slide rule and logarithm table. He was not actually making a forecast. He was making a hindcast. Richardson already knew the result because he was working with surface- and upper-air data from May 20, 1910, that had been analyzed by Vilhelm Bjerknes. Richardson wanted to see whether he could get the same answer by using equations.

The "primitive equations" that must be solved to predict the future state of the atmosphere cannot be solved analytically by using calculus;

they must be solved by using numerical analysis techniques. The mathematical problem is broken down into small increments, an initial solution is proposed, and then the mathematician solving the problem gradually narrows down the answer to a solution. It is unbelievably tedious without an electronic computer.

Because the observations were not evenly spaced across France, Richardson placed a "checkerboard" with squares 124 miles (200 km) on a side over the plotted map. Then he divided the upper atmosphere into five layers with the surfaces at sea level and then aloft at 1.2, 2.5, 4.3, and 7.5 miles (2, 4, 7, and 12 km) above sea level. There were 25 squares. He computed wind velocity in the black ones, and tem-

Lewis Fry Richardson divided western Europe into checkerboard-like squares and then computed wind velocity for the dark squares and atmospheric pressure for the light squares.

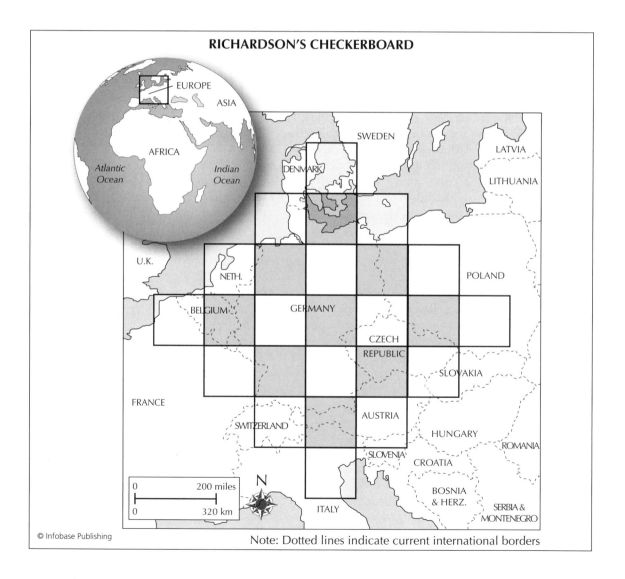

RICHARDSON'S CHECKERBOARD

Note: Dotted lines indicate current international borders

perature or pressure in the white ones so the values would be evenly spaced. Richardson then calculated the pressure change in two of the squares (doing so far all 25 would have taken too long). After six weeks of calculations, Richardson forecasted a pressure increase of 145 millibars (mb). The actual increase was almost zero! Richardson's attempt had failed.

Most people do not tell others when they fail. Richardson wrote about his experiment in his 1922 book *Weather Prediction by Numerical Process.* The book was filled with difficult mathematics but in the conclusion Richardson wrote about his vision for a "forecast factory" where 64,000 "human computers" calculated the weather for their assigned part of Earth. He thought they might be able to keep up with the weather as it occurred if they worked 24 hours a day but would never be able to forecast in advance. Actually, not even 64,000 people would have been enough to keep up with the weather—200,000 is closer to being correct.

While Richardson's method was not the least bit practical in 1922 and attracted little attention from his fellow meteorologists, in the late 1940s the creation of electronic digital computers provided meteorologists with the opportunity to explore numerical weather prediction. They looked at Richardson's book for ideas on how to avoid the problems he had encountered. Lewis Fry Richardson was on the right path—he was just 25 years ahead of a way to bring it to life. In the meantime, work on a practical forecasting method was continuing at the Bergen School.

Creating the Polar Front

With the 1919 summer forecasting season successfully concluded, the Norwegian government authorized Vilhelm Bjerknes and his assistants to issue storm warnings for the west coast during the fall and winter. The Bergen School members would be able to track and analyze the more intense fall and winter cyclones. They could also expand their research into cyclone structure. The decision by many European nations to take up to four observations daily in support of aviation also provided extra data needed by the Bergen team. Since a cyclone could significantly strengthen within 24 hours, the extra data would allow them to determine conditions favoring intensification and connect changing weather conditions to intensification stages.

During the summer, the Swedish meteorologist Halvor Solberg noticed that new cyclones appeared to "wave off" the remnants of the *squall* surface trailing the cyclone. This phenomenon was more pronounced in the stronger fall season cyclones. The cyclones lined up and linked—the Bergen meteorologists called them "families"—as they moved across the Norwegian coastline. British meteorologists had also noticed that "unsettled weather" developed from these mature squall

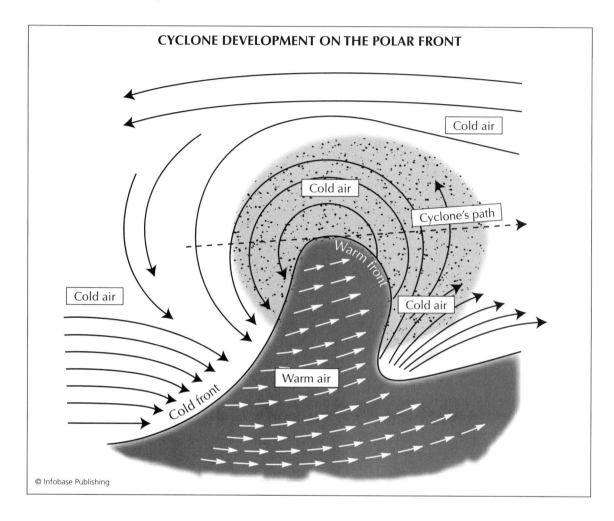

CYCLONE DEVELOPMENT ON THE POLAR FRONT

Cold air

Cold air

Cyclone's path

Cold air

Warm front

Cold air

Cold front

Warm air

© Infobase Publishing

According to the Bergen School, skirmishes of cold and warm air across the boundary between two air masses (the polar front) led to the creation of a cyclone. (Based on figure 21, Robert Marc Friedman, *Appropriating the Weather*)

surfaces but failed to make the connection between the new disturbance and the original cyclone.

Late in 1919, while arguing about the day's weather patterns, the Bergen meteorologists first considered the idea that a single line they termed a "battle line" might stretch around the Northern Hemisphere. Vilhelm Bjerknes had first used the analogy to battle in mid-1919. Returning to that theme in his 1920 paper "The Structure of the Atmosphere When Rain Is Falling," Bjerknes wrote, "We have before us a struggle between a warm and cold air current." Cold polar air was the "enemy" and it was launching attacks against warmer equatorial air. The warmer air launched counterattacks. The line of battle separating these two warring masses of warm and cold air was the *polar front*. As cold and warm air masses launched raids across the front, they created a cyclone on the front.

The polar front was both a three-dimensional surface that represented the boundary between cold and warm air masses that stretched into the upper atmosphere and a two-dimensional line that appeared on surface maps where the boundary intersected the ground. They renamed the steering surface the *warm front* (drawn in red) because warm air was "attacking" cold air. They renamed the squall surface the *cold front* (drawn in blue) because cold air was attacking the warm air.

The Bergen meteorologists needed additional data to determine whether their proposed polar front actually existed in nature. Weather maps in the 1920s covered relatively small areas, not entire hemispheres.

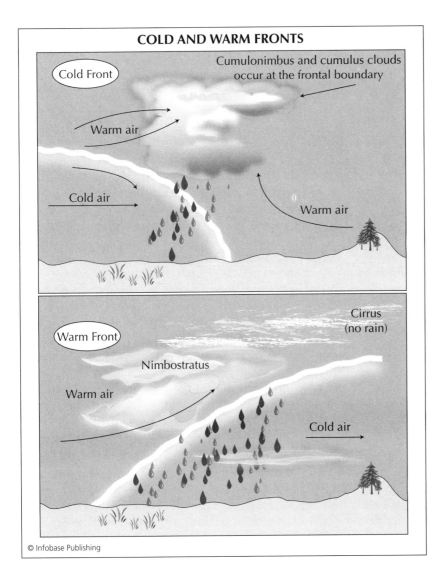

COLD AND WARM FRONTS

Cold Front

Cumulonimbus and cumulus clouds occur at the frontal boundary

Warm air

Cold air

Warm air

Warm Front

Cirrus (no rain)

Nimbostratus

Warm air

Cold air

© Infobase Publishing

Cold and warm fronts exhibit distinct cloud patterns and weather phenomena that Bergen School members used to forecast the weather.

The addition of ship observations taken in the North Atlantic aided German and Danish meteorologists in constructing a series of weather maps that extended beyond land-based areas. Solberg reanalyzed the data and created a map that stretched from North America to northern Europe. Even these additional ship data were not sufficient to define the polar front. When Jacob Bjerknes presented the polar front theory at professional meetings, his audience walked away unconvinced. The Bergen meteorologists needed to "sell" the polar front to their skeptical colleagues.

Vilhelm Bjerknes's sales pitch promoted the polar front concept as being important to both accurate weather prediction and meteorological theory. The challenge for meteorologists was to predict "weather," and for most people "weather" was synonymous with "bad weather"—precipitation, wind, and/or cold temperatures. Knowing the polar front's location would give forecasters a place to look for weather-producing perturbations. Unfortunately, there were insufficient weather observation stations providing the necessary data. In order for meteorologists to locate the cyclones on the polar front—the "pearls on a string"—the international meteorology community would need to collect and share additional data.

The Bergen meteorologists also needed to determine how cyclones were born, lived, and died, and the weather associated with each stage. Once again, they were aided by more and better weather observations. Instead of just reporting "clouds," weather observers began noting cloud type, altitude, and order of appearance. Careful sky observations allowed Jacob Bjerknes to discern the atmospheric changes that occur within a cyclone's life. Knowledge of these orderly changes improved forecasts as meteorologists analyzed weather data from their own and upstream stations. They could advise their customers about expected winds, temperatures, and precipitation over the upcoming 24 hours.

Not all weather events could be blamed on polar front perturbations. After years of study, the Bergen meteorologists proposed the air mass analysis concept. An air mass is a large body of air (greater than 621 miles [1,000 km] in diameter) that has remained in one place long enough to take on the characteristics of the underlying land. For example, an air mass that has stagnated over northern Canada or Siberia for several weeks in the winter will be cold and dry. As the cold, dry air mass moves from its origin, the lowest layers of the air mass are modified and become warmer and more humid. The upper levels change little because they are not in contact with Earth's surface. For this reason meteorologists use the upper-level characteristics to determine the air mass's origin. By tracking air masses, weather forecasts can determine when the weather will change. When an air mass "collides" with another air mass, weather occurs at their boundary (air mass discontinuity). For example, if cold, dry air collides with warm,

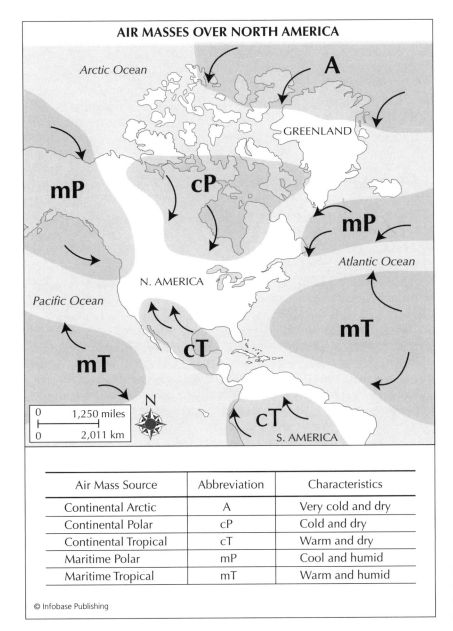

AIR MASSES OVER NORTH AMERICA

Arctic Ocean

A

GREENLAND

mP

cP

mP

Atlantic Ocean

N. AMERICA

Pacific Ocean

mT

cT

mT

| 0 | 1,250 miles |
| 0 | 2,011 km |

N

cT

S. AMERICA

Air Mass Source	Abbreviation	Characteristics
Continental Arctic	A	Very cold and dry
Continental Polar	cP	Cold and dry
Continental Tropical	cT	Warm and dry
Maritime Polar	mP	Cool and humid
Maritime Tropical	mT	Warm and humid

© Infobase Publishing

Different types of continent-sized masses of air contribute to weather patterns over North America.

moist air, the heavier, denser cold air pushes the warmer air up. As the warm air rises and cools, the moisture condenses and forms clouds, and rain may result.

Other meteorologists had recognized the existence of air masses, but the Bergen School meteorologists were the first to connect them to weather prediction. After several years of work to perfect the method, by the mid-1920s air mass analysis became their standard forecasting technique. From Norway, it would spread around the world.

Forecasting Lags Theory

The Bergen meteorologists had developed new and useful techniques for tying observational data to better forecasts, but not everyone adopted polar front theory and air mass analysis methods. The news about air mass analysis did spread quickly around the world, in no small part as a result of the efforts of Bergen School members who traveled to Russia, the United States, and throughout Europe to teach their techniques to every meteorologist who would listen.

The American meteorologist and long-range-prediction expert Jerome Namias (1910–97) told the popular meteorological magazine *Weatherwise* in a 1984 interview, "The concepts made order out of the apparent chaos of weather. They provided a practical method that the forecaster could use in his daily work." They also upset the accepted forecasting practices in some national weather services, some of which refused to adopt air mass analysis until the 1930s.

The British did not put fronts on their weather maps until 1933. The U.S. Weather Bureau did not introduce air mass analysis techniques until it was forced to do so in 1934. The ditching of the airship USS *Akron* into the frothy waves of the Atlantic Ocean during a major unforecasted storm in 1932 led to a review of Weather Bureau practices by the Science Advisory Board (SAB) in 1933. The SAB, whose

Forecasters at the U.S. Weather Bureau Forecast Office, Washington, D.C., 1926 (NOAA Photo Library)

Shortcuts to Prediction

Efforts to develop "calculating aids" to convert between different temperature scales, correct barometer readings, and compute atmospheric variables that could not be measured directly had started in the 19th century. By the beginning of the 20th century, calculating aids were being used to compute wind values from pressure data and rates of pressure change from temperature and pressure, and to make specialized calculations better solved with graphs.

Stations reported temperatures in Celsius, Fahrenheit, and Reamur depending on their location, and the temperatures had to be converted to Celsius before making calculations. Barometers often registered different air pressure values depending on air temperature, so there were special calculations to account for temperature before computing the final pressure. Humidity had to be calculated from simultaneous measurement of *wet-* and *dry-bulb temperatures.* For all of these calculations, meteorologists created special tables that allowed users to connect their observation data with the desired value.

The Bjerkneses created a graphical calculus that allowed meteorologists to determine the vertical velocity of air strictly on the basis of the horizontal wind speed and direction over a large area. The Japanese meteorologist Sakuhei Fujiwara (1884–1950), chief of the Central Meteorological Bureau in Tokyo, Japan, created a special scale printed on clear plastic film that helped to compute the *vorticity* (amount of spin) in the atmosphere. The gradient wind scale was placed over the weather map and adjusted until the distance between the lines on the scale matched the distance between the lines of equal pressure on the map. The vorticity could then be read off the overlay.

In 1925, the British meteorologist Shaw created a thermodynamic diagram called the tephigram (TEFF-ee-grahm). Weather balloons carrying instruments aloft recorded pressure, temperature, and humidity values. The data were plotted on the tephigram, and the resulting lines could be interpreted to determine cloud heights, relative amounts of moisture in the atmosphere, maximum and minimum temperatures for the next day, and time when fog and low clouds would clear.

Other calculating aids called *nomograms* allowed forecasters to enter two or three different variables, connect the values with a ruler, and find the desired variable. For instance, one nomogram required the meteorologist to know the pressure gradient (difference in pressure), the latitude of the observation, and the radius of curvature of the closest constant pressure line. Once the values were entered into the nomogram, the forecaster could find the velocity of the wind resulting from the pressure gradient. In this way, meteorologists could determine the wind velocity in areas lacking observation stations. Nomograms were popular with forecasters because they saved time and increased accuracy but are less common now because of the use of computer-generated forecasts. Meteorologists still use thermodynamic diagrams like the tephigram to identify the altitude and vertical extent of cloud formations.

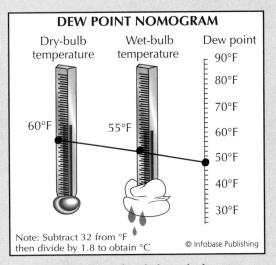

DEW POINT NOMOGRAM

Note: Subtract 32 from °F then divide by 1.8 to obtain °C

© Infobase Publishing

Nomograms, like this one for calculating the dew point temperature, provide convenient methods for calculating desired meteorological information.

creation was ordered by President Franklin D. Roosevelt (1882–1945), was composed of some of the most respected scientists in the United States, including Robert A. Millikan and the Massachusetts Institute of Technology (MIT) president, Karl T. Compton (1887–1954). In late 1933, they recommended that the Weather Bureau adopt Bergen School methods. By the next year, the Weather Bureau had hired three young meteorologists with Ph.D.'s to train its forecasters. Fronts appeared on U.S. weather maps for the first time in 1936.

Although the use of Bergen School techniques could have led to improved forecasts, often they did not. Air mass analysis and frontal analysis depend on accurate data from closely spaced weather stations. Furthermore, forecasters had to be extremely skilled in their use of data to locate frontal and air mass boundaries. When stations are hundreds of miles apart, as they are in the United States, the location of the front may be difficult to find. Without the benefit of satellite pictures and radar, forecaster judgment was the most critical component of successful predictions.

Keeping Planes in the Air

Commercial aviation expanded at a much faster rate than national weather services were equipped to support it during the 1920s. The rapid acceptance of air mass and frontal analysis throughout Europe attests to the desire to provide better flight forecasts for passenger and airmail flights. Upper-air data collection by means of pilot balloons, balloon-sondes, and aircraft assisted in this effort.

Weather services in the United States remained at a disadvantage compared to those in European nations. With a limited budget and a lot of territory, aviation forecasts were completely inadequate before 1926. The Weather Bureau could not afford to increase the number of daily observations or the number of surface and upper-air observation stations. To keep track of critical flight weather conditions, the bureau estimated that it needed one station every 250 miles (402 km) along air routes, known as airways. These special weather offices, called airways stations, needed to be connected by telephone so that information could be called ahead to the next station if conditions were deteriorating when a pilot was in the air. Existing telegraph circuits, operated by Western Union, needed to be adjusted to carry the weather observations at 6 A.M. instead of during the 90-minute time block reserved for weather reports after 8 A.M.

As all of these technical and financial problems stacked up, the Weather Bureau drew withering criticism for contributing to a number of high-profile aviation accidents because pilots had not received adequate warning of adverse flying conditions. On May 20, 1926, Congress passed the Air Commerce Act, requiring the Weather Bureau to provide aviation forecasts necessary for flight safety. A

An airmail pilot prepares to take off. (NOAA)

funding bill passed in July provided the bureau with the financial resources necessary to assign experienced meteorologists to all major landing fields and establish 22 pilot balloon stations on the New York–San Francisco flight route. Additional funding in 1928 added 18 more meteorologists to extend the airways system for another 6,000 miles (9,656 km).

By 1928, airways stations were relocated from city offices to major airports. They also operated 24 hours a day instead of between 8 A.M. and 11 P.M.—a huge advantage for pilots who wanted to get an early start in the morning. With the financial backing of the Guggenheim Fund for Meteorology, the bureau added a new Pacific airway extending from San Diego, California, to Seattle, Washington. The fund also enabled the Weather Bureau to send one of its meteorologists to Bergen to study the effects of fog, haze, and thunderstorms on flight safety.

Aviation forecasting got a significant boost when teletype replaced telegraph in 1928. By 1930, the Weather Bureau had extended teletype

Criticism of aviation forecasts made by the world-famous pilot Charles Lindbergh helped lead to the passage of the Air Commerce Act of 1926.
(Library of Congress)

over 8,000 miles (12,875 km) of airways, connecting all airways stations with the Washington, D.C., headquarters and allowing for complete data exchange. Equipment breakdowns were common in the early years of the program and meteorologists relied on telephone and telegraph in emergencies. Major airport control towers used radio to communicate weather information to pilots while they were still airborne, transmitting updated weather observations every 30 minutes.

As meteorologists and pilots gained more experience with weather conditions that could adversely affect flight safety, additional data and rules were introduced. In 1929, the Weather Bureau added ceiling and visibility information to observations. Beginning in 1930, the Department of Commerce restricted pilots from taking off when the ceiling was lower than 500 feet (152 m). Weather observers were then under pressure to determine the exact ceiling, particularly when the ceiling was close to the limit. Sometimes pilots would fly anyway and sometimes they would be upset because they could not fly. The Weather Bureau always made the point that they just made the observations; they did not tell pilots whether to fly or not—a situation that prevails to this day.

As the decade closed, meteorologists were providing considerably more information via teletype. In addition to normal temperature, pressure, and wind measurements, hourly teletype reports, dubbed aviation hourlies, provided information on how snow, rain, thunderstorms, or gusty squalls were affecting landing field conditions. Aviation forecasting showed tremendous improvement throughout the 1920s, only to be curtailed by fiscal problems caused by the Great Depression of the early 1930s.

Building a Profession

Physicists, chemists, and biologists were all considered professional scientists at the turn of the 20th century. Meteorologists and climatologists still labored on the fringes of the scientific community. Germany, Austria, and Scandinavia all had academic programs in meteorology and climatology with professors trained in those areas as the 20th century started, but the entire British Commonwealth did not have its first meteorological professorship until the appointment of Sir William Napier Shaw to Imperial College, London, in 1920. The United States was even further behind. All of the training for Weather Bureau meteorologists was conducted "in-house," and graduate training was provided by Weather Bureau employees at Columbian University (now called George Washington University) in Washington, D.C.

By the end of the decade, there were still no meteorology departments in American colleges and universities. The U.S. Navy Aerological Service, desperate for graduate-level trained meteorologists to provide weather support for its rapidly expanding aviation program, arranged with the Aeronautical Engineering Department at MIT to create a meteorology program. Financed with a $34,000 grant from the Guggenheim Fund, the navy provided the first six students in the summer of 1928. The program's director was the Swedish meteorologist and former Bergen School member Carl-Gustav Rossby, who had coordinated the Pacific Coast model airway.

With his Bergen School background, Rossby quickly focused the MIT program on atmospheric research and applications that continued the use of polar front and air mass analysis investigations. Faculty members and graduate students, who would eventually include some of the biggest names in U.S. meteorology, conducted empirical studies of air mass characteristics as well as physical and mathematical treatments of atmospheric phenomena. Within a few years, the California Institute of Technology and New York University both established meteorology programs within their aeronautics programs. By the 1930s, meteorology had finally attained academic respectability in the United States.

Scientist of the Decade: Jacob Bjerknes (1897–1977)

The Norwegian meteorologist Jacob Aall Bonnevie Bjerknes was born November 2, 1897, to modern meteorology's founder, Vilhelm Bjerknes, and Honoria Sophia Bonnevie in Stockholm, Sweden, where his father was a physics professor. Young Jacob was surrounded by an academic family—his aunt Kristine Bonnevie (1872–1948) was a zoologist and the first female professor in Norway.

Moving with his family to Christiania (later Oslo), where his father had been offered a professorship, Jacob remained in Norway to finish school when his father accepted the directorship of the Leipzig Geophysical Institute in Germany. When Vilhelm needed Jacob's assistance in Leipzig, the 19-year-old took over research on wind field convergence and published his first scientific paper ("Über die Fortbewegung der Konvergenz—und Divergenzlinienjust" [On the movement of convergence and divergence lines]) before turning 20. Returning to Norway in 1917, Jacob took over forecasting for the west coast of Norway as he continued his research on convergence lines. Within the year, he published yet another important paper, this one on cyclone structure ("On the structure of moving cyclones"). His research on cyclone structure and development, and associated weather phenomena, continued throughout the 1920s and culminated in yet another often-cited paper ("Life cycle of cyclones and the polar front theory of atmospheric circulation"), which

detailed his ideas on air mass and frontal analysis. Before he was 30, Jacob Bjerknes had an international reputation in meteorology.

Leaving forecasting behind in the 1930s, Bjerknes became a meteorology professor at the Bergen Museum so that he could concentrate on theoretical research. He was in demand as a speaker and traveled throughout Europe and to the United States lecturing on frontal dynamics. One of these lecture trips to the United States took place in July 1939. Bjerknes, his wife, Hedvig, and their children had anticipated being in the United States for eight months. Less than two months after their arrival, World War II started. Shortly thereafter, Germany invaded Norway. The Bjerknes family remained in the United States and became U.S. citizens.

Unable to return to Norway, Bjerknes needed a job in the United States. At the same time, the United States military needed thousands of trained meteorologists. Bjerknes was asked to lead a meteorological training program for the U.S. Air Force at the University of California, Los Angeles. Taking over the meteorological section of the physics department, he oversaw the training of servicemen and served as a consultant to the U.S. Army Air Corps.

After the war ended, the meteorology section expanded to become the meteorology department. With Bjerknes in charge, the department

As formal meteorological education became more available, national and international professional organizations became more organized. The International Meteorological Organization (IMO) had been active on an informal basis since 1880. By the end of the 1920s, the IMO was working to standardize the meteorological codes that were used to record and transmit observations via telegraph and teletype, the units of measure for observational elements such as pressure and temperature, and the symbols that were used on weather maps. Code standardization was a major achievement in promoting

grew very rapidly and was soon a leading international center for teaching and research in the atmospheric sciences. He continued his work on cyclones and expanded it to include research on the general circulation of the atmosphere. By the end of the 1950s, Bjerknes decided to turn his attention to a relatively new field: air-sea interaction.

In his first investigations, Bjerknes examined the changes in sea surface temperature in the North Atlantic Ocean and determined that the sea surface temperature was tied to the strength of the westerly wind. In years when the westerlies were particularly strong, the water south of Iceland and Greenland would be exceptionally cold and the Gulf Stream outside the Grand Banks would be much warmer. After publishing several studies on the Atlantic, Bjerknes turned his attention to the Pacific.

The eastern Pacific Ocean, particularly the coastal waters near Peru, was known to be subject to an oceanographic phenomenon called El Niño—the change in sea surface temperature from cool to warm every two to five years. The nutrient-rich cool waters supported a strong fisheries industry, but when they were replaced by sterile warm waters the industry temporarily collapsed. Bjerknes turned his attention to determining the mechanism behind El Niño. He discovered that the local change in sea surface temperature was actually part of a change that affected the ocean and atmosphere of the entire equatorial Pacific.

Bjerknes also discovered that a very large expanse of the middle and eastern equatorial waters of the Pacific became almost 3.6°F (2°C) warmer than normal. This was a major difference. The increased temperature added heat and moisture to the atmosphere, significantly increasing rainfall on nearby land. The effects extended well beyond a few ocean islands. El Niño increased westerly winds in the northern Pacific that affected weather all across North America and into Europe.

As he continued his investigations of the connections between El Niño and global weather, Bjerknes discovered a tie between El Niño and the Southern Oscillation. The Southern Oscillation, originally discovered in the 1920s by the British scientist Sir Gilbert Walker (1868–1958), is a pulse of atmospheric pressure that occurs irregularly between the Pacific and Indian Oceans. Because of Bjerknes's investigations, meteorologists and oceanographers have a basic understanding of how the Southern Oscillation and El Niño processes affect the equatorial Pacific. Furthermore, the theoretical ideas behind these processes continue to affect the development of climate change theories.

Although he made lasting contributions in many areas of meteorology, perhaps Jacob Bjerknes made his most enduring, and lifesaving, contribution with his frontal cyclone model and its associated forecasting techniques. He continued his work as an active scientist until his death at age 77 on July 7, 1975.

the international nature of a discipline that does not respect political boundaries.

In the United States, the American Meteorological Society (AMS) had been established in 1920; it was open to both professional meteorologists and amateurs, who included anyone who had an interest in the weather. The mission of the AMS was to promote research and instruction in meteorology. Shortly after its founding, members formed 11 committees to address two areas: "the advancement and diffusion" of meteorology and "the development of numerous applications of meteorology to human affairs." As reported in the first issue of its official publication, the *Bulletin of the American Meteorological Society*, committee chairmen actively sought to put both meteorology and climatology on a firm scientific footing through education from primary through graduate school.

Compared to more established scientific communities, meteorology and climatology remained small in the early 20th century. Basic and applied research on the atmosphere took on increased importance as the general public became more aware of commercial and military aviation, automobile travel, commercial shipping, agriculture, and the health-related effects of the weather. As the 1920s ended, research on atmospheric problems was about to pay off.

Further Reading

Ashford, Oliver M. *Prophet—or Professor? The Life and Work of Lewis Fry Richardson.* Bristol, England, and Boston: A. Hilger, 1985. This biography of Richardson describes his departure from meteorology and concentration on peace studies in his later years.

Bjerknes, J., and Halvor Solberg. "Life Cycle of Cyclones and the Polar Front Theory of Atmospheric Circulation." *Geofysiske publikasjoner* 3(1) (1922): 1–8. This paper explains how cyclones develop, mature, and die.

Bjerknes, J. "Atmospheric Teleconnections from the Equatorial Pacific." *Monthly Weather Review* 97(3) (1969): 163–172. Bjerknes describes how weather phenomena in the Pacific influence weather all over the world.

Bjerknes, Vilhelm. "The Structure of the Atmosphere When Rain Is Falling." *Quarterly Journal of the Royal Meteorological Society* 46 (1920): 119–130. Vilhelm Bjerknes describes the precipitation associated with lines of convergence.

Eliassen, Arnt. "Jacob Aall Bonnevie Bjerknes." In *Biographical Memoirs.* Vol. 68. Washington, D.C.: National Academy of Sciences, 1996. Eliassen provides a short biography of Jacob Bjerknes.

Hayes, Brian. "The Weatherman." *American Scientist* 89 (2001): 10–14. In this short article, Lewis Fry Richardson's attempt at numerical weather prediction is detailed.

Hughes, Patrick. *A Century of the Weather Service: A History of the Birth and Growth of the National Weather Service, 1870–1970.* New York and London: Gordon and Breach, 1970. In this nicely illustrated volume the National Weather Service meteorologist Hughes discusses changes in the nation's meteorological support from its days as part of the Army Signal Corps.

Moore, Henry Ludwell. "The Origin of the Eight-Year Generating Cycle." *Quarterly Journal of Economics* 36(1) (1921): 1–29. Moore argues that the position of Venus influences the weather and economics.

Richardson, Lewis Fry. *Weather Prediction by Numerical Process.* New York: Dover, 1965. This reprint of Richardson's 1922 book explains his experiment in forecasting the weather by using equations that define atmospheric processes.

Shaw, Sir Napier. *Manual of Meteorology.* 4 vols. Cambridge: Cambridge University Press, 1926. Shaw summarizes the history and current state of the meteorology discipline.

Whitnah, Donald A. *A History of the United States Weather Bureau.* Urbana: University of Illinois Press, 1961. The historian Whitnah provides a detailed look at the evolution of the Weather Bureau and the way it supported pilots in the early days of aviation.

4

1931–1940:
Big Steps in Cloud Physics and Climatology

The decade just prior to the start of World War II saw major advances in two different areas of atmospheric studies, climatology and cloud physics. As in the previous three decades, European scientists led in theoretical and empirical atmospheric research. In the United States, weather forecasting continued to be meteorology's focus. Although the U.S. Weather Bureau finally introduced Bergen School methods into its forecasting repertoire, consistent underfunding precluded an active research program. As the decade closed, once again a nonmeteorologist raised the possibility that industrialization was changing the global climate—a little-understood scientific issue that would become more controversial throughout the century.

Climate: The Köppen Scheme

Wladimir Köppen's climate classification scheme, in various stages of development from its beginning in 1884, arrived at its ultimate form during the 1930s with the writing and publication of the five-volume *Handbuch der Klimatologie* (Handbook of climatology). Edited by Köppen with his colleague Rudolph Geiger, these volumes presented the results of the latest climatological studies from around the world. They also presented the final version of Köppen's personal classification scheme.

Climate classification schemes generally fall into one of two categories: genetic or empirical.

- Genetic classification schemes group climate types on the basis of their cause. That is, the scheme develops by asking the question, Why do climate types occur where they do? The cause may be a geographic feature (for example, the presence or absence of a large body of water), the result of net solar energy at the surface (that is, the difference between the amount of radiation that arrives at a given location and the amount that leaves), or the result of air mass analysis (that is, the presence of a predominant air mass type).

- Empirical classification schemes analyze the presence of readily identifiable characteristics that represent the effect of climate. For example, the types and quantities of vegetation that occur or the extent to which exposed bedrock erodes is an indication of persistent weather patterns. The Köppen scheme was a combination of both genetic and empirical schemes.

Because of his early academic training in botany, Köppen was first drawn to the relationship between plant growth and temperature. Using vegetation as a naturally occurring indicator of climate regimes, he combined information on the geographical extent of vegetation types, average monthly temperature and precipitation, and average annual temperature to define climate boundaries. He assigned letters, (*A*) tropical rainy; (*B*) dry; (*C*) midlatitude rainy, mild winter; (*D*) midlatitude rainy, cold winter; and (*E*) polar, to designate the five main climate groups found around the world. All of the groups except (*B*), which was controlled by the amount

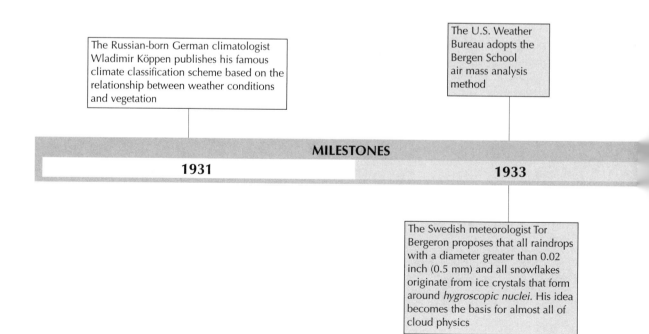

The Russian-born German climatologist Wladimir Köppen publishes his famous climate classification scheme based on the relationship between weather conditions and vegetation

The U.S. Weather Bureau adopts the Bergen School air mass analysis method

MILESTONES

1931

1933

The Swedish meteorologist Tor Bergeron proposes that all raindrops with a diameter greater than 0.02 inch (0.5 mm) and all snowflakes originate from ice crystals that form around *hygroscopic nuclei.* His idea becomes the basis for almost all of cloud physics

of available moisture, were controlled by air temperature. Köppen then assigned a second letter to subdivide these groups further into climate types. For example, in group A, the temperature of the coolest month is greater than or equal to 64.4°F (18°C). If an area within (A) receives at least 2.36 inches (60 mm) of rain in its driest month (subgroup [f]), it is designated as *Af*. If significant variations appeared within the climate types, a third letter refined the definition.

The Köppen scheme had its detractors. Climate is the principal determining factor in the types of plants and animals that find their ecological niche in a particular area, but it is not the only one. For example, soil types and their ability to hold moisture are also important to vegetation. Plants may be able to survive in areas where there is limited rainfall as long as the soil holds the moisture that does fall. The same plants may also be found where there is more rainfall and the soil has good drainage characteristics that prevent the root system from drowning. In either case, the ability of plants to survive also directly affects the ability of animals dependent upon them for food or shelter to survive. Köppen's scheme did not take weather extremes into account. The average conditions may be punctuated by periods of extreme drought or cold that are

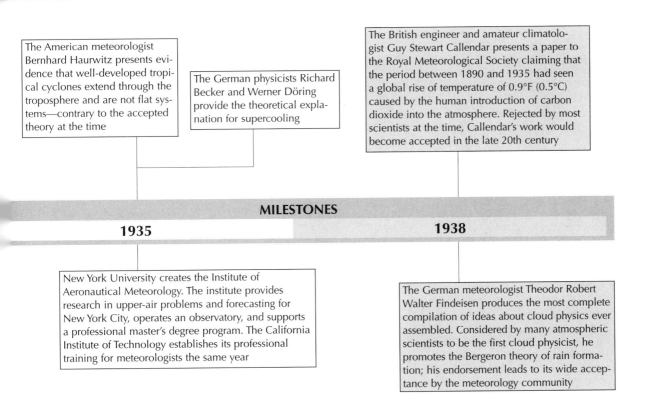

The American meteorologist Bernhard Haurwitz presents evidence that well-developed tropical cyclones extend through the troposphere and are not flat systems—contrary to the accepted theory at the time

The German physicists Richard Becker and Werner Döring provide the theoretical explanation for supercooling

The British engineer and amateur climatologist Guy Stewart Callendar presents a paper to the Royal Meteorological Society claiming that the period between 1890 and 1935 had seen a global rise of temperature of 0.9°F (0.5°C) caused by the human introduction of carbon dioxide into the atmosphere. Rejected by most scientists at the time, Callendar's work would become accepted in the late 20th century

MILESTONES

1935

1938

New York University creates the Institute of Aeronautical Meteorology. The institute provides research in upper-air problems and forecasting for New York City, operates an observatory, and supports a professional master's degree program. The California Institute of Technology establishes its professional training for meteorologists the same year

The German meteorologist Theodor Robert Walter Findeisen produces the most complete compilation of ideas about cloud physics ever assembled. Considered by many atmospheric scientists to be the first cloud physicist, he promotes the Bergeron theory of rain formation; his endorsement leads to its wide acceptance by the meteorology community

just as critical to vegetation as the averages. Wind is another weather factor that affects vegetation and yet does not appear in the classification scheme. Critics also pointed out that vegetation boundaries and climate boundaries are not always the same, making it difficult to determine where one climate type stops and another begins. Despite these issues, currently used climate schemes are almost exclusively revisions of the original Köppen classification scheme.

During this same period, the American geographer C. W. Thornthwaite (1899–1963) expanded on the relationship between vegetation and climate by analyzing the movement of moisture from the soil into the atmosphere by either direct evaporation or passage through the leaves of plants (*evapotranspiration*) and by measures of soil moisture. His work extended the applicability of climatological studies to agriculture but was so complex that it did not gain the wide following of the Köppen scheme.

The most commonly used Köppen-based scheme in use today is that presented by the biogeographers Glenn T. Trewatha (1896–1984) and Lyle H. Horn (1924–89) in their book *An Introduction to Climate*.

This illustration of Köppen's climate classification scheme shows the primary climate types found around the world.

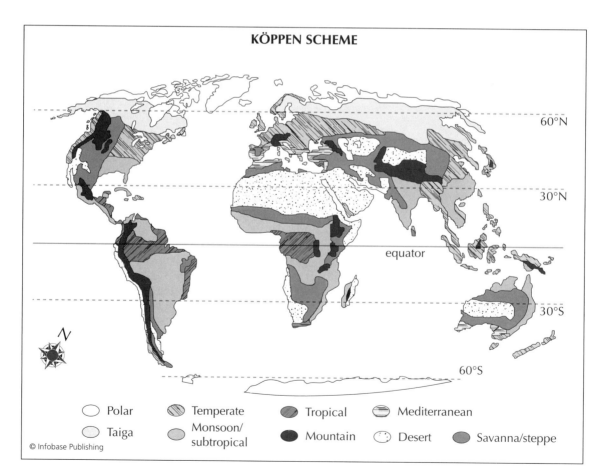

KÖPPEN SCHEME

60°N
30°N
equator
30°S
60°S

Polar   Temperate   Tropical   Mediterranean
Taiga   Monsoon/subtropical   Mountain   Desert   Savanna/steppe

© Infobase Publishing

They use seven climate groups, instead of Köppen's five. Added were a boreal climate group—a climate zone that only exists in the Northern Hemisphere between 50°N or 55°N and 65°N latitude—and a highland climate group, which acknowledges that higher-elevation areas in different climate groups have more in common with each other than with the lowland areas surrounding them. This climate scheme appears in the accompanying illustration.

Although climatology studies were only tangentially related to weather prediction, the knowledge of climate types was used by architects and engineers to build the most suitable, safe structures for a geographical area; by agricultural experts to recommend appropriate crops for the greatest farming success; and by water managers to make informed decisions about proper water systems to support resident populations in their areas. Regional climate studies were also important to countries such as Great Britain, France, Germany, and the United States that controlled far-flung territories as they considered the health implications of climate for their transplanted citizens sent to oversee their empires. As important as the climate classifications of the 1930s were, they would neither meet the needs of the worldwide military effort expended during World War II nor address the issue of climate change. Those developments would await the transformation of climatology from a geographical endeavor to a physical science undertaking.

Norwegian Methods in the United States

The U.S. Weather Bureau had proved extremely resistant to the Bergen School methods that swept European meteorology in the 1920s. The Swedish meteorologist Carl-Gustav Rossby, trained at the Bergen School and awarded a Scandinavian-American Association fellowship, had arrived in the United States in 1926 to work at the bureau. Rossby tried to convince bureau forecasters to use the frontal and air mass analysis techniques developed by the Bjerkneses; he so irritated bureau leaders with his ideas that they forced him to leave.

There is little doubt that some members of the bureau were just too attached to their ways of operating to see the usefulness of Bergen School methods. Others were probably resentful that Europeans were trying to tell them how to make forecasts in the United States. The primary reason that the Bergen School methods were not immediately accepted was the significant difficulty of applying polar front and air mass analysis methods in a country as large as the United States. Unlike densely populated European countries, the United States had large expanses where no one lived. West of the Mississippi River, large tracts of land contained only a few hardy farmers, ranchers, or lumbermen. Even if they could have reported weather data back to Weather Bureau headquarters for inclusion in the daily map analysis and subsequent forecast for the next day, the observations would have been so widely spaced as to be meaningless.

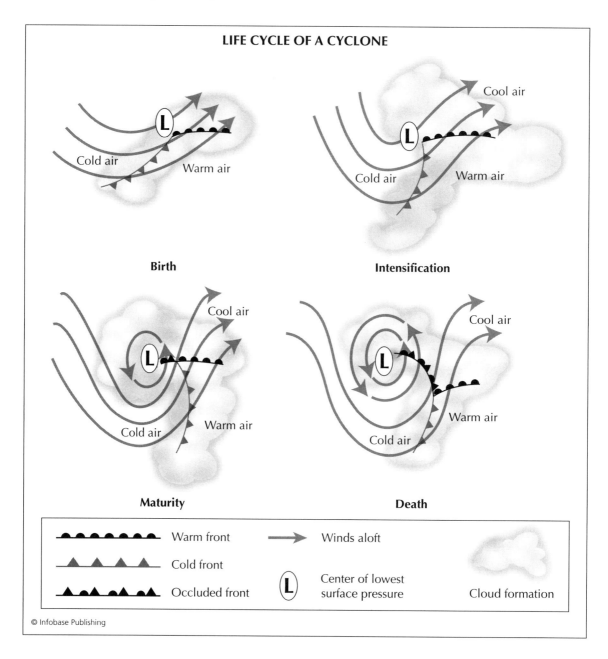

LIFE CYCLE OF A CYCLONE

Cool air

Cold air

Warm air

Birth

Cool air

Cold air

Warm air

Intensification

Cool air

Cold air

Warm air

Maturity

Cool air

Cold air

Warm air

Death

●●●● Warm front

▲▲▲ Cold front

▲●▲● Occluded front

→ Winds aloft

(L) Center of lowest surface pressure

Cloud formation

© Infobase Publishing

In this series of drawings, the cyclone starts to develop, intensifies, begins to form a closed circulation aloft, and then, with its energy cut off, slowly dies.

Recall that Jacob Bjerknes was able to create his theory of frontal development in large part because of the closely spaced observation stations hugging the Norwegian coastline. He was able to get additional observations from the United Kingdom, Germany, and Denmark—observations that taken together gave him a good "snapshot" of the current weather conditions. The cost of implementing such an observational network in the United States would have been huge. The cash-strapped Weather Bureau had neither the money nor the manpower to establish and maintain the number of surface and upper-air stations that would allow full implementation of Norwegian methods. Weather Bureau forecasters continued to cling to their old, ineffective techniques.

This condition continued into the early 1930s when two embarrassing incidents served as the catalyst for change at the Weather Bureau. The first came about when the American Society of Civil Engineers (ASCE) launched a formal complaint against the Weather Bureau in 1932. The civil engineers, involved in building roads, bridges, and dams, were clamoring for special climatological data in a format that would be easiest for them to use. The Weather Bureau was happy to provide the information to the engineers—just as it was happy to provide the data to anyone who asked—but they did not have the time or the manpower to arrange the data in a way that was most useful to the engineers. After several months of investigations, the ASCE published a nasty condemnation of the Weather Bureau, accusing its leaders of incompetence and proclaiming its methods to be unscientific and behind the times. In making recommendations for "fixing" the Weather Bureau, the engineers suggested that the chief of the Weather Bureau be replaced by a stronger leader—one who *was not* a meteorologist.

The second occurred on April 4, 1933, when the navy airship USS *Akron* (ZRS-4) crashed into a raging sea off the coast of New England during a violent storm. All 73 people aboard died, including the navy's chief of the Bureau of Aeronautics. During the investigation that followed, the navy charged that the Weather Bureau's bad forecast had endangered *Akron*. Had the pilots received an accurate weather forecast, *Akron* would not have taken off and its passengers and flight crew would not have perished. So serious was this accident that President Franklin D. Roosevelt, who had been inaugurated for his first term in office just a few weeks before, took a personal interest in addressing the problem. What could be done about the Weather Bureau?

President Roosevelt ultimately appointed a group of distinguished scientists to form the Science Advisory Board (SAB). The SAB, which was affiliated with the premier scientific organization in the country—the National Academy of Sciences in Washington, D.C.—was directed to examine the complaints of the engineers, analyze the results of the *Akron* investigation, and make a formal recommendation for improvements. Within a few months, the board issued its first report. The board found that the engineers' complaints were without merit. The Weather Bureau was not obligated to make their work easy for them. However, the *Akron* crash might have been prevented if they had used the Norwegian techniques. To aid the Weather Bureau in the introduction of those techniques, it needed to establish additional surface and upper-air stations that would take observations four times instead of just two a day. Since

The U.S. Navy's airship Akron
(U.S. Navy)

no Weather Bureau meteorologists had training in the Norwegian techniques, the board recommended the bureau hire people who had. Three such meteorologists had just received their Ph.D. from MIT's graduate program, and they were hired to train a small group of people at the Weather Bureau who would, in turn, train others.

By 1935, training was under way. Norwegian methods were not fully integrated into the Weather Bureau's operations until the end of the decade. The bureau's training program would later extend to the military services and have a major impact on the provision of weather services during World War II.

The additional upper-air observations made possible by improved radiosonde equipment in the thirties provided an extensive collection of new data for both meteorologists and climatologists. The meteorologists could use the data as they came in, but climatologists needed to wait until the data could be compiled and averaged with previously collected pressure, temperature, and wind velocities for higher altitudes. Compiling climatological data was a tedious, labor-intensive job, and the U.S. Weather Bureau rarely had sufficient employees to process all of the data arriving monthly in their climatology division. The fiscal cutbacks of the Great Depression had significantly reduced the bureau's manning levels, leaving it unable to cope with current data, much less the accumulated backlog. This situation could have worsened as the Depression dragged on. Instead, the bureau was able to make use of recently enacted federal programs that were putting unemployed people to work. Out of the depths of the Great Depression, the Weather Bureau was able to process valuable climatological data with the help of a recently acquired technology: card-reading machines.

Little Radios and Big Balloons

Upper-air observations were critical to the successful application of Bergen School methods. Although tethered balloons and kites, free-floating balloons, and aircraft had been used to gather upper-air data since the early 20th century, they were all deficient in some way. Tethered balloons and kites could not fly as high in the atmosphere, and free-floating balloons carrying equipment packets had to be found before the data could be retrieved. (One set of instruments launched from Harvard's Blue Hill Meteorological Observatory landed in a pasture in Amherst, Massachusetts, only to be eaten by a hungry cow—both cow and sensors suffered fatal injuries.) Data from aircraft were used when available, but aircraft could not be launched in stormy weather, just when meteorologists most needed the data. The solution would be to create a free-floating balloon that could carry not only meteorological equipment but also a radio transmitter that would send the data back to a receiving station as they were measured.

In 1930, the Russian meteorologist Pavel A. Moltchanoff was the first to sound (gather information from) the stratosphere successfully with his 4.4-lb. (2-kg) "radio-meteograph" launched from Sloutsh in the Soviet Union (USSR). His instrument was called a "Kammgerat" because of the comblike metal strips that created the signal. On December 30, 1931, in Helsinki, the Finnish mathematician-turned-meteorological-instrument-inventor Vilho Väisälä (1889–1969) launched his new radiosonde for the first time. Unlike the Kammgerat, Väisälä's radiosonde transmitted data by using radio signals. The original prototypes only measured temperature, but by 1935 his radio-

sondes could also measure pressure and humidity. Used routinely at Finnish meteorological observation stations, they quickly spread throughout the Scandinavian countries. Väisälä started shipping radiosondes to the United States in 1936.

While this work was taking place in Finland, meteorologists and technicians at Harvard's Blue Hill Observatory were developing their own radiosonde. They had two main problems: making the equipment small enough and finding balloons with enough lift to get the equipment off the ground. The scientists attacked both problems simultaneously. The first successful launch of a two-pound (890-g) radio transmitter carried by three small hydrogen-filled balloons took place in October 1935. They were able to receive a signal from a height of 43,000 feet (13.1 km) and a distance of 60 miles (96 km). To launch both the radio transmitter and the meteorological instruments, the team needed larger balloons. Working with balloon manufacturers, they were able to obtain balloons with diameters of four to six feet (1.2–1.8 m) that could carry loads weighing between 1.8 and 2.6 lb. (800–1,200 g). Their first successful radio-meteograph launch took place on December 23, 1935. The four balloons carrying the instruments took 1.5 hours to reach an altitude of approximately 52,500 ft. (16 km).

By the end of the decade, improvements in radiosonde construction had made them much easier to use and they were widely utilized at upper-air stations around the world. The data obtained from these devices were critical for meteorologists who were providing aviation forecasts and would play an even larger role in flight safety during World War II.

Ice Crystals and Raindrops

By the end of the 19th century, scientists had a good grasp of how clouds formed. As a parcel of moist air rose, it expanded as a result of reduced air pressure and cooled, and the moisture condensed. The resulting water vapor droplets—with 4×10^{-9}-inch (10^{-9}-m) diameters—formed a cloud as

The Great Depression Aids Climatological Study

The U.S. Weather Bureau had made a good start on compiling useful climatological data from stations throughout the United States through the end of World War I. Funding reductions in the immediate postwar years, however, led to the steady deterioration of climatological services after 1920. Lack of station reports was not the problem. Over 5,000 unpaid cooperative observers submitted reports of maximum and minimum temperatures, air pressure readings, and precipitation totals by mail to bureau headquarters at the end of each month. These reports, combined with the detailed observational data collected by official Weather Bureau "first-order" stations, provided valuable information about weather conditions. But, data must be analyzed to be useful, and all too often the data arrived only to be filed away. Observational data that could have yielded scientific insight into climatological problems languished in boxes. The relatively limited averages available in weekly crop bulletins, pamphlets issued by state agricultural offices, or supplements to the Weather Bureau's in-house journal *Monthly Weather Review* were not sufficiently detailed for wide-scale use by land planners, water resource managers, building construction companies, aircraft designers, or public health workers. The bureau was sitting on a wealth of information and had no way to make it usable by the broader public.

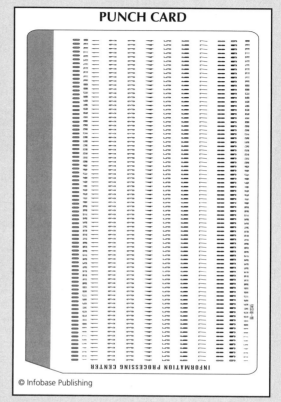

PUNCH CARD

INFORMATION PROCESSING CENTER

© Infobase Publishing

The U.S. Weather Bureau used punch cards like this one to record thousands of climatology records during the Great Depression.

long as there was something to which they could cling. For example, sea salt particles, fine dust, or sulfuric acid droplets formed from combustion were all suitable *hygroscopic* particles because they were from 100 to 1,000 times larger than the individual water molecules. These droplets needed to have diameters of at least 0.04 inch (1 mm) to fall from the cloud. That meant a million of the tiny droplets had to join before they could fall out. Once one droplet attached itself to a *cloud condensation nucleus* then others would join it. It would take days or weeks for the droplet to grow large enough to fall. Clearly that was not the way rain formed.

There were two possible ways that a drop could form faster. The first way, called drop capture, assumed that larger drops fall faster than

By the 1920s, Great Britain, France, Germany, and the Netherlands had all adopted systems using punched cards to record and sort climatological data. At the time, that was really the only way to process large volumes of information. The bureau did not take steps to add punch card machines and techniques to its central office in Washington, D.C., until the Science Advisory Board recommended that it do so in 1934. Punch card machines would not solve the data analysis problem if there were no people to punch the data onto the cards. Since all government agencies had seen severe budget reductions as a result of the Great Depression, the Weather Bureau had fewer people available to compile climatological records than in the past.

That problem was solved later the same year when the Civil Works Administration—a depression-era government agency that created work for over 4 million unemployed men and women desperate for jobs—appropriated enough money to the Weather Bureau to allow the hiring of several hundred people to tackle the backlog. As a result, more than 50 years of marine-weather data (ship and coastal reports), eight years of fire-weather service data, and 35 years of routine climatological data were punched onto cards and sorted by machine. In 1936, the Weather Bureau received another appropriation of funds from the Works Progress Administration (WPA)—another make-work organization—that it used to compile, record, and sort both surface and upper-air (radiosonde and pilot balloon) observational data from approximately 400 airways stations.

Once the data were on cards, they could be analyzed and examined for possible occurrences of weather cycles that could be used in long-range weather forecasting. As the drought that produced the dust bowl continued, the ability to predict the return of a wetter pattern accurately was foremost in the minds of the Weather Bureau's meteorologists. In addition to U.S. data, observational records from other countries were entered onto hemispheric weather maps, which were reanalyzed to show large-scale weather patterns that influenced U.S. weather. Furthermore, the compilation of marine observations provided information for tropical areas that were the spawning grounds for tropical storms and *hurricanes*.

Although depression-era cuts had significantly hampered the Weather Bureau's research work and forecasting program, later infusions of funds to pay clerical workers to record the data on punch cards would provide a valuable boost to its climatological services. These studies would be critical for advances in atmospheric knowledge in the years ahead.

smaller ones and thus pick up all the water molecules they hit along the way. The second way, due to vapor transfer, had been proposed by Alfred Wegener in 1911 as part of his hoarfrost studies. According to Wegener, if ice crystals were present in the vicinity of supercooled water, molecules from the latter would attach to the crystals until they became heavy enough to fall out. Although Wegener's frost work attracted some attention, its extension to precipitation processes was ignored at the time.

One meteorologist who remembered reading Wegener's work and subsequently applied it to the precipitation problem was Tor Bergeron. Bergeron had been fascinated by clouds since he was a boy. In February 1922, just before leaving Sweden to work with the Bjerkneses at the Bergen School, he had spent some time at a mountain resort. While walking along a path cut through the woods, he made an interesting observation. If the air temperature was below freezing, then the supercooled stratus layer that shrouded the hillside did not fill the path—a clear tunnel appeared between the trees, as shown in the illustration below. When the temperature was above freezing, the "tunnel" disappeared as the cloud reached the ground and became fog. Mulling this over, Bergeron thought that when the temperature was below freezing, the ice on the tree limbs pulled the moisture away from the cloud, thus dissipating the cloud below the

BERGERON'S WALK IN THE FOREST

Stratus

t < 32°F (0°C)

Stratus

t > 32°F (0°C)

Tor Bergeron noticed that supercooled stratus did not drop to the ground and become fog when the temperature was below freezing but did become fog when the temperature rose above freezing.

tree line. When there was no ice on the trees, then the cloud filled in the space to the ground.

Once Bergeron was in Bergen he was too busy making weather forecasts to spend much time on ice crystals and clouds, but whenever he had a chance he collected additional information about how ice crystals affected the development of both cumuliform (puffy) and stratiform (flat) clouds. In his doctoral dissertation, completed in 1927, Bergeron gave a detailed account of his ideas on ice crystals. Published in the Norwegian journal *Geofysiske publikasjoner* (Geophysics publications) in 1928 as "Die dreidimensional verknüpfende Wetteranalyse" (Three-dimensionally combining synoptic analysis), his dissertation received limited attention in the United States and England.

Selected to represent Norway at the International Union of Geodesy and Geophysics (IUGG) meeting in Lisbon, Portugal, in 1933, Bergeron used this opportunity to present a detailed paper on his ice crystal theory. He argued that if there are a few ice crystals within a supercooled cloud, the ice crystals will grow at the expense of the supercooled droplets until they are large enough to fall out. Bergeron thought, therefore, that all raindrops originally started as snowflakes (even in the summer) and either continued as snow if the air temperature were cold all the way to the surface or fell as rain if the air temperature were above freezing.

Bergeron's paper attracted much attention in the meteorological world, becoming the topic of discussion at major meetings and much cited in the academic literature. Although there was widespread agreement from those who worked in the middle and high latitudes, those working in tropical areas vehemently disagreed that ice crystals were a major factor in rain production. The German meteorologist Walter Findeisen (1909–45) provided additional measurements and calculations in the late 1930s that helped to refine Bergeron's theory. The ice crystal process of rain formation became known as the Bergeron-Findeisen process and was widely (although not completely) accepted as the dominant precipitation mechanism until additional observations from aviators flying in tropical regions during World War II caused meteorologists to look for another method for forming raindrops.

Even at their tops, tropical clouds are "warm"—their temperatures are higher than 23°F (-5°C). Bergeron's vapor transfer mechanism, which worked so well in supercooled clouds, did not work in these warm clouds. Since aviators reported heavy rains in the Tropics, there had to be another raindrop-creating mechanism at work. Meteorologists began considering other possible causes of drop development, which led to the discovery of the collision-coalescence mechanism of rain creation. In collision-coalescence, approximately one in 1 million droplets has to be larger than the others in its vicinity. This difference allows it to fall faster and pick up additional droplets as it falls. The larger it grows, the faster it falls, and the more droplets it

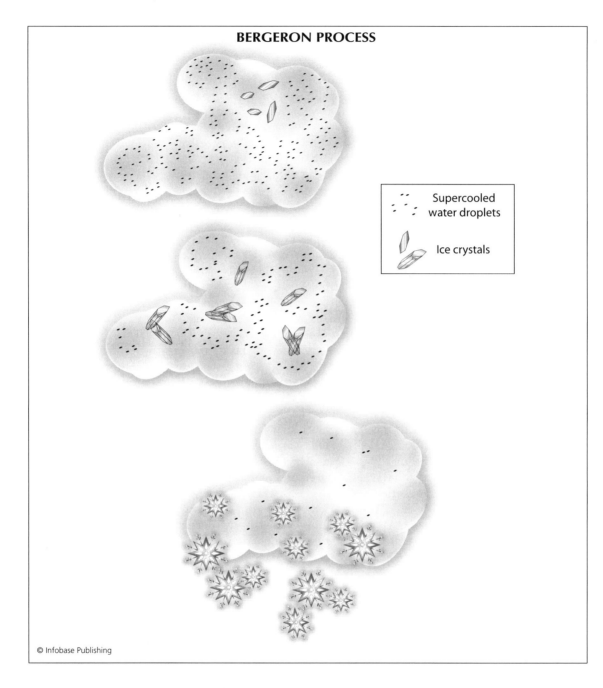

BERGERON PROCESS

Supercooled
water droplets

Ice crystals

© Infobase Publishing

The Bergeron process shows how a few ice crystals in minute supercooled water droplets can lead to snow formation.

accumulates. Once large enough, the droplet falls out. Later work in cloud physics confirmed that midlatitude summer rains are formed by collision-coalescence, while winter rains are formed by the Bergeron-Findeisen mechanism. Research on precipitation mechanisms would continue throughout the 20th century as weather radar became more sophisticated, providing detailed information on cloud formation and behavior. Additional research focused on air pollutants and the influence of *topography* on cloud physics.

Carbon Dioxide and Global Warming

Research on climate change had languished since the early 20th century work of Svante Arrhenius and others who were trying to determine what factors might lead to atmospheric warming or cooling. Climatologists remained convinced that although climate had indeed been different in the past, it was not currently changing. Meteorologists were still focused on producing the next day's forecast. Research on the connection between atmospheric carbon dioxide (CO_2) and atmospheric warming again fell to a man working outside the atmospheric sciences.

In a paper published in 1938 ("The Artificial Production of Carbon Dioxide and Its Influence on Climate"), Guy Stewart Callendar (1897–1964) argued that the naturally occurring chemical composition of the atmosphere was being altered by the more than 9,000 tons (8.1 million kilograms) of CO_2 that was being pumped into the atmosphere every minute by carbon-based fuels (oil, gas, coal, wood) burned to run industry, provide electricity and heat, and power automobiles. He calculated that over 75 percent of the CO_2 that had been spewed into the atmosphere since 1888 had remained in the atmosphere—a total of 100 bil-

Guy Stewart Callendar argued that industrialization, represented here by the fossil fuel–burning Monroe Power Plant, had raised the carbon dioxide level in the atmosphere. (EPA)

lion tons (9×10^{13} kg). As a result, the CO_2 level in the atmosphere had increased by 6 percent since the turn of the century.

According to Callendar, this additional CO_2 could be responsible for 60 percent of the 0.9°F (0.5°C) increase in temperature over the previous century. He calculated that if the carbon dioxide level doubled (from 0.032 percent to 0.064 percent of the atmosphere), the increase in reradiation of heat back to Earth would result in a 3.6°F (2°C) temperature increase. In 1938, a warmer atmosphere still did not appear to be a bad trade-off for increased CO_2 emissions. Not only would the air temperature be warmer, thus reducing heating requirements in winter, but the increased CO_2 would help plants to grow larger, allow increased cultivation in northern latitudes, and prevent glaciers from growing. As the world's population increased, all of these potential outcomes seemed to be good.

Meteorologists, however, did not accept Callendar's conclusions. Some disputed his data, arguing that CO_2 measurements from the late 19th century were not very accurate. In addition to data issues, the British meteorologist Sir George Clark Simpson (1878–1965) viewed the global warming scenario as being too simplistic because Callendar had neglected to consider how air moved throughout the entire atmosphere. Callendar, however, defended the reliability of CO_2 levels measured since the beginning of the 20th century and argued that global warming was a very real phenomenon.

In his 1939 article "The Composition of the Atmosphere through the Ages," Callendar further argued that people were conducting a "grand experiment" by pumping CO_2 into the air and interfering with the natural order of things. His analysis of weather data indicated that the years between 1934 and 1938 were the warmest of the previous 180 years. He concluded that the rise in temperature was directly related to industrial emissions of CO_2. (The relatively small number of automobiles—compared to today's levels—made their contribution negligible.) Meteorologists and climatologists continued to discount Callendar's work.

It would not be until 1941, when Callendar published yet another article in the *Quarterly Journal of the Royal Meteorological Society* ("Infra-Red Absorption by Carbon Dioxide, with Special Reference to Atmospheric Radiation") showing that the absorption of heat by CO_2 in the atmosphere was far more important than anyone had realized, that meteorologists finally took notice. Once they understood that warming could not be attributed exclusively to water vapor, the increase in CO_2 level took on special importance.

Interest in global warming—and cooling—would wax and wane during the next two decades. As data started to accumulate and computer models became more accurate, debates over global warming and climate change would become more intense in the latter part of the century.

Guy Stewart Callendar (1897–1964): Amateur Meteorologist

The British steam engineer Guy Stewart Callendar was the second son of the steam expert Hugh Longbourne Callendar (1863–1930)—a fellow of the Royal Society of London. The younger Callendar followed in his father's footsteps, working as his assistant in conducting research on steam at high pressures and temperatures at the Royal College of Science. After his father's death in 1930, Callendar took over his father's classes and continued his own steam research experiments with funding provided by turbine manufacturers.

Although he was a steam engine specialist, Callendar devoted a considerable amount of free time to his hobby, meteorology. Intrigued by news reports that air temperature had been rising since the 19th century, he decided to examine observational records closely and make his own computations. Others had made similar attempts, but the records were scattered and in disarray, frustrating most would-be researchers. Not only did Callendar confirm that there had indeed been a temperature increase, he revived the early 20th-century theory that the cause was increased atmospheric CO_2. Publishing his first paper in 1938, and despite opposition from the meteorological community, Callendar continued to examine the connections among industrialization, CO_2 emissions, and atmospheric warming. His articles appeared in such distinguished scientific journals as the *Quarterly Journal of the Royal Meteorological Society, Tellus,* and *Weather* through the early 1960s. As additional data confirmed his original conclusions, Callendar's work was seen with new appreciation by the meteorological community. He was honored as a fellow of the Royal Meteorological Society and served as member of its leadership council.

Callendar died suddenly in 1964, living long enough to see his work validated by the broader scientific community, but not long enough to witness the dramatic increase in climate research that occurred at the end of the 20th century. In retrospect, Guy Stewart Callendar can be seen to have played a critical role in focusing attention on the effects of the industrial age on Earth's climate.

In the first half of the 20th century, research on climate changed seemed to fall to those who were not climatologists: physical chemist Svante Arrhenius at the turn of the century, mathematician Milutin Milankovitch in the second decade, and then, starting in the late thirties, steam engineer Guy Stewart Callendar boldly proclaimed that rising carbon dioxide levels have been and will continue to raise global temperatures. While climatologists such as Wladimir Köppen concerned themselves with defining climate, these non-climatologists were postulating reasons behind climate—a very different undertaking. Their work more closely paralleled that of the meteorologists of this era who were struggling to understand the physical mechanisms underlying atmospheric phenomena such as rain, hail, and frost in hopes of aiding the production of more accurate forecasts. This new generation of meteorologists, unlike those of thirty years before, was more likely to have been attracted by weather phenomena at a young age and have been focused on atmospheric studies in graduate school. Norwegian Tor Bergeron was one of those meteorologists.

Scientist of the Decade: Tor Bergeron (1891–1977)

The Swedish meteorologist Tor Bergeron was born in England but returned to Sweden with his family at a young age and completed his education there. After receiving his bachelor's degree in 1916, he joined the Swedish Weather Service as a meteorologist. Bergeron spent much of 1919 helping Vilhelm and Jacob Bjerknes establish their new forecasting program in Bergen. Jacob Bjerknes had introduced his now-famous cyclone model in 1918, but the complete model—including the life cycle of the cyclone—depended upon Bergeron's critical discovery of the occlusion process that leads to the decline and death of the cyclone. (In simplest terms, an occluded front develops when a cyclone's cold and warm fronts collide.) Bergeron returned to Bergen in 1922, becoming a full-time meteorologist with the Bergen Weather Service, a position he held intermittently until 1929. From 1923 to 1925 he worked at the Leipzig Geophysical Institute collaborating with German researchers who were applying Bergen School analysis techniques to European weather scenarios.

Returning to Norway, Bergeron completed his doctoral dissertation in 1928. Although earlier scientists, including Jacob Bjerknes, had addressed the concept of air masses and their relationship to weather patterns, Bergeron was the first to make a systematic study of air masses, the source regions that spawned them, and ways they were subsequently transformed as they moved. Classifying air masses as equatorial, tropical, polar, and arctic, he looked for the characteristics (for example, temperature and humidity) that tended to be retained by the air masses even after they left their source regions. These characteristics—termed quasi-conservative—allowed meteorologists to track air masses around the world. Bergeron described how the transformation of the air masses resulted in distinctive cloud and precipitation patterns, temperature structure, visibility, and turbulence activity. So consistent were these results that they could be used to draw conclusions about the vertical distribution of air temperature and to predict the weather. In the decade before the widespread use of radiosonde equipment, Bergeron's methods were especially important for aviation forecasting. This work explained the existence of the world's main frontal development zones and provided a method for determining the location of cold and warm frontal zones on weather maps.

After completing his doctorate, Bergeron became a "missionary" for the Bergen School. He spent a year at the Meteorological Office on the island of Malta in the Mediterranean, providing training on Bergen School methods. He then spent two years in Moscow lecturing on air mass analysis and polar front theory. There Bergeron met his future wife, Vera Romanovskaja, who served as one of his student assistants. Bergeron greatly influenced the development of Soviet meteorology. His lectures provided the basis for a textbook used for training Russian meteorology students in meteorological theory.

Returning to Norway, Bergeron served as a meteorologist and consultant to the Norwegian Meteorological Institute in Oslo. While there, he worked on the famous ice crystal precipitation paper described earlier. Moving to Sweden in 1936, he became a senior meteorologist and later the scientific chief of the Swedish Meteorological and Hydrological Institute. He held the latter position until 1947, when he became professor of synoptic meteorology at the University of Uppsala, a position he held until his retirement in 1961. At Uppsala he started Project Pluvius—an effort to determine the influence of topography on the distribution of precipitation. Realizing that rain gauge networks were generally too coarse to determine the geographic variation of rainfall accurately, he directed the installation of 350 rain gauges in a 154-square-mile (400-km^2) region surrounding Uppsala. The resulting data showed that even modest 131- to 230-foot (40- to 70-m) hills could induce a surprising increase in rainfall as a result of *orographic* lifting. Bergeron continued his research even after retirement, and several of his works on the subject were published after his death.

Further Reading

Bergeron, Tor. "Some Autobiographic Notes in Connection with the Ice Nucleus Theory of Precipitation Release." *Bulletin of the American Meteorological Society* 59 (1978): 390–392. Bergeron explains how he developed his ice nucleus theory.

Braham, Roscoe R., Jr. "Formation of Rain: A Historical Perspective." In James Rodger Fleming, editor, *Historical Essays on Meteorology, 1919–1995: The Diamond Anniversary Volume of the American Meteorological Society.* Boston: American Meteorological Society, 1996. Braham presents a short discussion on research into precipitation processes.

Callendar, Guy Stewart. "The Artificial Production of Carbon Dioxide and Its Influence on Climate." *Quarterly Journal of the Royal Meteorological Society* 64 (1938): 223–240. Callendar's first paper argues that the burning of fossil fuels was changing the climate.

———. "The Composition of the Atmosphere through the Ages." *Meteorological Magazine* 74 (1939): 33–39. The article argues that atmospheric chemistry can change.

———. "Infra-Red Absorption by Carbon Dioxide, with Special Reference to Atmospheric Radiation." *Quarterly Journal of the Royal Meteorological Society* 67 (1941): 263–275. Callendar explains why increased carbon dioxide levels contribute to warming by absorbing Earth's radiation.

Eliassen, Arnt. "Tor Bergeron 1891–1977." *Bulletin of the American Meteorological Society* 59 (1978): 387–389. This article provides a short biography of Bergeron by a colleague.

Fleming, James Rodger. *The Callendar Effect.* Boston: American Meteorological Society, 2007. Fleming explains the life and work of the steam engineer who established the carbon dioxide theory of climate change.

Liljequist, Gosta H. "Tor Bergeron: A Biography." *Pure and Applied Geophysics* 119 (1981): 409–442. Liljequist provides a biography of Tor Bergeron.

Moran, Joseph M., and Michael D. Morgan. *Meteorology: The Atmosphere and the Science of Weather.* 4th ed. New York: Macmillan College, 1994. Chapter 18 presents a clear description of the Köppen climate scheme.

Weart, Spencer R. *The Discovery of Global Warming.* Cambridge, Mass.: Harvard University Press, 2003. This is a readable book about the people behind the discovery of global warming.

5

1941–1950:
Military Needs—Disciplinary Advancement

During this decade, war would once again lead to scientific advances just as science would lead to advances in war-fighting techniques. The rapid increase in military aviation among all combatants required a corresponding increase in meteorologists, climatological studies, surface and upper-air observations, and new forecasting techniques. The boost in manpower and funding received by the atmospheric sciences during the war years would prove crucial to disciplinary advancement and professionalization in the coming decades.

Forecasters by the Thousands

In the United States, military meteorology units had been disbanded at the end of World War I in conjunction with an overall reduction in military forces. Just a handful of meteorologists remained, primarily to provide aviation support services. The Weather Bureau's ranks of forecasters had been decimated by the Great Depression—many senior meteorologists had been forced to retire and others had been laid off when there was no money to pay them. By 1940, as war in Europe started to look inevitable, the United States had approximately 400 professional meteorologists. U.S. meteorologists, and those in European countries threatened by Nazi Germany, realized that they would not have enough forecasters to meet their nations' domestic or military needs.

The full extent of the problem became apparent when President Franklin D. Roosevelt announced in May 1940 that he was requesting the delivery of 50,000 new military aircraft. The newly trained pilots flying those planes would need accurate weather forecasts before taking to the air. At the time of this announcement, there were only three graduate-level meteorology programs in the country: an academic program at MIT and professional programs geared to training meteorologists to work with the airline industry at New York University and the California Institute of Technology. By fall 1940, academic programs were getting started at the University of Chicago and at UCLA. In a very short time, the numbers of students enrolled skyrocketed. For example, in fall 1940, Chicago's program had 20 students. The number doubled every quarter until it had 1,000 students by 1943. More people received meteorological training in the fiscal year ending June 30, 1943, than had been trained in the previous 10 years combined—and that was before the largest classes convened. The British were also busy training meteorologists; the British Meteorological Office was 10 times larger (a total of 6,000 people) by the end of the war.

Carl-Gustav Rossby, who had been coordinating research and training at the U.S. Weather Bureau, moved to Chicago and formed the University Meteorology Committee (UMC)—a group representing members of the "Big Five" meteorology schools. The UMC's mission was to train the thousands of meteorologists needed, to do so quickly, and to ensure they could operate on an extremely professional level. Every academic meteorologist in the nation, including Jacob Bjerknes, who had been trapped in the United States after the war broke out, and Bernhard Haurwitz (1905–86), who had escaped Nazi Germany, was

Until 1945, virtually all normal scientific work is disrupted by World War II. Military requirements lead to research in fog and fog dissipation, low ceilings and visibility, aircraft icing, turbulence, contrail formation and suppression, microwave propagation and scattering, spherics (the use of radio static to find storms), and lightning. Data requirements lead to the expansion of surface and upper-air stations around the world

The U.S. Nobel Prize–winning chemist Irving Langmuir and his colleague Katherine B. Blodgett calculate drop collision efficiencies while working on smoke screens and aircraft icing for the military. Their work provides the theory underlying the formation of rain without ice crystals

Under the leadership of Carl-Gustav Rossby, the "Big Five" meteorology programs—University of Chicago; University of California, Los Angeles (UCLA); California Institute of Technology; Massachusetts Institute of Technology; and New York University—start training thousands of young scientific-minded men and women as meteorologists to serve the war effort

MILESTONES

1941	1943	1945

The German meteorologist Ludwig Weickmann initiates data collection on ice phases during flights in open-cockpit reconnaissance aircraft. He eventually makes over 100 meteorological flights—some to elevations over 6.2 miles (10 km). After the war, he publishes a major work on cloud physics, *Die Eisphase in der Atmosphäre* (Atmospheric ice phase) (1947)

British weather observers become the first to use radar to track a rain shower to a range of 2.5 miles (7 km) off the coast of England

The U.S. Weather Bureau's primary hurricane forecasting office moves to Miami, Florida

The U.S. Weather Bureau meteorologist Harry Wexler, using data gathered from radar and airplane observations during the war, discovers that the vertical motion in a hurricane takes place in the eyewall

devoted to training new meteorologists. All military officers entering the one-year accelerated graduate training program had to have degrees, or almost-completed degrees, in physics or mathematics. Those who had other majors were accepted as long as they had a significant background in mathematics and physics. After a year of nonstop study, graduates were shipped out to air stations and military bases around the world to provide aviation forecasts, forecasts for ships at sea, and specialized forecasts for amphibious landings. The very best students were often retained at the universities to train the next class of students. By the time training was completed in 1943, over 7,000 young men (and a handful of women) had been trained as meteorologists. In addition, the UMC directed the training of an additional 20,000 men and women as meteorological observers and technicians.

This influx of new meteorologists—there were almost 20 times as many professional meteorologists after the war as before it—would radically change the discipline. These new additions to the profession had math-

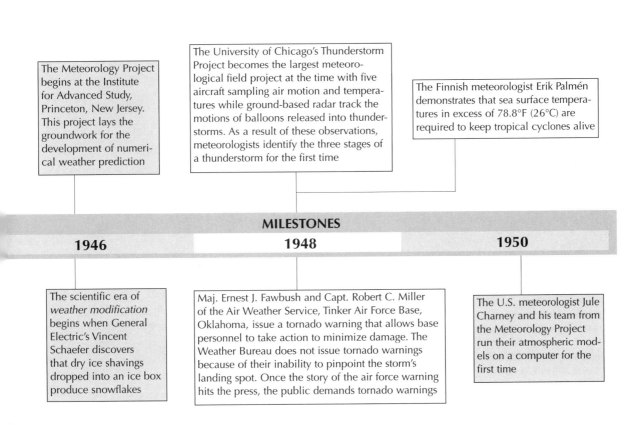

The Meteorology Project begins at the Institute for Advanced Study, Princeton, New Jersey. This project lays the groundwork for the development of numerical weather prediction

The University of Chicago's Thunderstorm Project becomes the largest meteorological field project at the time with five aircraft sampling air motion and temperatures while ground-based radar track the motions of balloons released into thunderstorms. As a result of these observations, meteorologists identify the three stages of a thunderstorm for the first time

The Finnish meteorologist Erik Palmén demonstrates that sea surface temperatures in excess of 78.8°F (26°C) are required to keep tropical cyclones alive

MILESTONES

1946   **1948**   **1950**

The scientific era of *weather modification* begins when General Electric's Vincent Schaefer discovers that dry ice shavings dropped into an ice box produce snowflakes

Maj. Ernest J. Fawbush and Capt. Robert C. Miller of the Air Weather Service, Tinker Air Force Base, Oklahoma, issue a tornado warning that allows base personnel to take action to minimize damage. The Weather Bureau does not issue tornado warnings because of their inability to pinpoint the storm's landing spot. Once the story of the air force warning hits the press, the public demands tornado warnings

The U.S. meteorologist Jule Charney and his team from the Meteorology Project run their atmospheric models on a computer for the first time

emetics and physics skills that many of their predecessors had never had. Because of their backgrounds, they approached the science in a significantly different way. Entering meteorology from the physical sciences and mathematics, they were determined to turn it into a "real science," moving forecasting from the realm of art to one of numerically based objectivity.

Expanding the Observational Network

Besides drawing thousands into the meteorological discipline, World War II's requirements for operational data profoundly affected the growth of the atmospheric sciences. With aircraft operating in the Tropics of the Pacific theater, in the Caribbean, and in support of ships transiting the

An upper-air observer prepares to launch a radiosonde during World War II. (NOAA Photo Library)

Panama Canal, meteorologists needed an expanded network of surface and upper-air stations to provide accurate flight forecasts.

Military operations in high northern latitudes also required an expansion of observation stations. Greenland and Iceland became important way stations for transporting men and material to and from the European theater. Stations in northern Canada provided information critical for identifying developing weather systems. Small islands in the Atlantic, including the Azores, were critical refueling spots for aircraft squadrons. Data from their weather stations were critical to analyzing the current atmospheric situation and making predictions for the next 24 to 48 hours. The army alone expanded their weather stations from a total of 40 before the war to 700 by war's end in 1945.

The German military as well as the Allies maintained fixed land stations and "weather stations on wheels" that followed military units. They also invested heavily in weather reconnaissance flights despite losing aircraft in enemy action. The Allies maintained over 20 weather ships in both the Atlantic and the Pacific. Collecting both surface and upper-air data, they were critical to transoceanic flight safety. The Germans used submarines to place automated weather recording instruments in the Atlantic and repeatedly landed in Greenland to maintain a weather station there. The Allies also worked to gather weather information from behind enemy lines. Spies, aircraft, and commando units penetrated enemy territory and sent back coded weather information.

Although cost prohibited the maintenance of the new wartime stations in the postwar period, there were still many more active stations at the end of the war than at its beginning. These new data points would be critical to the successful introduction of numerical weather prediction methods in the late 1940s.

War-Driven Research

The tactical and strategic needs of the military forces compelled meteorologists to postpone their personal research projects during the war. Academic meteorologists turned their attention to the most difficult problems first. Chemical warfare, which had been such a critical component of the war-fighting arsenal in World War I, was less important in World War II. The Chemical Warfare Service realized they needed very specific meteorological information if they were to use chemicals effectively. Navy meteorologists took on this problem, establishing a special training unit that provided techniques for determining weather conditions just a few feet above the ground—the area that experiences the greatest impact from chemical weapons.

As the military services gathered data from around the world, meteorologists worked to understand weather conditions in combat areas. Facing serious deficiencies in the understanding of tropical weather, the University of Chicago and the University of Puerto Rico established the Institute for Tropical Meteorology in Puerto Rico. Researchers at the

An SCR-658 radio direction finder ("bedspring" antenna) tracks a radiosonde in this photograph from around 1945. (NOAA Photo Library)

institute developed forecasting rules for tropical regions that could be used by military forecasters, particularly those on remote islands who had access to very little information. Some senior academic meteorologists, including Sverre Petterssen and Jacob Bjerknes, traveled to Newfoundland, Greenland, Iceland, Labrador, Alaska, and India to gather information on weather conditions that could be passed on to the military officers receiving weather training.

Long-term projects were divided up among the Big Five meteorology programs. Meteorologists started analysis and atlas projects to study large-scale atmospheric patterns and the resulting weather. Researchers in climatology projects compiled large amounts of data from critical military stations and calculated long-term averages of temperature, precipitation, and air pressure. On the basis of these climatological data, military planners determined the best locations and orientations of landing strips and the best (or worst) times for launching particular military operations. Projects dealing with the collection and study of upper-air observations were particularly important because it was impossible to determine the atmosphere's dynamic structure from surface data alone. The increased availability of upper-air reports gave meteorologists their first opportunity to study the general circulation of the atmosphere better. Their findings gave forecasters greater knowledge for predicting flight conditions and for making longer-range forecasts (several days instead of just one or two). New techniques for measuring ozone and its relationship to circulation patterns were especially important to military planners, who needed at least a tentative forecast a week in advance.

The importance of war-driven meteorological research to the advances of the atmospheric sciences in the 20th century cannot be overstated. New techniques, new instrumentation, and new knowledge, combined

Radar: A Military Tool for Meteorology

Since the 1930s, British scientists had been working on ground-based radar techniques. The very long wavelengths they employed combined with very broad beams made them difficult to use and provided very little directional accuracy. By 1940, the invention of the magnetron had provided a technique for creating very short wavelengths. Sir Henry Tizard (1885–1959), a prominent British physicist, showed his colleagues in the United States and Canada how the magnetron could enhance the usefulness of radar as the race to create a military tool that would allow Allied forces to "see" incoming ships and aircraft intensified. The scientists at the Massachusetts Institute of Technology's Radiation Lab, impressed with the potential of the magnetron, adopted its use in their radar development program and were soon working on building microwave radar.

These shorter wavelengths allowed users to locate their own and enemy combat forces with much greater accuracy, but microwave radars had their own set of problems. Whereas old radars had been able to "look through" rain and snow, the new microwave radars returned images of rain and snow that masked the presence of ships and aircraft. On February 20, 1941, a radar team tracked a rain shower some 2.5 miles (7 km) off the English coast—the first confirmed use of "weather radar."

Hearing this news, wartime meteorologists were quick to exploit the use of microwave radar to track storms, especially those that could be hazardous to ships and aircraft. Although the principal efforts in radar advancement during the war were aimed at locating enemy assets, work continued on radar specifically designed for weather forecasting purposes. The British Meteorological Office established a radar research site near London before the end of the war, and the Canadian Army Operational Research Group carried out Project Stormy Weather in 1944, making time-lapse photographs of radar returns to study storm movement. Radar was especially helpful in tropical regions because observational data were extremely limited and rain showers were very heavy, providing excellent radar images. Furthermore, heavy rain showers were a flight hazard for the smaller, lighter World War II aircraft. In busy flight areas such as the Panama Canal Zone, U.S. Army Air Corps meteorologists used radar to locate and track the movement of heavy showers, allowing pilots to avoid them while flying into, and out of, the area.

In the immediate postwar years, MIT's Weather Radar Project concerned itself not only with improving equipment, but with using radar returns to determine precipitation processes and internal storm structure. As weather radar became more sophisticated, researchers used these instruments to study thunderstorms, and forecasters—who learned to recognize the distinctive patterns made by thunderstorms, tornadoes, and hurricanes—used them to guide aviators away from dangerous flight areas.

The first specially designed weather radar, built by Raytheon Corporation for the U.S. Air Force's Air Weather Service, appeared in 1949. In the half century since its introduction, weather radar has become an important tool for meteorological prediction and atmospheric research.

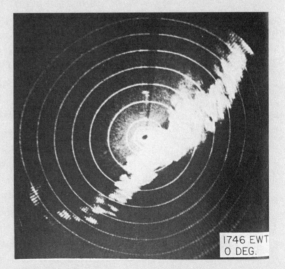

This radar image shows a frontal thunderstorm near Spring Lake, New Jersey, on July 16, 1944. (NOAA Photo Library)

with the influx of new meteorologists, would be critical to rapid disciplinary advances after 1950.

Numerical Dreams—Numerical Reality

The idea of using mathematics to solve the weather forecasting problem was not a new one in 1946—Vilhelm Bjerknes had made a case for such an undertaking in the early 20th century and Lewis Fry Richardson of Great Britain had made an abortive attempt to do so during World War I. Both Bjerknes and Richardson realized that numerical weather prediction would not be practical until calculations could be made much more quickly than was possible with pencil, paper, and adding machines and/or slide rules.

Electronic calculating machines capable of handling complex problems first made their appearance during World War II, primarily to solve ballistics problems. Army units needed a way to compute "fire control solutions," that is, to take into account the size and weight of the ordnance being fired, the wind at its multiple flight levels, and the terrain in which it was being fired. At this time, computers with little computational capability took up entire rooms. Furthermore, they were individually designed and built to solve a given problem. Each army unit would not have a computer, but a single computer could produce tables that could be used to extract the fire control solution on distant battlefields.

Electronic digital computers emerged from this starting point in 1946. The brilliant Hungarian-born mathematician John von Neumann (1903–57) of the Institute for Advanced Study in Princeton, New Jersey, was ready to design and build such a machine. He had garnered support from the Office of Naval Research, which was eager to have access to such a computing machine for a variety of military purposes. Von Neumann still needed a project for his computer. With a significant background in fluid dynamics, von Neumann did not need much encouragement from his friend Vladimir Zworykin (1889–1982), a physicist best known for inventing the scanning television camera at the RCA Laboratory (just a short distance away from von Neumann's offices in Princeton), to apply the computer to the weather forecasting problem.

When Francis W. Reichelderfer (1895–1983) chief of the Weather Bureau, visited Princeton at the end of 1945, he heard about Zworykin's recommendation to use computers to forecast the weather. This sounded like a terrific idea to Reichelderfer. The Weather Bureau, always strapped for money and personnel, could use an *objective* method for forecasting the weather. If Zworykin's idea worked, then all meteorologists would start out with a machine-produced forecast map that would only take into account the equations that defined the atmosphere and data collected from observation stations. These maps would replace the *subjective* method of chart production in which meteorologists would plot the data, look at past weather information, and then try to picture the future atmosphere in their minds before representing it on a weather map. Subjective prognostic charts were created from a feel for the atmosphere. In Reichelderfer's opinion, computer-generated charts would not only save money, but lead to better forecasts.

Reichelderfer pursued this idea by asking von Neumann and Zworykin to present their work at a confidential meeting of Weather Bureau, air force, and navy meteorologists at Weather Bureau headquarters in January 1946. The participants all agreed that numerical weather prediction held great promise. Academic meteorologists such as University of Chicago's Carl-Gustav Rossby were approached to advise on the theoretical aspects of such a problem. By the end of 1946, the navy had once again provided money to von Neumann—this time for the Meteorology Project that would create the mathematical models to run on the new computer being developed by von Neumann's Computer Project.

Although von Neumann had anticipated that his new computer would be built and operational within two years, it would not actually come alive until the early 1950s. That was just as well, because the meteorological problems were extremely difficult to solve and the models were ready only a year before von Neumann's computer. The American mathematician-turned-meteorologist Jule Charney (1917–81)—one of the many men who entered the atmospheric sciences as a result of the war—joined the Meteorology Project in 1948 and played a critical role in developing the equations that would define the atmosphere. With the help of an international team of meteorologists, particularly those from Scandinavian countries, the Meteorology Project took the first steps toward a more thorough understanding of the atmosphere and set the stage for operational numerical weather prediction in the next decade.

Although it might appear that the purpose of numerical weather prediction would have been to predict the weather, in fact the ultimate goal of Zworykin and von Neumann was not weather prediction, but weather control. Both of these distinguished scholars thought that if they could program the computer to produce the weather that people wanted by changing different meteorological variables in the machine, then others could change those same variables in the real world and produce weather on demand. They were not the only ones with this idea. While they were busy with their projects in Princeton, scientists at the General Electric Laboratory in Schenectady, New York, were developing and applying weather modification techniques.

Weather Modification

In the immediate postwar years, political leaders, the general public, and many scientists embraced the idea that almost anything could be "fixed" with science and technology. World War II, the feeling went, had been won for the Allies by the skillful use of scientific development and technological achievement that had created the atomic bomb, radar, proximity fuses, rockets, and advanced aircraft designs. No longer content with damming streams for power and irrigation, tunneling through mountains, or draining and filling swamps, science turned its attention to controlling nature. The biggest challenge: controlling the weather.

The scientists who took the lead in weather modification were not meteorologists. On the contrary, they were usually physicists like Zworykin or chemists like Irving Langmuir (1881–1957) who entered the weather modification field through other work. At the RCA Laboratory where Zworykin worked, technicians and engineers were under contract to design and build advanced meteorological equipment for measuring

The Nobel Prize–winning chemist Irving Langmuir applied his knowledge of "smokes" to inducing rain from clouds. (AIP)

atmospheric properties. At General Electric, Langmuir had been under contract to the army for a number of years, researching ways to produce smoke that would provide cover for troops from enemy aircraft and analyzing the growth of ice crystals on aircraft bodies, a critical problem that could cause airplanes and helicopters to crash.

Langmuir's work in both smokes and icing had led him to analyze the properties of precipitation nuclei. In 1946, while Langmuir was in California, his assistant, Vincent Schaefer (1906–93), was conducting experiments to determine under what circumstances ice crystals appeared in clouds. Installing a home freezer in the laboratory, he lined it with black velvet so that any ice crystals would show up in light beams against the black background. Exhaling into the freezer, Schaefer created his own cloud—just as one does when exhaling on a very cold day. Even though the temperature in the freezer was below -4°F (-20°C), there were no ice crystals—just water droplets. Schaefer dropped in small quantities of fine dust created from a variety of chemicals, but they produced few, if any crystals. One day in July, when the freezer was not cold enough, he decided to drop a block of dry ice into the bottom of it. Almost instantaneously, the air in the freezer filled with ice crystals and the crystals remained there even after he pulled the dry ice back out. Schaefer was intrigued. Again and again, he experimented with dropping small amounts of dry ice shavings into the supercooled cloud in the freezer. Each time, he introduced a few less shavings than the time before. Even the smallest grain of dry ice, Schaefer found, could trigger the formation of ice crystals in a supercooled cloud.

Experimenting with other very cold objects and substances—for example, a chilled sewing needle—Schaefer discovered that it was possible to induce crystal formation as long as the temperature of the introduced material was -40°F (-40°C) or colder. Upon his return to the lab in August, Langmuir started making theoretical calculations to determine the effects of "seeding" an actual cloud with dry ice pellets. As snow and ice particles formed within the cloud, the cloud's temperature would increase, causing the air within it to rise. The rising air would cause the cloud to billow even higher and the seeds would be further scattered by the turbulence. By Langmuir's calculations, if they seeded a stratiform cloud along lines one to two miles (1.5–3.2 km) apart, the resulting air movement would spread the precipitation nuclei throughout the entire cloud within 30 minutes. He and Schaefer decided to see whether it would work on a real cloud.

On November 13, 1946, Schaefer took six pounds (2.7 kg) of crushed dry ice up in a small rented plane, looking for a suitable cloud to seed. Finding one about 50 miles (80 km) from the Schenectady airport, Schaefer dropped the first three pounds (1.4 kg) from the plane's window as they flew through the cloud and watched as snow started to fall from its base. Looping back around for another try, Schaefer dropped another three pounds and watched the ice crystals forming around the plane and the snow falling once again from the cloud. Langmuir, watching from the airport, was thrilled. They had successfully caused a nonprecipitating cloud to snow.

After several more months of experimentation, General Electric decided to pursue government funding for weather modification research. Creating rain and snow was not really part of the company's usual line of work, but since it had the potential of being extremely beneficial for the nation the effort was continued. Within a year, Project Cirrus was born. Funded by the Army Signal Corps and the Office of Naval Research, with aircraft and personnel assistance from the U.S. Air Force, it had as its purpose testing the efficacy of cloud seeding.

There were a number of government agencies who were interested in cloud seeding. The military, which was providing the money, was interested in the possibility of using weather control as a weapon. If the U.S. military could muddy an enemy's fields before a major tank battle, that would be an advantage. If enemy runways could be fogged in, that could keep their aircraft on the ground. Alternatively, if U.S. runways were fogged in, the fog could be cleared and the planes could be launched. In addition to the military, the Department of Agriculture was interested because rainmaking on demand opened the possibility of growing crops in arid regions. The Department of the Interior was interested because that capacity could also alleviate water problems for urban areas in arid regions. There seemed to be no shortage of good uses for weather control.

Within a few months of Schaefer's flight experiment, private consulting meteorologists were using his techniques to "augment rain" for farmers, ranchers, and utility companies (for hydroelectric power) and to clear fog from airport runways. By the end of the decade, hundreds of thousands of dollars were being spent annually on weather modification covering millions of acres (square kilometers) of land in the United States. The techniques spread all over the world and were being tried in Central and South America, Australia, Europe, and Africa. Lawsuits resulted when farmers for whom rain meant crop losses sued farmers who needed rain for their crops. States sued other states for "stealing their water" from clouds.

From this beginning in the late 1940s, research into weather modification and control developed into projects costing tens of millions of dollars by the 1970s. Using special seeding techniques, the U.S. military secretly used weather as a weapon during the Vietnam War in the late 1960s and early 1970s. A variety of government agencies pursued weather control to boost water resources, prevent lightning-induced fires, and create rain to put out forest fires. Although research funding started to drop off in the 1980s, private firms have continued to seed clouds for ski resorts, municipal water supplies, and farmers. As the world's population grows and the demand for freshwater increases,

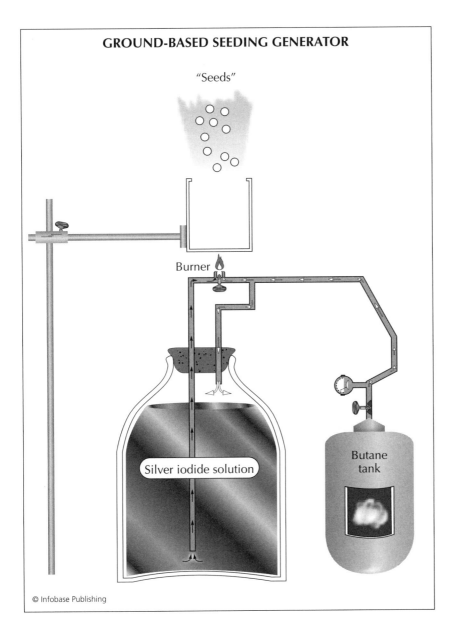

GROUND-BASED SEEDING GENERATOR

"Seeds"

Burner

Silver iodide solution

Butane tank

© Infobase Publishing

Silver iodide "seeds" were injected into clouds from both aircraft and ground-based seeding generators, as shown in this example; the method was based on a design tested at the New Mexico Institute of Mining and Technology, Socorro, in the early 1950s. (Based on Holmes and Hume, "Final Research Report to the State of New Mexico Economic Development Commission, Water Resources Development," 1951)

attention will be focused once again on fixing the problem with weather modification technology.

Figuring Out Hurricanes

Hurricanes, also known as typhoons in the western Pacific and tropical cyclones in the Indian Ocean, were giant, deadly, and unpredictable weather systems until the middle of the 20th century. In large part this was because they were difficult to study. Forming over equatorial waters out of sight of land, unless a ship happened to be unlucky enough to travel underneath one or the hurricane ran over an island in its path, they could be born, develop, and die without anyone ever knowing of their existence. Without satellites watching from space, they could literally move ashore with high winds, accompanying tornadoes, and the wall of water known as the storm surge with absolutely no warning. Thousands of people living in coastal areas died when these monsters landed. Outrage sparked by deaths caused by large hurricanes prompted changes in hurricane forecasting and encouraged additional research into their structure and behavior.

By the mid-1930s, meteorologists agreed that well-developed hurricanes extended vertically through the entire troposphere and were maintained by the release of latent heat caused by convection near the storm center. By the early 1940s, they had developed a fairly accurate description of the life cycle of a hurricane. In the first stage of a tropical system, the storm became organized (exactly what triggered this event was unclear). If conditions favored development, the system would intensify as the barometric pressure plummeted and the winds increased in the second stage. In the third stage, the winds did not increase appreciably, but the storm itself expanded to cover a larger geographic area. In the last stage, the system would dissipate or fall apart.

Early ideas on hurricane genesis had centered on a tropical comparison to Jacob Bjerknes's polar front theory, but data obtained from additional observations eliminated this possibility. By early in this decade, researchers had shown that the most likely trigger for these storms was the presence of a "wave" or perturbation in the easterly flow of the atmosphere moving off the African coast.

Efforts to determine hurricane structure were aided by the availability and use of upper-air observations. The number of pilot balloon stations and the frequency of observations had increased rapidly in the Caribbean during the 1930s, primarily through the efforts of Pan American Airways. Radiosonde stations had also been added. As a result, the flow patterns of upper-level winds were routinely plotted and found to be more useful than surface reports for determining hurricane movement.

Although the upper-air observations had provided new insight into hurricanes during the late 1930s and very early 1940s, a significant advance was made in July 1943, when the U.S. Army Air Corps' Colonel Joseph P. Duckworth (1902–64) became the first person to fly into a hurricane's eye intentionally. Regular missions to hunt down and penetrate hurricanes began in 1944, with army and navy pilots taking part. Their purpose, of course, was not so much to accurately forecast where hurricanes would go ashore, as to keep ships out of their way. Early in the war, the navy had suffered massive damage to its seagoing assets during

Pacific typhoons. Weather reconnaissance flights allowed navy personnel to locate and determine the intensity of these storms. It is impossible to forecast a hurricane's movement without knowing its position and strength. Aircraft provided the fastest method of finding out. Although expensive and dangerous, the process was less expensive than losing ships at sea in high winds and waves.

Radar also provided the first look at complicated hurricane structure. Meteorologists using radar combined with aircraft observations discovered that the upward vertical motion in hurricanes resided in the eyewall—the thick, doughnut-shaped circle of convective clouds that surrounds the clear eye in the storm's center. Additional data also over-

The introduction of sophisticated instruments on hurricane-penetrating aircraft allowed scientists to determine how air moves within tropical storms.

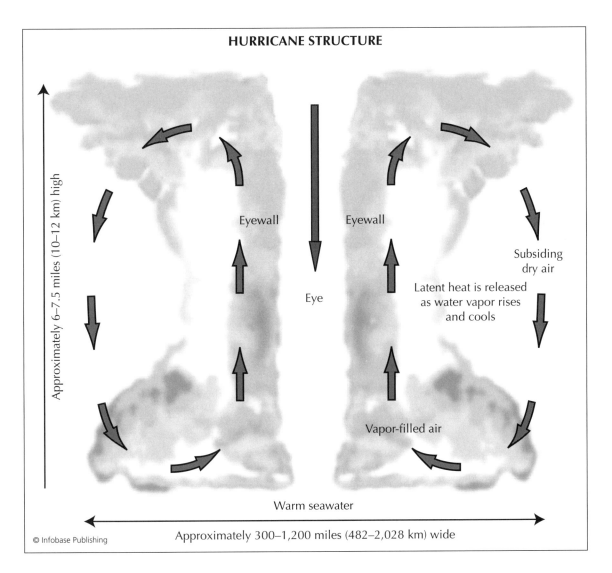

HURRICANE STRUCTURE

Approximately 6–7.5 miles (10–12 km) high

Eyewall

Eyewall

Eye

Subsiding dry air

Latent heat is released as water vapor rises and cools

Vapor-filled air

Warm seawater

© Infobase Publishing

Approximately 300–1,200 miles (482–2,028 km) wide

Taming a Tempest

Meteorologists may have been uncertain about the causes of hurricanes and the circumstances under which they strengthened, but that did not discourage people outside the discipline from making recommendations on ways to reduce the severity of hurricanes. Some people viewed the atomic bomb as the answer to controlling hurricanes. The power of the bomb, they thought, should be enough to offset the power of the hurricane. A nuclear weapon detonated within a nascent hurricane would sufficiently disrupt its structure, causing the storm to dissipate. The nuclear weapon-as-hurricane-buster theory had some serious problems. First, the average hurricane stores considerably more energy than a nuclear bomb. Second, once the bomb exploded, the radioactivity associated with the blast would then be blown around with the storm's wind and fall out of the sky with the storm's rain. The hurricane, which would cause a few days of mayhem, would be turned into long-term environmental disaster.

Another idea at the time, which resurfaces periodically, was to pour oil over the surface of the ocean under the offending hurricane. Proponents of this method pointed to the requirement for moisture to be evaporated from the sea surface in order to feed the large cloud system associated with the hurricane. The method had problems: It would require a huge amount of oil,

the oil slick would not remain one coherent mass in rough seas, and the oil slick would create a huge ecological disaster.

Vladimir Zworykin, concerned with weather control as well as numerical weather prediction, suggested to Weather Bureau personnel that they float the oil on the sea surface and then ignite it to make a giant fire under the hurricane. He had concluded that the burning oil slick would pull heat energy away from the tropical system, thus causing it to dissipate quickly. The Weather Bureau declined to give Zworykin's method a try.

There was one serious attempt to control hurricanes during this decade. The General Electric team, fresh from its triumph of seeding clouds in Massachusetts, decided to drop 200 pounds (90 kg) of dry ice onto an Atlantic hurricane in October 1947. Instead of dissipating, the hurricane made a hard right turn and struck Savannah, Georgia. Although the dry ice actually had nothing to do with the hurricane's track change, scientists knew so little about hurricane steering at the time that many people assumed that the seeding had caused the hurricane to change course. Savannah's residents were furious and General Electric's lawyers prohibited Langmuir's group from making any more seeding runs without company permission. Attempts to tame hurricanes would be put aside until the 1960s.

turned the idea that hurricanes stopped intensifying after a certain point in their life. Meteorologists found out that hurricanes could alternately strengthen and weaken throughout their life cycle.

By the end of the decade, researchers had determined that the sea surface temperature had to remain above 78.8°F (26°C) in order for tropical systems to stay alive. In the presence of too much vertical shear, which prevents air from flowing out the top of the hurricane, the tropical system falls apart.

Tropical meteorologists, aided by advances in radar, the addition of numerous surface and upper-air stations throughout the Tropics, and the availability of weather reconnaissance aircraft, made significant discoveries about tropical systems during the 1940s. Forecasting the movement of these large, violent, and complex systems has remained a difficult problem despite the use of satellites and high-speed computers.

Unmasking Thunderstorms

Throughout the 1930s, meteorologists often referred to thunderstorms as "heat thunderstorms" because they thought they were usually triggered by intense surface heating. That heat would cause thunderstorms actually made sense. Thunderstorms were typically most severe on summer afternoons after the ground had been baked by the Sun all day. As the hot air rose, taking moisture with it, large cumulus clouds would begin to form. Within a few hours, the cumulus would continue to grow vertically, forming bright, billowing white tops, called towering cumulus, stretching tens of thousands of feet (several kilometers) into the atmosphere. When their tops bumped into the tropopause and flattened out, they became cumulonimbus—commonly known as thunderclouds.

The relatively small size of thunderstorms was one reason meteorologists possessed only rudimentary knowledge of their structure and behavior. They often occurred near mountains as warm air rushed up the hillsides and were obscured by trees. Furthermore, unless a trained observer happened to be present while the thunderstorm clouds were building, it was impossible to get a good sense of what was happening.

The observational problem was reduced after World War II when the availability of radar and aircraft made it possible to examine thunderstorm mechanisms closely. The University of Chicago's Thunderstorm Project, largely funded by the airline industry, whose airborne assets were most likely to be affected by the driving rain, hail, icing, and turbulence associated with thunderstorms, undertook to unmask thunderstorms.

As a result of their research, University of Chicago researchers identified the three stages of a thunderstorm. In the first, or cumulus, stage, the air only moves up within the cloud. This leads to precipitation only at the top of the cloud, where the vertical velocity is at a minimum. At lower levels within the cloud, the air is moving up so rapidly that it holds droplets in it. In the second, or mature, stage, water droplets become too heavy to be carried within the cloud and rain starts to fall. As the rain falls, it carries air with it and forms a downdraft. Now air is moving both up and down within the cloud. At the highest levels (the anvil top), ice crystals form in the extremely cold temperatures, and as discussed earlier, grow at the expense of the water droplets. Moving up and down within the clouds, these ice crystals pick up more moisture and freeze again and again. Hail forms one layer at a time, much as onions are formed by layers of plant tissue. When the updrafts can no longer hold them, the hail falls out. Although most hail is small, if the cloud is very tall (up to 60,000 feet [18 km]) and the hailstones have made many trips, they can grow to become grapefruit-sized—and very

Scientist of the Decade: Carl-Gustav Rossby (1898–1957)

Born on December 28, 1898, in Stockholm, Sweden, the meteorologist Carl-Gustav Rossby was one of the most influential atmospheric scientists in the 20th century. After earning his *filosofie kandidat* (that is, bachelor's degree) at the University of Stockholm in 1918 with specializations in mathematics, mechanics, and astronomy, Rossby left Stockholm and moved to Norway to join the Bergen School. He worked with the Bjerkneses on the development of the polar front and air mass theories until 1921. After two years in Bergen, he realized he did not have the necessary mathematics and physics background to undertake the theoretical work in meteorology that he thought necessary to solve atmospheric problems.

Moving back to Stockholm, Rossby studied mathematical physics at the university until 1925, ultimately earning his *filosofie licenciat* (a degree between a master's and a doctorate). While finishing his degree, he worked as a forecaster for the Swedish Meteorological and Hydrological Service and took part in oceanographic expeditions. After completing his degree, Rossby was awarded an American-Scandinavian Foundation fellowship through which he traveled to the United States to work with the U.S. Weather Bureau. Within a year, his efforts to introduce Bergen School methods to U.S. meteorology began to significantly influence the way meteorologists considered atmospheric processes.

In addition to completing several scientific articles during his stay with the bureau, Rossby tried to convince officials to incorporate the new Bergen School techniques into their forecasting. He met with great resistance. Most bureau personnel did not have college degrees and were suspicious of this enthusiastic Swede, who was trying to tell them to change their way of doing business. One person at the bureau was attracted to his message: the navy lieutenant Francis W. Reichelderfer. Reichelderfer became a good friend of Rossby's and introduced the Bergen School methods to his navy colleagues. (In 1938, when Reichelderfer became the chief of the Weather Bureau, Rossby joined his team to introduce the latest meteorological theory to forecasters.) While at the bureau, Rossby also made his first attempt at building a rotating tank (the "dishpan") to study atmospheric circulation. Although he was unsuccessful at the time, the apparatus was successfully employed 25 years later while he led the University of Chicago's meteorology department.

Rossby irritated his Weather Bureau hosts and they wanted him out of the way within a year of his arrival. At the same time, the leaders of the Daniel Guggenheim Fund for the Promotion of Aeronautics were looking for an energetic meteorologist to help them establish a "model airway" along the West Coast of the United States. Rossby took on the job, setting up weather stations that took observations and provided aviation forecasts for pilots flying from Los Angeles to Seattle. After completing this task, he was tapped to organize, with Guggenheim funds, the new meteorology program at MIT—the first graduate program in the nation.

Rossby, who was always looking for a way to promote modern meteorology in the United States, attracted the best students in the country and sent them out to advance both research and practice further. They filled positions at the Weather Bureau, spent time in Norway with the Bergen School, and helped to establish a meteorology program at New York University.

After 10 years of building the MIT program and producing his famous papers on the movement of long waves in the upper-level westerlies, including his 1940 paper "Planetary Flow Patterns in the Atmosphere," he accepted Reichelderfer's invitation to pull the Weather Bureau into the modern meteorological era. Rossby's time at the bureau was short. The opportunity to develop yet another meteorology department, this one at the University of Chicago, called. While at Chicago he surrounded himself yet again with an incredible group of talented young scientists. Organizing the largest meteorological training program in history for the war effort, he personally recruited a number of distinguished meteorologists who executed his vision of a rigorous theoretical

Carl-Gustav Rossby, seen here in 1926, used this "dishpan" to study atmospheric motion. (NOAA Photo Library)

education combined with practical forecasting experience. Working at the highest levels of government, he arranged for teams of these scientists to travel throughout the world to analyze the meteorological needs of the military services and offer solutions to their atmospheric problems.

As the war came to a close, Rossby recognized that the meteorological community had a unique opportunity to strengthen the discipline's scientific advances if it could retain at least some of the thousands of new meteorologists trained during the war. Becoming the president of the American Meteorological Society, he transformed it from an organization that had been composed of both amateurs and professionals into a wholly professional society equivalent to those representing engineering and other sciences. Concerned that there was no peer-reviewed journal for publishing meteorological research, he established the *Journal of Meteorology*. Rossby was also influential in a number of research projects, most notably the Meteorology Project at the Institute for Advanced Study that developed numerical weather prediction techniques.

Although he had become a naturalized American citizen, Rossby returned to Sweden to help the government reorganize its meteorological research, services, and education; he established his third meteorology department, the International Meteorological Institute at the University of Stockholm, Sweden. This unique research and educational organization drew scientists from both the West and from behind the iron curtain—a rarity in a time of cold war tensions. In Stockholm, he founded another scientific journal (*Tellus*) and created the first numerical weather prediction center in Europe. Turning his attention to atmospheric chemistry, he was a leader in using the radioactive isotopes left over from nuclear tests as an aid to understanding atmospheric circulation.

Carl-Gustav Rossby was not only personally productive, he was the father of uncounted "academic children," who carried his message of meteorological theory throughout the world. A prodigious worker, Rossby was less careful about his health than about his atmospheric studies. In 1957, he died of a heart attack while in Stockholm.

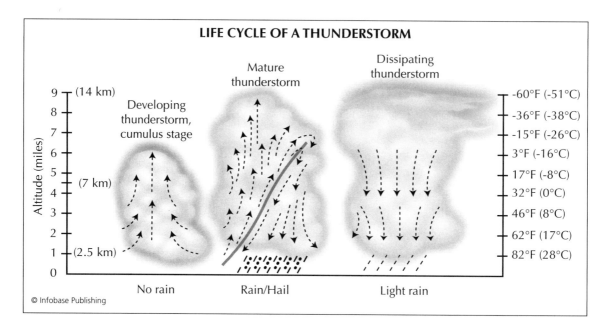

LIFE CYCLE OF A THUNDERSTORM

Developing thunderstorm, cumulus stage

Mature thunderstorm

Dissipating thunderstorm

Altitude (miles)

9 — (14 km)
8
7
6
5 — (7 km)
4
3
2
1 — (2.5 km)
0

-60°F (-51°C)
-36°F (-38°C)
-15°F (-26°C)
3°F (-16°C)
17°F (-8°C)
32°F (0°C)
46°F (8°C)
62°F (17°C)
82°F (28°C)

No rain   Rain/Hail   Light rain

© Infobase Publishing

Vertical air movement, cloud behavior, and types of precipitation change throughout the life cycle of a thunderstorm.

dangerous. In the third, or dissipating, stage the updraft disappears; dry air is pulled in from outside the cloud, causing the cloud to evaporate; and sometimes only the anvil top remains.

Surface heating does contribute to thunderstorm development, but these small-scale systems will not grow to large heights unless there is air converging from all sides into the area of surface heating, and air diverging (or moving out of) the top of the cloud. In mountainous areas, the mechanical lifting of warm, moist air over the mountains often contributes to the building of large thunderstorms. In the United States, one of the most common areas for severe thunderstorm development is the Florida peninsula. Not only is there significant afternoon heating combined with lots of available moisture, but as the air rises, it pulls in more moist air from coastal regions. The thunderstorms peak out late in the afternoon and heavy downpours follow.

Radar improvements, combined with the use of specialized satellite sensors and computer models, have allowed meteorologists to gain additional knowledge of thunderstorm mechanics and have given forecasters the tools they need to guide airplanes around these dangerous systems. Research continues on the most complex of these thunderstorm systems.

Further Reading

Bates, Charles F., and John F. Fuller. *America's Weather Warriors: 1814–1985*. College Station: Texas A&M University Press, 1986. This book

provides details about the importance of weather forecasting during
World War II and the introduction of weather radar.

Harper, Kristine C. "Research from the Boundary Layer: Civilian
Leadership, Military Funding and the Development of Numerical
Weather Prediction (1964–55)." *Social Studies of Science* 33(5) (2003):
667–696. This article discusses how the U.S. Navy, Air Force, and
Weather Bureau joined forces with academic meteorologists from the
United States and Europe to develop numerical weather prediction.

Holmes, C. R., and William Hume II. "Final Research Report to the
State of New Mexico Economic Development Commission, Water
Resources Development." Socorro: New Mexico Institute of Mining and
Technology (Research and Development Division), September 19, 1951.
This research report discusses developments in weather modification.

Koelsch, William A. "From Geo- to Physical Science: Meteorology and
the American University, 1919–1945." In James Rodger Fleming, editor, *Historical Essays on Meteorology, 1919–1995: The Diamond Anniversary
Volume of the American Meteorological Society*. Boston: American
Meteorological Society, 1996. This article is a short discussion on the
changes in meteorological education as a result of World War II.

Nebeker, Frederik. *Calculating the Weather: Meteorology in the 20th Century*.
San Diego, Calif.: Academic Press, 1995. This book presents the development of von Neumann's computer just after World War II and discusses the early work of the Meteorology Project.

Petterssen, Sverre. *Weathering the Storm: Sverre Petterssen, the D-Day
Forecast, and the Rise of Modern Meteorology*. Edited by James Rodger
Fleming. Boston: American Meteorological Society, 2001. This autobi-
ography of the Norwegian meteorologist Sverre Petterssen, one of the
most distinguished atmospheric scientists of the 20th century, discusses
his meteorological work during World War II.

Rogers, R. R., and P. L. Smith. "A Short History of Radar Meteorology."
In James Rodger Fleming, editor, *Historical Essays on Meteorology, 1919–
1995; The Diamond Anniversary Volume of the American Meteorological
Society*. Boston: American Meteorological Society, 1996. This article
describes the development and implementation of weather radar in the
years during and after World War II.

Rossby, C.-G. "Planetary Flow Patterns in the Atmosphere." *Quarterly
Journal of the Royal Meteorological Society* 66 (1940): 68–77. This is
Rossby's famous paper about the role of atmospheric long waves, which
are now known as Rossby waves.

Spence, Clark C. *The Rainmakers: American "Pluviculture" to World War II*.
Lincoln: University of Nebraska Press, 1980. This is a history of weather
modification in the first half of the 20th century.

Townsend, Jeff. *Making Rain in America: A History*. Lubbock, Tex.:
ICASALS, 1975. This is a short history of weather modification in the
United States.

6

1951–1960:
The Rise of Atmospheric Modeling

The 1950s were years of fiscal retrenchment for the U.S. government, but the military services—fighting the cold war—had ample funds for basic research. The Office of Naval Research provided significant funding for numerical weather prediction, cloud physics, and a variety of weather control techniques. The National Science Foundation, established in 1950, would become the primary provider of basic research funds, while the military concentrated on applied research. The money that flowed into atmospheric research was critical for the computer-driven advances in meteorology and climatology of this decade. Efforts by the two cold war giants—the United States and the Soviet Union—to outshine each other in science and technology and thereby demonstrate the superiority of their political system, also led to the beginning of the "space race" at the end of the decade. The attention to space and artificial satellites paid dividends for the atmospheric sciences, which finally had an "eye in the sky" to observe remote weather systems. Advances in hardware and instrumentation such as computers, radar, and satellites were critical to meteorological progress throughout the decade.

The Cold War and Research Funding

In many ways, the 1950s was a period of financial retrenchment for much of science. European nations, still rebuilding after the war's devastation, had little in the way of spare funds for scientific research. Fiscal restraint was also a feature of the Eisenhower administration in the United States. While the Weather Bureau was trying to prepare for the introduction of numerical weather prediction techniques, which would require the acquisition of a computer and related peripheral equipment, its budget was cut. One part of the federal budget had not seen significant reductions: the military.

Hostilities in Korea and tense relations between the United States and the USSR over atomic weapons and Soviet expansionism in Eastern Europe kept military budgets high. Funds for research and development, primarily handled by the Office of Naval Research, were available to scientists who were prepared to pursue research in both *basic* and *applied* science that could potentially aid the nation's defense. As seen earlier during times of war, weather and climate play an important role in the successful prosecution of military strategy and tactics. Accurate domestic weather forecasts during periods of conflict are also important for agricultural and industrial production, transportation of material and personnel, and optimal provision of heating fuel. Because of their importance, therefore, atmospheric sciences were well funded by the military services.

Atmospheric studies and forecasts in support of aeronautics continued to be of importance. In the immediate postwar years, the air force pursued its development of rockets, missiles, and high-altitude, high-performance jet aircraft. All of these hardware developments needed to take into account the influence of weather systems during launch, flight, and recovery stages. Most U.S. Air Force–funded meteorological research focused on the upper atmosphere; some was also related to oceanograph-

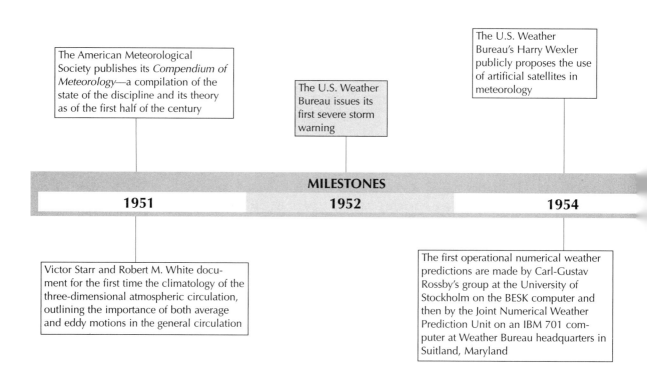

The American Meteorological Society publishes its *Compendium of Meteorology*—a compilation of the state of the discipline and its theory as of the first half of the century

The U.S. Weather Bureau issues its first severe storm warning

The U.S. Weather Bureau's Harry Wexler publicly proposes the use of artificial satellites in meteorology

MILESTONES

1951   **1952**   **1954**

Victor Starr and Robert M. White document for the first time the climatology of the three-dimensional atmospheric circulation, outlining the importance of both average and eddy motions in the general circulation

The first operational numerical weather predictions are made by Carl-Gustav Rossby's group at the University of Stockholm on the BESK computer and then by the Joint Numerical Weather Prediction Unit on an IBM 701 computer at Weather Bureau headquarters in Suitland, Maryland

ic research related to the recovery of pilots who were forced to ditch their planes at sea. Although the army had ceded most of its weather services to the air force, the Signal Corps remained active in meteorological equipment research and development, and in studies addressing climatological and current atmospheric information as they related to chemical and biological warfare.

The military services, headquartered at the Pentagon, provided significant funding for scientific and technological research after World War II. (Arlington Historical Society)

Unlike the air force and army, the navy was more likely to fund basic research from which it hoped to derive a useful outcome eventually. The navy had been the first of the military services to fund the Meteorology

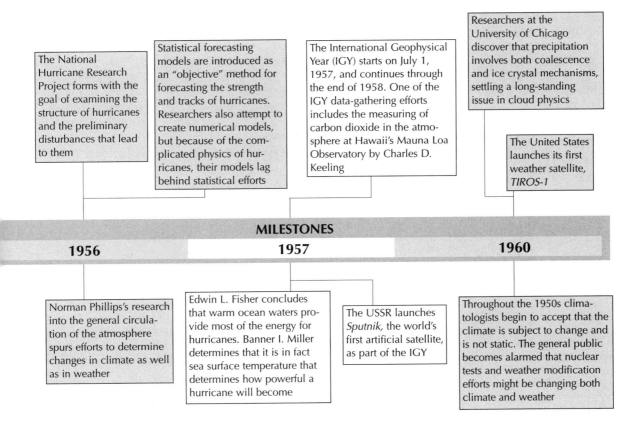

The National Hurricane Research Project forms with the goal of examining the structure of hurricanes and the preliminary disturbances that lead to them

Statistical forecasting models are introduced as an "objective" method for forecasting the strength and tracks of hurricanes. Researchers also attempt to create numerical models, but because of the complicated physics of hurricanes, their models lag behind statistical efforts

The International Geophysical Year (IGY) starts on July 1, 1957, and continues through the end of 1958. One of the IGY data-gathering efforts includes the measuring of carbon dioxide in the atmosphere at Hawaii's Mauna Loa Observatory by Charles D. Keeling

Researchers at the University of Chicago discover that precipitation involves both coalescence and ice crystal mechanisms, settling a long-standing issue in cloud physics

The United States launches its first weather satellite, TIROS-1

MILESTONES

1956   **1957**   **1960**

Norman Phillips's research into the general circulation of the atmosphere spurs efforts to determine changes in climate as well as in weather

Edwin L. Fisher concludes that warm ocean waters provide most of the energy for hurricanes. Banner I. Miller determines that it is in fact sea surface temperature that determines how powerful a hurricane will become

The USSR launches Sputnik, the world's first artificial satellite, as part of the IGY

Throughout the 1950s climatologists begin to accept that the climate is subject to change and is not static. The general public becomes alarmed that nuclear tests and weather modification efforts might be changing both climate and weather

Project on numerical weather prediction and was an active supporter of weather modification efforts. It also funded research taking place at McMurdo Station on Antarctica, staffing the station year-round with military and civilian scientists and technicians. As the tensions escalated between the United States and the USSR, and it appeared that the next war might be fought over the North Pole, the navy also funded research in the Arctic. A research station established in the far northern Alaska territory examined both meteorological and oceanographic conditions, collected data for climatological studies, and developed knowledge on war-fighting techniques and provisions necessary to win a war in a region more familiar to the Russians.

The Russians also expended large sums on meteorological research during this period and for the same reasons as the United States. Each side was convinced that the other had better meteorological forecasting capabilities and either had mastered, or was close to mastering, the control of weather as a weapon. The lack of communication between scientists on opposite sides of the iron curtain heightened suspicion on both sides as they sought ways of obtaining research results for in-depth analysis.

Despite the suspicion, meteorologists from around the world would join during the International Geophysical Year to obtain data needed to determine the nature of the general circulation of the atmosphere. While all participants were supposed to share all of their data, each nation withheld some of its data for national security reasons. Although scientists almost always promote internationalism and the free exchange of scientific information and discoveries, national security almost always takes precedence. With the military funding much of the research, some of it secretly, clearly its needs had greater priority than purely scientific needs. The military-dependent numerical weather prediction project was unclassified and its success would dramatically change 20th-century meteorology.

A Virtual Atmosphere and Real Weather

Progress in numerical weather prediction continued throughout this decade. By 1952, Jule Charney and his Meteorology Project team had reached the point where it was time to talk about going "operational." In all scientific research projects there is a time when the technique under development needs to leave the controlled world of the laboratory, where scientists have virtually unlimited time to analyze and perfect data, adjust their methodology, and consult other scientists. A new methodology may work very well in the laboratory or computer center, but the true test of its worth occurs when it enters the "real world," where it must produce a usable product in limited time, with imperfect data and balky equipment. In the early 1950s, it was time for the virtual reality of numerical weather prediction to meet the real world.

Besides the need to convince theoretical and applied meteorologists that numerical weather prediction techniques accurately portrayed the future state of the atmosphere, meteorologists such as Charney in the United States and Rossby in Sweden faced three primary challenges. First, they needed a computer that would withstand the rigors of everyday use. John von Neumann's new computer (dubbed Johnniac) in Princeton could run the atmospheric models, but it had persistent hardware problems. The Swedish machine BESK, modeled on von Neumann's computer architecture, had similar problems but had been

Jule Charney, Norman Phillips, Glenn Lewis, Norma Gilbarg, and George Platzman of the Meteorology Project at the Institute for Advanced Study, Princeton, New Jersey, 1952 (Photography by project member Joseph Smagorinsky; AIP Emilio Segrè Visual Archives)

built with an operational use in mind. Second, they needed to be able to obtain data from around the world, sort out and remove the faulty observations, and feed the rest into the computer in a short amount of time. In the development phase, this often took weeks; for an operational forecast, meteorologists would only have a few hours to prepare data. To solve this nontrivial problem, meteorologists worked with both communications specialists and computer specialists developing automated data processing techniques. Third, they needed more than just a handful of people to deal with the input of data and the interpretation of the results. This new breed of meteorologist needed a sense of the atmosphere and the mathematical skills to adjust atmospheric models until the computer-created virtual atmosphere looked like the real weather outside the window.

The Joint Numerical Weather Prediction Unit, a combined effort of the U.S. Weather Bureau, Air Force, and Navy, started producing its first operational weather maps in 1955, several months after Rossby's team and BESK started producing the same kinds of maps for Sweden. These first prognostic charts looked meteorological, but they were not as good as those produced by experienced weather forecasters. Instead of producing surface forecasts, which must take friction, and therefore topography, into account (a very difficult and time-consuming problem), the first models produced a chart for the 500-millibar (about 18,000-ft. [5,5000-m]) level. Meteorologists chose this level because it is considered to be the midpoint in the atmosphere—half of the total mass of air in the atmosphere is above this level and half below. Motion at this level determines what happens at the surface and was the flight level for most airplanes at the time. With each computer run, meteorologists found additional problems with the models, which they revised and then put back into operation. Although it was not a fast process, continuous improvement allowed the gradual phasing out of hand-drawn charts in favor of the computer-generated versions that were sent electronically to civilian and military weather stations around the country and at sea.

Atmospheric models remained comparatively rudimentary throughout the 1950s because computers were not sophisticated enough to handle the large numbers of variables required to describe the atmosphere completely. Throughout the 20th century, computer models of weather, and later climate, were limited by the size of available computers. The ability to test theoretical ideas about atmospheric behavior "quickly" (days instead of months) made numerical weather prediction a valuable tool for understanding the atmosphere. By the end of the decade, the USSR, Japan, Great Britain, and Germany had all established modeling groups in addition to those at U.S. and Swedish centers. Their combined efforts led to rapid advances in scientific knowledge of atmospheric conditions and behavior.

Big Machines with Tiny Brains

The ENIAC—Electronic Numerical Integrator and Computer—had made its appearance in 1946, the first of many electronic calculators to be known as computers. (Before this time, the term *computer* was applied to people who did mathematical calculations.) By the 1950s, these vacuum tube–filled giants occupied entire rooms (and had far less memory than today's cell phones), had been dubbed "brains" by the press, and were expected to perform an amazing array of tasks. Among the uses anticipated by the end of the decade: the complete translation of books from one language to another, the "control" of the Missouri River, and, of course, weather prediction.

The first UNIVAC machine (1951) took up a 140-square-foot (13-m^2) space, contained over 5,000 vacuum tubes, and performed 465 multiplications per second. IBM's first commercial machine, the 701 (1952), was about four times faster, at 2,000 multiplications per second. That may sound fast, but the average desktop computer today handles about 100 million instructions per second and 2004's fastest supercomputer handled 70 trillion instructions per second—35 billion times faster than IBM's 701, which was used to compute the Weather Bureau's first operational weather maps in 1955.

These early computers, with their blinking lights and miles of wire, did make computations faster, and more accurately, than could be accomplished with adding machines and slide rules. Their unreliability was a continuing problem. The vacuum tubes burned out quickly and when one died, the "brain" stopped working until it was replaced. It was difficult to detect and solve both hardware and software problems. Getting data in and out of the machines took a long time. When the early weather modelers were trying to run their programs, they took three weeks to process the data to load into the computer and just three hours to compute the forecast. Considering that people could compile the data on pieces of paper and in their heads and make the forecast in less than 12 hours, the electronic "brain" was not an improvement over the human brain.

Engineers working for the large computer companies continuously developed methods of increasing the memory, data handling, and computational capabilities of their machines to meet the needs of business, government, and academic customers. In the 21st century, computers and the small handheld electronic devices that everyone takes for granted will continue to become more powerful and be used to solve increasingly complex problems. It remains to be seen whether they ever become the "brains" anticipated by 1950s-era media accounts. After all, the human brain handles about 10 quadrillion instructions per second.

The General Circulation of the Atmosphere

Wind patterns—the physical manifestation of the general circulation of the atmosphere—have been known since people starting sailing long distances across the oceans. Some, such as the Viking Erik the Red, found out about persistent westerly winds the hard way during failed attempts to sail from Iceland to Greenland. Others, such as Christopher Columbus, found that easterly winds would carry them across the Atlantic if they sailed down the west coast of Africa before trying to head west. By the late 1600s, these wind systems had been plotted on sailing charts and were used to advantage by ships' captains. The first conceptual model of atmospheric circulation did not appear until 1735, when the English scholar George Hadley (1685–

1768) suggested that the conservation of angular momentum explained the easterly flowing *trade winds*. By the middle to late 19th century, the Americans William Ferrel (1817–91) and James Henry Coffin (1806–73) had both developed the familiar three-cell model. As the illustration shows, the model describes air rising at the equator and at 60° of latitude, sinking at 30° latitude and at the poles, and flowing along the surface from west to east between 30° and 60° of latitude, and easterly elsewhere. Their conceptual model showed what happened—not why it happened.

Scientists continued to work on this problem off and on, gathering observational information and attempting to make sense of it. The lack of upper-air observations meant that they were only able to see what was happening at the surface. An accurate description of the general circulation needed to include air movement throughout the atmosphere. Scientists would also need simultaneous measurements over a large area of the Earth's surface—an unlikely event given the limited availability of transportation, balloons, and instrument packets. The first attempt to gather a geographically smaller and yet massive amount of upper-air information took place in the mid-1930s, when Jacob Bjerknes and Erik Palmén arranged the launch of a "swarm" of 120 radiosondes from 11 European countries into a developing midlatitude cyclone. A similar event would not take place again until the International Geophysical Year.

By the mid-1940s, meteorologists were really no further ahead in determining the general atmospheric circulation. As the British meteo-

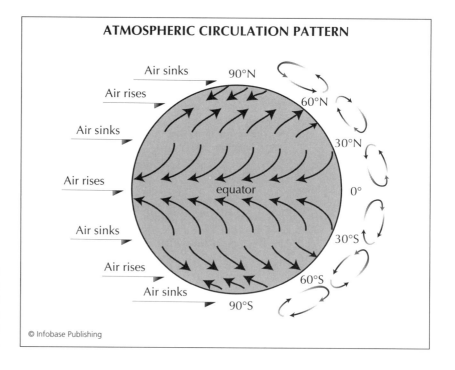

The three circulation cells in each hemisphere present a simple view of atmospheric motion that is made more complicated by topography and heat-transfer processes.

rologist Sir David Brunt (1886–1965) noted in 1944, the only way to figure out the wind pattern was to start with the temperature distribution, derive the corresponding pressure pattern, and only then draw a conclusion about the most logical wind circulation. Meteorologists were working on the problem; they just had no way of reaching a final decision on how the atmosphere transferred energy to support circulation. The problem might have remained unanswered except for the introduction of numerical weather prediction.

Original work in numerical weather prediction was not directly connected to the general circulation problem. Models and computers could not handle multiple layers and large geographical areas. The initial runs in the United States did not even cover all of North America—there was not enough memory or calculating power. The purpose of numerical weather prediction was to make a forecast for a defined geographic area, not for the entire Northern Hemisphere and certainly not for the whole globe. Meteorologists were sure that as computer size increased they would be able to do so. In the meantime, the meteorologist Norman A. Phillips (1923–   ), who had worked with the Meteorology Project, decided to create a general circulation model over a geographical space approximately 6,200 miles by 3,700 miles (10,000 km by 6,000 km) and to integrate the defining equations every hour for as many days as he could—that is, until the model started producing nonsense. His atmospheric model was simpler than the real atmosphere. Phillips's "world" did not distinguish among land, water, and frozen ocean areas, and he started with a predefined initial atmosphere. Running for 12 computer hours, Phillips's model churned out charts 31 days into the future. The resulting maps provided a reasonable approximation of atmospheric behavior, showing that disturbances (that is, "storms") would be created, live, decay, and ultimately die over a several-day period. This success meant that unlike weather prediction, which only needed to be calculated for a few days, prediction of atmospheric changes over many years would be possible in the future. It would be possible to create not just weather models, but climate models.

Phillips's work, published in 1956, became the basis for all future climate models. Many such models run today. Significantly more complex than the first general circulation model, today's models include detailed topography, changing atmospheric chemistry, and atmospheric variables such as moisture content. Environmental policies based on the output from these models have the potential to shape the way Earth will look in the next century and beyond.

Statistical Meteorology

Numerical weather prediction was not the only forecasting technique to face opposition in the 1950s. Meteorologists who advocated the use of statistics as a prediction tool also confronted significant opposition from their synoptic meteorology colleagues. The synopticians—those meteorologists who met the daily challenge of preparing weather forecasts—viewed statistical methods with virtually the same disdain with which they had viewed the *dynamic meteorology* of Vilhelm Bjerknes some 50 years before. Certainly dynamic meteorology had been critical for gaining a more detailed understanding of atmospheric processes, but did it help forecasters determine the next day's weather? For most synopticians, the answer was no. Similarly, early 20th-century attempts to use statistics in forecasting had not given forecasters much useful information. On the contrary, statistics had often just confused the issue. When statistical methods were divorced from dynamic considerations—for instance, when some statisticians attempted to connect the position of the planets with weather on Earth—they lost all credibility.

By the 1950s advances in statistical theory and increasing computer capability made the use of statistics for weather forecasting seem more promising. The large amount of observational data streaming in every day gave atmospheric scientists an instant "snapshot" of the world's weather. This snapshot was what statisticians would refer to as a data sample. Although the data sample could be used to calculate atmospheric disturbances, some of them would be too small to be handled by numerical weather prediction—which "filtered out" such small-scale effects to keep the solution under control. These small perturbations did appear to be statistically distributed, as meteorologists could see by looking at precipitation charts. Some geographic areas consistently received more rain than others even when affected by the exact same weather system. Using statistics and making probability forecasts for precipitation (for example, 30 percent chance of rain) seemed to be the best choice.

To succeed, meteorologists and statisticians had to work together since neither group was likely to have full knowledge of the other's field. Meteorologists could provide advice on which physical properties were dynamically related and statisticians could "crunch the numbers." For example, there is a strong correlation between air mass type and air temperature. If the air mass changed (the front passed by) suddenly, then the statistical prediction would fall apart. Statistical techniques had to be used together with a subjective analysis of the atmospheric situation to be effective.

As promising as it seemed, in the 1950s the use of statistics in meteorology was actually restricted to the use of statistics in climatology. Climatological studies began during World War II and continued after the war, allowing meteorologists to compute probabilities for temperature and precipitation in a given locality for a given week, month, or season. These climatological statistics offered the promise of clues to general atmospheric circulation and short-term forecasts.

Improved data collection and analysis, as well as statistical techniques, gradually made statistical meteorology more acceptable. Increased computer capability allowed the inclusion of more atmospheric variables, which heightened the physical reliability of the result. Particularly in hurricane and tornado forecasting, statistical methods would become critical for determining where these severe weather systems were most likely to strike.

The International Geophysical Year

The International Geophysical Year (IGY), which ran from July 1, 1957, through December 31, 1958, was a period of concentrated international scientific cooperation in the spirit of the two International Polar Years (1882–83 and 1932–33). This particular 18-month period was selected because it was the 25th anniversary of the Second International Polar Year and because it would be a period of unusually active solar activity. Although 13 different scientific programs investigated the geophysical relationships between Earth and space, and between different locations on Earth, the primary purpose of the IGY was to gather and analyze simultaneously data from around the world in fields where conditions changed rapidly. Meteorology, which focuses on the constantly changing atmosphere and its interactions with Earth, was one of those fields.

More than 60 nations and thousands of scientists participated in the IGY. Participants focused most of their research at stations located in the Antarctic and Arctic, along the equator, and along the longitude lines of 10°E, 110°E, 70°W, and 140°W. A special committee assembled and sponsored by the International Council of Scientific Unions (ICSU) provided uniform instructions to all participating nations. Each nation determined its own research program. The IGY's

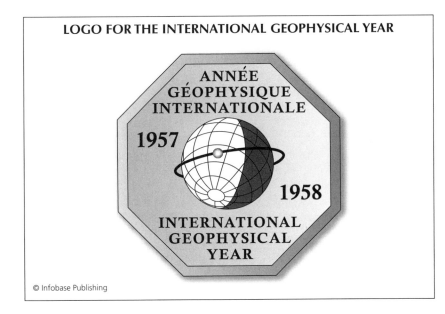

LOGO FOR THE INTERNATIONAL GEOPHYSICAL YEAR

ANNÉE GÉOPHYSIQUE INTERNATIONALE

1957

1958

INTERNATIONAL GEOPHYSICAL YEAR

© Infobase Publishing

The International Geophysical Year's (IGY's) logo clearly shows the intent to launch the first artificial satellite in history.

meteorology program, which focused most of its attention on the problem of the general circulation of the atmosphere, depended heavily on the international sharing of observational data. Establishing a chain of observation stations along three of the four longitudinal lines (10°E [Europe/Africa], 70°W [North/South America], 140°W [Japan/Australia]), which effectively divided the globe into three roughly equal parts, participants simultaneously collected data on "Regular World Days" and "World Meteorological Intervals." Researchers launched rockets to high altitudes and developed balloons that could ascend to the outer reaches of the atmosphere to gather information on radiation, ozone, and carbon dioxide (CO_2). These measurements aided scientists conducting research on the global energy budget (that is, the inbound solar radiation compared to the outbound Earth radiation). The resulting data were deposited in three World Data Centers (United States, USSR, and either Japan or Europe), which remain major repositories for global climatological information. (There are currently 52 centers holding data from 33 earth science disciplines.)

Through data collected during the IGY, meteorologists confirmed the presence of the jet stream that encircles the globe and identified the long-term trend in increasing atmospheric CO_2 concentration (see the sidebar "The Keeling Curve"). The project's simultaneous collection of atmospheric information marked the first time that data required to meet the needs of new numerical weather prediction models had been available. The installation of new observation stations around the world and heightened international cooperation in meteorological research during the IGY set the stage for future global collection efforts, including the World Weather Watch of the 1960s and the Global Atmospheric Research Program (GARP) of the 1970s. The continued international efforts set in motion by the IGY would be critical as scientists focused on air pollution and climate change problems in the second half of the 20th century.

Triggering Climate Change

The evidence was beginning to mount in the 1950s that climate was not a static geographic feature. Callendar's warnings from the late 1930s and early 1940s seemed to be more realistic with each passing year. The climate specialist Helmut E. Landsberg (1906–85) noted that there had been a noticeable warming trend on both sides of the northern Atlantic since the turn of the century. The Swedish glaciologist and climatologist Hans Ahlmann (1889–1974) pointed to the retreat of Iceland's Áobrekke glacier as evidence of warming. The MIT meteorologist Hurd C. Willett (1903–92) had examined global temperature data and reported that most of the warming occurred north of 50°N latitude. Between 1890 and 1940 scientists had recorded a 30 percent decrease in the thickness of ice covering the Arctic Ocean and a decrease in horizontal extent of almost 15

The Keeling Curve

The systematic measurement of atmospheric CO_2 was one of the many data gathering efforts begun during the IGY and it has continued to the present time. The Weather Bureau's Harry Wexler (1911–62), who led the atmospheric science efforts for the United States, obtained funding to install an infrared gas analyzer to make continuous readings of CO_2 at the Mauna Loa Observatory on the "Big Island" of Hawaii. The observatory was chosen because of its location in the middle of the Pacific, far removed from industrial pollution, and because its elevation of 11,140 feet (3,397 m) guaranteed the availability of clean air. The task of collecting and analyzing the CO_2 data fell to a young atmospheric chemist, Charles D. Keeling (1928–2005) of the Scripps Institution of Oceanography in San Diego, California.

Keeling had been studying atmospheric CO_2 since 1954. Before starting his project he had consulted Guy Stewart Callendar, obtaining data on CO_2 levels extending back to the 19th century. Examining the combination of the continuous readout of CO_2 data from the Mauna Loa Observatory and readings obtained in Antarctica during the IGY, Keeling realized that the percentage of CO_2 in the atmosphere had increased from 1958 to 1959. In contrast to the commonly held assumption that once a good measurement had been made there would not be enough variation to warrant additional measurements, Keeling discovered that the CO_2 level changed with the seasons—a significant 3 percent change in the Northern Hemisphere between spring and fall. Had the results shown no overall increase and no intraannual variation, the CO_2 measuring

(continues)

The Mauna Loa Observatory on the island of Hawaii (NOAA Photo Library)

(continued)

program might have ceased at the end of the IGY. Since Keeling's initial findings confirmed Callendar's argument that the concentration of atmospheric CO_2 had been steadily increasing since the industrialization of the early 19th century, the measurements continued. In 1961, Keeling published the first version of what came to be known as the Keeling curve. The now-familiar sawtoothed curve shown in the accompanying illustration indicates a steady increase in CO_2 levels since 1958.

The intraannual variation in the Northern Hemisphere is due to the effect of plant life on CO_2 levels. In the spring, when plants leaf out, they absorb large quantities of CO_2 for photosynthesis and produce large quantities of oxygen. The CO_2 level drops as this process continues until the fall. When leaves die and fall back to the ground, the process of decay releases the CO_2 back to the atmosphere, and the level increases once again.

The overall increase in CO_2 levels concerned scientists and spurred additional research into the climatic effects of CO_2. In the almost 50 years since Charles Keeling made his first measurements at Mauna Loa, the Keeling curve has become one of the most recognizable symbols of the global warming debate.

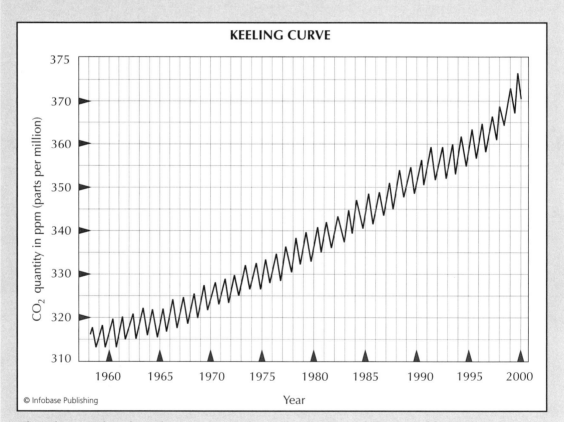

The Keeling curve shows the steady increase in atmospheric carbon dioxide since the beginning of the International Geophysical Year (IGY) collection program in 1958.

percent. Sea level was rising and schools of cod were moving north from their usual habitats. No one was really sure what was causing the change. Most meteorologists steadfastly refused to believe that CO_2 could be the cause. They were convinced that Callendar had not taken into account the amount of CO_2 that could and would be stored in the world's oceans. Some members of the general public connected the rising air temperature with the testing of nuclear weapons. Meteorologists quickly disputed that claim, but it was no longer possible to dismiss possibilities without finding one that would work.

By the mid-1950s, some meteorologists favored changes in the Sun's radiation as a cause, but there was really no evidence to back up this claim. Meteorologists did not accept climate change as being attributable to the rearrangement of Earth's continents and oceans proposed by Alfred Wegener and known as continental drift. Nor did they accept the

Some people mistakenly thought that nuclear bomb tests, such as this nuclear explosion during Operation Teapot at the Nevada Test Site in 1955, were changing the weather. (National Security Administration, Nevada Site Office)

Scientist of the Decade: Jule Gregory Charney (1917–1981)

The mathematician-turned-meteorologist Jule Charney was born in San Francisco, California, to Stella and Ely Charney—both Russian émigrés. Raised in Los Angeles, he was attracted to mathematics by the time he was in high school and had familiarized himself with the basics of differential and integral calculus before enrolling in the University of California, Los Angeles. Graduating from UCLA in 1938 with an A.B. (with honors) in both mathematics and physics, he turned his sights on graduate school. Remaining at UCLA, within two years he had a master's degree in mathematics, and it appeared that he would earn the first mathematics Ph.D. awarded at the university. When World War II intervened, Charney's life took a different path.

While attending a seminar discussing fluid turbulence, Charney heard a talk by the Norwegian meteorologist Jörgen Holmboe (1902–79) from UCLA's physics department. A new meteorology program under Jacob Bjerknes's leadership was just getting established and Holmboe invited Charney to join him as an assistant in spring 1941 as the new military meteorology training program was taking shape. After discussing with his mentors the relative merits of turning his attentions to aeronautical engineering or to meteorology in support of the war effort, Charney decided to apply his considerable mathematical abilities and theoretical interests to the atmosphere.

While learning about the atmosphere, Charney was also teaching about the atmosphere, staying just slightly ahead of his students. The synoptic meteorology of Bjerknes and Holmboe, with its emphasis on hand-drawn weather maps to determine current and future atmospheric conditions,

did not appeal to the mathematical Charney. Once exposed to Carl-Gustav Rossby's theoretical writings, Charney could envision making a real contribution to the discipline. His doctoral dissertation on the behavior of unstable waves in westerly flow, including how wind, temperature, and pressure were distributed within them, was published shortly after its completion and was widely accepted as an explanation for this phenomenon, although the mathematics he used was well beyond the understanding of most meteorologists at the time. Not only did Charney make a significant contribution to the field with his first major meteorological project, he did so without the assistance of fluid dynamics experts.

After receiving a Ph.D. in 1946, Charney was awarded a National Research Council fellowship, and he decided to use it to study with the meteorologist Halvor Solberg in Oslo, Norway. While he was en route to Norway, Charney fortuitously stopped off to visit Rossby at the University of Chicago. With an extremely active research program in progress, Rossby used his considerable charm and powers of persuasion to convince Charney to remain in Chicago. Postponing his fellowship for almost a year, Charney was with Rossby when discussions concerning the new Meteorology Project and the possibilities for numerical weather prediction first began in the summer of 1946. Using mathematics and computers to describe the atmosphere appealed greatly to Charney, and when he finally left for Norway in 1947, he was considering how to adapt the physical equations of motion, in addition to the thermodynamic and hydrodynamic equations, into an atmospheric model solvable by numerical

possibility that orbital changes could have a significant influence. Even while acknowledging that CO_2 levels had risen as a result of industrialization, most meteorologists doubted that CO_2 had sufficient absorptive properties to produce a notable temperature increase. It appeared that

The numerical weather prediction pioneer Jule Gregory Charney, from the cover of Eos 57 *(August 1976) (© Nora Rosenbaum)*

Project in 1948, leading the effort to develop numerical weather prediction as both a theoretical and an applied research tool. The combined efforts of everyone on the modeling team led to operational computer forecasting in 1955, as described earlier, and Charney then turned his attention to the establishment of a center to examine the general atmospheric circulation. The Geophysical Fluid Dynamics Laboratory, now part of the National Oceanic and Atmospheric Administration (NOAA), in Princeton continues as a world leader in cutting-edge atmospheric research.

Charney, who had accepted a professorship at MIT in 1956, spent increasing amounts of time on geophysical fluid dynamics, addressing problems in the atmosphere and oceans. He was in demand as an adviser and consultant on scientific programs and in 1966 became the leader of the Global Atmospheric Research Program (GARP), a position he held until 1971. Charney's research interests also led him to examine issues related to *desertification*—a problem that worsened in the last half of the century.

In addition to his personal achievements—Charney was elected to the National Academy of Sciences and was awarded the most prestigious medals in meteorology—he had a tremendous influence on a generation of new meteorologists because of his outstanding characteristics as a mentor. His supervision of some of the brightest young meteorological minds during his 25 years at MIT led to many significant advances in atmospheric modeling and theoretical meteorology. Charney's death of cancer in 1981 at the age of 64 was a tremendous loss to both the meteorological and oceanographic communities as well as to the scientific community at large.

techniques. Within a year, he had found a way to "filter" out the "noise" from these equations: That is, he had found a way to separate out the large-scale atmospheric motion that influenced the weather from the smaller acoustic and gravity waves that had caused L. F. Richardson's numerical calculations during the First World War to give a wildly wrong forecast for the next day.

Offering his solution to John von Neumann in Princeton, Charney joined the Meteorology

volcanic ash in the atmosphere was the most likely trigger for climate change. Of course, the spewing of large quantities of ash into the atmosphere would have been the trigger for cooling and an ice age—not for global warming.

Then, in his 1956 article "Effects of Carbon Dioxide Variations on Climate," the physicist Gilbert Plass (1920–   ) argued that increasing amounts of CO_2 entering the atmosphere could lead to huge problems if it continued. Plass wrote, "If at the end of the century, measurements show that the CO_2 content of the atmosphere has risen appreciably and at the same time the temperature has continued to rise throughout the world, it will be firmly established that CO_2 is an important factor in causing climate change." He also noted that by the time scientists had sufficient data to determine the outcome of the increasing CO_2 it would be too late to reverse the process. Within two years, Charles Keeling would have the evidence that CO_2 was increasing. By the end of the century it would be an established fact. Between the late 1950s and the end of the century, the debate would rage over climate change. Was climate cooling down or warming up?

Further Reading

Ahlmann, Hans W. *Glacier Variations and Climatic Fluctuations.* New York: American Geographical Society, 1953. The Swedish glaciologist probes the meaning of glacial retreat in climate fluctuation.

Aspray, William. *John von Neumann and the Origins of Modern Computing.* Cambridge, Mass.: MIT Press, 1990. Aspray discusses von Neumann's role in computer architecture, and the role of computers in numerical weather prediction in chapter 6.

Ceruzzi, Paul E. *A History of Modern Computing.* Cambridge, Mass.: MIT Press, 1998. In this scholarly yet accessible book, Ceruzzi traces the development of computing (both hardware and software) from the first electronic digital computer through the beginnings of the World Wide Web.

Landsberg, Helmut E. "Trends in Climatology." *Science* 128 (1958): 749–758. In this article Landsberg, one of the premier climatologists of the 20th century, discusses how the science of climatology had changed and what the prospects were for climate change.

Lindzen, Richard S., Edward N. Lorenz, and George W. Platzman, editors. *The Atmosphere—a Challenge: The Science of Jule Gregory Charney.* Boston: American Meteorological Society, 1990. This edited volume of Charney's most important papers also provides information about his life and influence on meteorology.

Malone, Thomas F. *Compendium of Meteorology.* Boston: American Meteorological Society, 1951. A huge undertaking, this 1,334-page volume captures the latest in meteorological thought in the 1950s.

Phillips, Norman A. "The General Circulation of the Atmosphere: A Numerical Experiment." *Quarterly Journal of the Royal Meteorological Society* 82 (1956): 123–164. Phillips's groundbreaking article discusses the results of his numerical simulations of atmospheric motion.

Plass, Gilbert N. "Effect of Carbon Dioxide Variation on Climate." *American Journal of Physics* 24 (1956): 376–387. Plass argues that carbon dioxide will significantly influence the global climate.

Sullivan, Walter. *Assault on the Unknown: The International Geophysical Year.* New York: McGraw-Hill, 1961. Sullivan, a prominent and famous *New York Times* reporter, wrote this book as a result of his experiences covering the IGY story.

Willett, Hurd C. "Temperature Trends of the Past Century." In *Royal Meteorological Society Centenary Proceedings*, pp. 195–206. London: Royal Meteorological Society, 1950. Willett examines how global temperature had changed since the mid-19th century.

7

1961–1970: Remote Sensing Impacts Weather and Climate Studies

It may have provided low-quality, grainy photographs, but *TIROS-1*, America's first weather satellite, was a boon to meteorologists and weather forecasters as it provided images of frontal systems and tropical storms at sea, far from surface observation posts. Over the course of the decade, more sophisticated weather satellites were launched, carrying additional sensors to measure global temperatures as well as to provide photographs of clouds.

Meteorologists continued to actively research techniques for weather modification and to advance numerical weather prediction. While neither was living up to its advertised capabilities, both were in operational use by the end of the decade.

Concerns about climate change were also heard during the 1960s. The meteorologist Edward N. Lorenz (1917–   ), father of chaos theory, pointed out the chaotic nature of Earth's climate system and documented the possibility that climate could suddenly switch from *glacial* to *interglacial* and back. As meteorologists expanded their modeling efforts to describe climate, they continued to add more atmospheric variables to their calculations in an attempt to generate a more accurate picture of Earth's future atmosphere.

Eyes in the Sky

Meteorologists have always known that they would have a much easier time forecasting the weather if they could see approaching weather systems. In the early 20th century, they addressed this problem by sending observational data via telegraph to stations downstream to advise them of heavy rain, snow, or wind en route. Knowing the upstream weather did not guarantee it would not change before arrival. Forecasters on coastlines were blind to weather moving in from the oceans because there were no observers sitting in the middle of the water radioing in observations.

Attempts to change this situation began in the late 1920s. The rocket expert Robert Goddard (1882–1945) launched an instrument packet containing a barometer, a thermometer, and a camera in 1929. Advances in rocketry during World War II led to the launching of more sophisticated meteorological equipment that produced the first composite photographs of clouds taken from the top of the atmosphere in 1949. These photographs were interesting and provided enticing evidence of their usefulness, but they reached forecasters too late to be operationally useful. The introduction of weather radar after World War II provided a better long-distance "eye" for meteorologists, but radar only "sees" a relatively few miles away. What was needed was a way to see an entire region of the Earth. Meteorologists needed weather satellites.

With the launch of the USSR's *Sputnik* in 1957 during the IGY, the race was on to launch additional artificial satellites into space. Weather forecasting would be an obvious beneficiary of such technology if scientists could attach sensors to collect and transmit data or photographs to meteorologists. The United States launched its first weather satellite, *TIROS-1*, on April 1, 1960. The TIROS series satellites took pictures with a television camera and transmitted them to a receiving station. These early photographs were not operationally useful because the satellite's spin axis pointed out into space. This meant the photographs included a lot of black space along with a few clouds. Once engineers

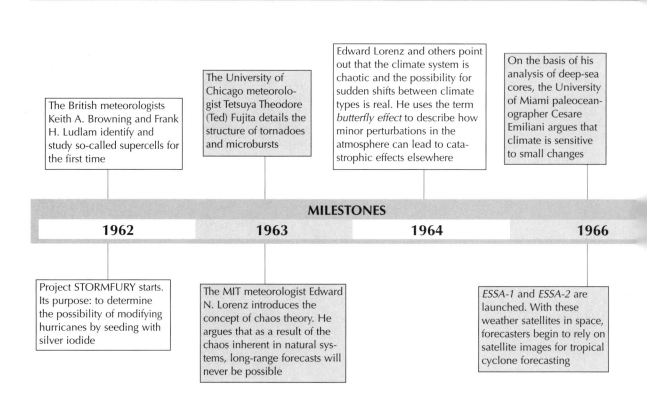

The British meteorologists Keith A. Browning and Frank H. Ludlam identify and study so-called supercells for the first time

The University of Chicago meteorologist Tetsuya Theodore (Ted) Fujita details the structure of tornadoes and microbursts

Edward Lorenz and others point out that the climate system is chaotic and the possibility for sudden shifts between climate types is real. He uses the term *butterfly effect* to describe how minor perturbations in the atmosphere can lead to catastrophic effects elsewhere

On the basis of his analysis of deep-sea cores, the University of Miami paleoceanographer Cesare Emiliani argues that climate is sensitive to small changes

MILESTONES

| 1962 | 1963 | 1964 | 1966 |

Project STORMFURY starts. Its purpose: to determine the possibility of modifying hurricanes by seeding with silver iodide

The MIT meteorologist Edward N. Lorenz introduces the concept of chaos theory. He argues that as a result of the chaos inherent in natural systems, long-range forecasts will never be possible

ESSA-1 and *ESSA-2* are launched. With these weather satellites in space, forecasters begin to rely on satellite images for tropical cyclone forecasting

realigned the cameras, the photographs became useful tools and meteorologists clamored for them.

NASA launched 10 experimental TIROS series satellites between 1960 and 1965 and followed them with nine operational ESSA satellites, and seven Nimbus research satellites. Unlike the ESSA satellites, which were strictly for meteorological measurements, the Nimbus series provided information across the wide range of earth science disciplines.

All of these satellites were polar orbiters. As the illustration at the bottom of page 128 shows, polar orbiting satellites continued on the same track from pole to pole while the Earth spun underneath them and took pictures of the same spot every 12 hours. Meteorologists needed information more often than twice per day when storms were moving quickly. The answer to the problem was the launching of the first Applications Technology Satellite (*ATS-1*) on December 6, 1966. It was the first geosynchronous satellite.

Geosynchronous satellites are placed in orbit about 22,000 miles (36,000 km) out in space directly above the equator. At this distance, they remain in the same position relative to a fixed spot on the surface. They send back a "full disk" photograph of Earth's surface, showing half

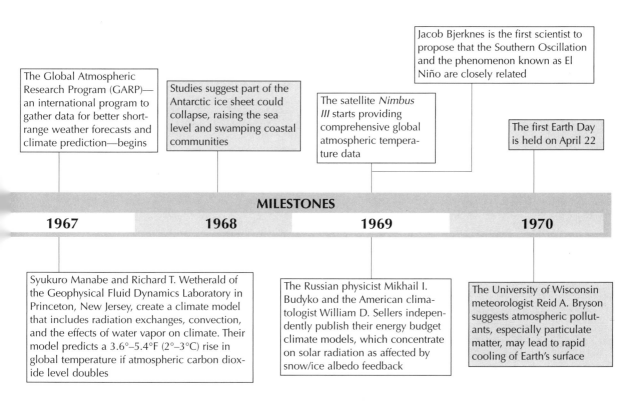

The Global Atmospheric Research Program (GARP)—an international program to gather data for better short-range weather forecasts and climate prediction—begins

Studies suggest part of the Antarctic ice sheet could collapse, raising the sea level and swamping coastal communities

The satellite *Nimbus III* starts providing comprehensive global atmospheric temperature data

Jacob Bjerknes is the first scientist to propose that the Southern Oscillation and the phenomenon known as El Niño are closely related

The first Earth Day is held on April 22

MILESTONES

1967   **1968**   **1969**   **1970**

Syukuro Manabe and Richard T. Wetherald of the Geophysical Fluid Dynamics Laboratory in Princeton, New Jersey, create a climate model that includes radiation exchanges, convection, and the effects of water vapor on climate. Their model predicts a 3.6°–5.4°F (2°–3°C) rise in global temperature if atmospheric carbon dioxide level doubles

The Russian physicist Mikhail I. Budyko and the American climatologist William D. Sellers independently publish their energy budget climate models, which concentrate on solar radiation as affected by snow/ice albedo feedback

The University of Wisconsin meteorologist Reid A. Bryson suggests atmospheric pollutants, especially particulate matter, may lead to rapid cooling of Earth's surface

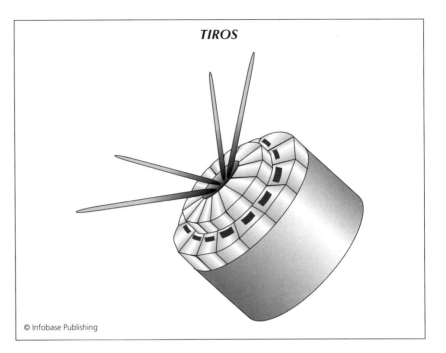

TIROS

© Infobase Publishing

The TIROS series satellites were the first used for weather forecasting.

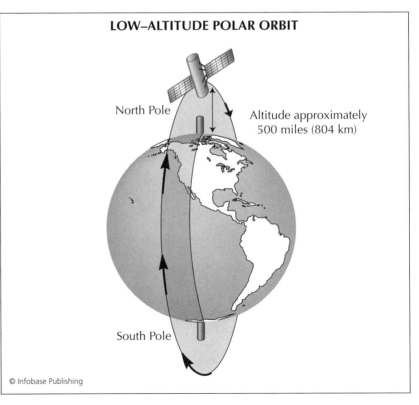

LOW–ALTITUDE POLAR ORBIT

North Pole

Altitude approximately
500 miles (804 km)

South Pole

© Infobase Publishing

Low-altitude polar orbiting satellites fly from pole to pole and back while Earth spins beneath them.

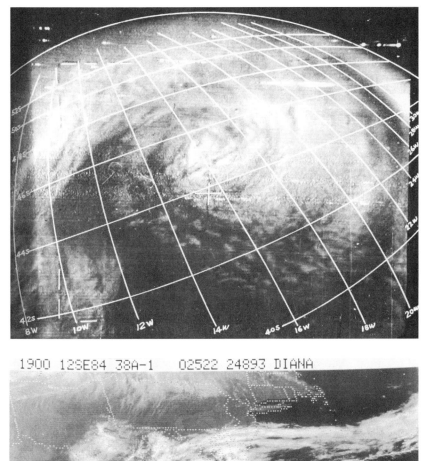

1900 12SE84 38A-1   02522 24893 DIANA

The TIROS-1 *image taken in 1960 is not nearly as clear and informative as the same image taken from* NOAA-15 *in 2000.* (NOAA)

the Earth. Receiving pictures every 30 minutes, meteorologists looped the pictures on film and saw clouds moving across the planet's face for the first time. The Geostationary Operational Environmental Satellite (GOES) series has provided the United States with continuous photographs that cover all of North America plus the Pacific and Atlantic Oceans. Other nations (Japan, Russia, India, and China) and Europe also have geostationary satellites. (More information on GOES satellites may be found in the sidebar "*GOES-1* Goes Up" in chapter 8.)

By the end of the century, meteorological satellite development had advanced to include a variety of specialized sensors that measured temperature, moisture content, precipitation rates, and winds on Earth and throughout multiple atmospheric layers. Meteorologists today depend on these weather eyes in the sky; without them, meteorology as we know it would not be possible.

A New Look at the Energy Budget

By the end of the 1950s, weather modification had evolved from being a matter of changes in local weather (clearing fog, preventing frost on tender young fruit, reducing hail damage, generating rain) to massive plans for climate control. One of the more grandiose schemes proposed by Russian scientists was to eliminate the Arctic ice cap in an attempt to warm up the northern (and very cold) regions of their country to improve their habitability. While the proposal itself may have been rather farfetched, it did inspire atmospheric scientists around the world to start asking the question, What would happen to the world's climate if the Arctic ice melted? The possibility of global warming due to an increase in critical atmospheric gases (carbon dioxide, water vapor, methane) raised the threat of shrinking glaciers and ice sheets. Increases in pollutants in the form of dust and debris (termed *aerosols*) in the atmosphere raised the issue of potential global cooling by blocking sunlight. The time was right for taking a fresh look at the global energy budget.

Scientists considered three primary energy budget–related mechanisms: changes in planetary *albedo* (the reflectivity of Earth's surface), the solar constant (the amount of energy emitted by the Sun), and atmospheric *turbidity* (the extent to which aerosols reduced incoming solar energy). Working independently, in the late 1960s the Russian meteorologist Mikhail I. Budyko (1920–) and the American meteorologist William D. Sellers both reached the same conclusions about these factors' roles in climate change.

Melting the Arctic ice sheet (not viewed as a very realistic option) or covering it with black powder to reduce its albedo (considered by some to be a realistic option), Budyko and Sellers discovered, would affect global temperatures. Their models showed melting or blackening the Antarctic ice sheet would have an even larger effect because its albedo was significantly greater than the Arctic's. With land beneath the ice instead of

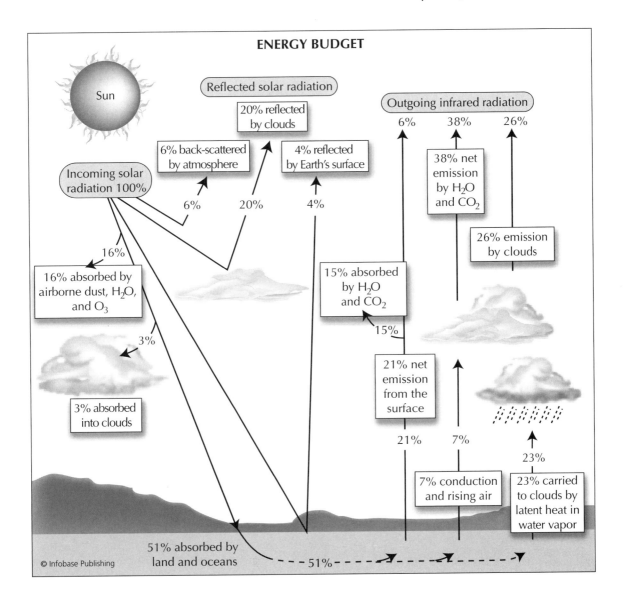

ENERGY BUDGET

Sun

Reflected solar radiation

Outgoing infrared radiation

20% reflected
by clouds

6%   38%   26%

6% back-scattered
by atmosphere

4% reflected
by Earth's surface

38% net
emission
by H_2O
and CO_2

Incoming solar
radiation 100%

6%   20%   4%

26% emission
by clouds

16%

16% absorbed by
airborne dust, H_2O,
and O_3

15% absorbed
by H_2O
and CO_2

3%

15%

3% absorbed
into clouds

21% net
emission
from the
surface

21%   7%

23%

51% absorbed by
land and oceans

7% conduction
and rising air

23% carried
to clouds by
latent heat in
water vapor

© Infobase Publishing

- - - 51% - - - →

water, an Antarctica free of ice would absorb much more energy and contribute to significant temperature increases everywhere but the equator.

Slight changes in the solar constant would also trigger significant climate change. Keeping other variables constant, a 2 percent reduction in solar energy would allow polar ice caps to grow equatorward to the 50° latitude line. A 3 percent increase would cause all the ice sheets to melt. Model experiments that kept the solar constant the same but changed the Earth's ability to transfer heat poleward from the equator also led to climate change. If the transfer rate doubled, the ice sheets would melt and the global temperature increase by 9°F (5°C). If the transfer

The energy budget describes the relationship between incoming and outgoing radiation.

rate were cut in half, temperatures in the Tropics would plunge by 31°F (16°C) and snow would almost reach the equator. On the basis of these outcomes, Budyko and Sellers determined that climate models needed to consider both the possibility of changes in heat transfer within the Earth/atmosphere system and changes in the solar constant, since they could effectively cancel each other out. Exactly how changes in incoming radiation might change the circulation pattern was unknown, but they certainly needed to be considered.

In a much-cited 1966 paper by Budyko and others entitled "Impact of Economic Activity on Climate," they pointed out that people were using increasing amounts of energy (in particular fossil fuels) that were converted to heat. The annual rate of increase was 4 percent. If that rate continued, Budyko argued, in less than 200 years people would actually be producing more heat through their everyday activities than would arrive from the Sun. People would be creating their own climate. Although Sellers thought this was a little extreme, he acknowledged that the effect was likely to be greatest in the middle to high latitudes of the highly industrialized and populated Northern Hemisphere. If people continued to make a significant impact on the atmosphere, Sellers conceded, the temperature increase could melt the polar ice caps. As the ice caps thin and glacier melting accelerates, the role of albedo in climate change is sure to take on a more important role.

Snuffing Out Nascent Hurricanes

Cloud physicists had continued to uncover the mechanisms for cloud development and precipitation during the 1950s. Some of those advancements had been crucial to the further understanding of hurricane development and behavior. Others had been critical to the development of more sophisticated weather modification techniques. Progress in all of these areas merged in a joint Department of Commerce, Environmental Science Services Administration, and U.S. Navy effort called Project STORMFURY. Its ultimate mission: to snuff out hurricanes.

The National Hurricane Research Laboratory had been studying hurricanes since 1956. Using aircraft, radar, and radiosondes to penetrate hurricane eyewalls, scientists had determined that these thick clouds contained a significant amount of supercooled water. Earlier cloud modification studies had shown that seeding such clouds could successfully produce rainfall. Scientists wanted to know whether seeding the supercooled eyewall clouds, the hurricane's primary energy cell, would modify the hurricane structure sufficiently to reduce its strength. In the meantime, cloud physicists at the Naval Ordnance Test Station in China Lake, California, had been experimenting with a new way to introduce silver iodide seeds into supercooled clouds. Their new technique introduced large quantities of subfreezing silver iodide nuclei into the tops of cumulus clouds extending thousands of feet into the atmosphere. This invention made hurricane modification experiments feasible.

Scientists intended to alter the balance of forces within a hurricane by seeding the eyewall clouds, precipitating the moisture, and causing the clouds to collapse. This would stop the "engine" and the storm would die. A preliminary test on Hurricane Esther (1961) caused part of the eyewall cloud to disappear. Although it re-formed within two hours, the test result was good enough to initiate STORMFURY, which, with National Science Foundation funding, was officially under way on July 30, 1962.

Led by the Weather Bureau's Dr. Robert H. Simpson (1912–   ) and advised by a number of prominent meteorologists, STORMFURY participants conducted scientific experiments exploring the structure and dynamics of hurricanes. They wanted to understand better, predict, and possibly eliminate some of the destructive power of these storms. Using a new silver iodide generator, they fired small canisters packed with propellant from a navy aircraft. The canisters would fall 20,000 feet (6,100 m) through a cloud, producing a plume of silver iodide seeds for about 40 seconds. Additional navy planes took meteorological observations and photographs.

Without a good knowledge of hurricane behavior, scientists could not take a chance on seeding a hurricane that was close to populated areas. They outlined a target area in the Atlantic and waited for a hurricane to pass through so they could begin seeding. The first seedable hurricane was Hurricane Beulah in late August 1963. The silver iodide seeds missed the active eyewall on the first attempt, but the second created a pressure increase within the eye and the maximum wind zone moved away from the eyewall. (A hurricane's central pressure is always very low, so if it increases, the hurricane loses strength.) There was no proof that the seeding had caused either of these changes.

These results had raised researchers' hopes, but hurricanes failed to reach the target areas for the next four years. Turning their attention to improving seed delivery and developing numerical hurricane models, they discovered that seeding the first rainband outside the eyewall (as shown in the illustration on page 134) would be more effective than seeding the eyewall itself. The faster-moving air would be drawn away from the center, thus weakening the hurricane. The seeding teams finally had the opportunity to try this new technique in August 1969 on Hurricane Debbie. As expected, the winds died down—on one day by 31 percent and on another by 15 percent. One hurricane experiment does not provide proof. In subsequent years, researchers found themselves without appropriate hurricanes to seed.

There were other problems. Attempts to move STORMFURY to the Pacific Ocean, where there were more hurricanes, led to political disputes with surrounding countries, which declined to risk their populations to modified hurricanes. Aircraft were aging and the navy withdrew its support to fulfill higher-priority defense requirements. On the scientific side, the inability to replicate the experiments meant that researchers could not distinguish between the effects of seeding and naturally occurring hurricane behavior. Additional observations had exposed a fatal flaw in the project: The clouds contained far too many ice crystals and too few

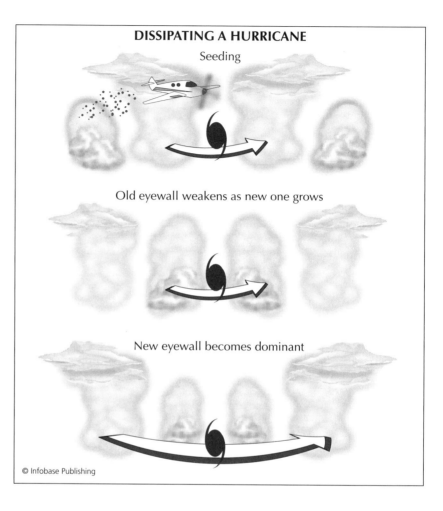

DISSIPATING A HURRICANE

Seeding

Old eyewall weakens as new one grows

New eyewall becomes dominant

© Infobase Publishing

By seeding the tropical cyclone before it grew to hurricane strength, STORMFURY meteorologists hoped to draw energy away from the circulating low-pressure center, causing it to dissipate.

supercooled droplets. Once the underlying assumption for the experiments proved false, the rest of the project collapsed.

STORMFURY may not have been a success in hurricane modification, but it did lead to improved meteorological instrumentation and two decades of exciting and productive hurricane research that would improve hurricane forecasting. Considering the billions of dollars in damage that can be inflicted when a major hurricane strikes a heavily populated coast, the dream of snuffing out these dangerous systems will never really die. Scientists are now more realistic about their ability to influence the strength and path of Earth's largest storms.

The Butterfly Effect

Numerical weather prediction techniques had continued to improve throughout the 1950s. As computer power grew and meteorologists continued to develop a more sophisticated theory of the general circulation of the atmosphere, numerical modelers designed increasingly complex forecasting models. In fact, it often appeared that computer architecture would prove to be the primary obstacle to accurate short- and long-term weather forecasts. As computers could handle more data and process them faster, meteorologists would be standing by to exploit their new capabilities.

This overriding theme in modeling met with a disconcerting halt in the early 1960s with a discovery made by the MIT meteorologist Edward N. Lorenz. Lorenz had been working on his own computer model of the atmosphere and had made numerous "runs" of the data. That is, he had written the program, given it data, and then run it on the computer to produce a forecast. Typically in this kind of work, after a given run the model is adjusted and run again. One day, Lorenz decided to save time by putting in data produced from a previous run and starting the calculation from the middle instead of the beginning. Doing other things while the machine computed the new results, Lorenz was stunned upon his return to see that the new answer was wildly different from his previous run. The newly forecast weather pattern was not even remotely similar to any of the previously calculated patterns—it was almost unrecognizable.

Puzzled, Lorenz looked back to see where he could have erred. To save paper, he had printed out the results from the earlier run to only three decimal places. After all, the calculation was probably only accurate to three decimal places and the remaining trailing digits should not have made a difference. Lorenz had been confident that there would be no problem with entering the three-digit numbers into the middle of the computer program. He was wrong. So was the prevailing idea that

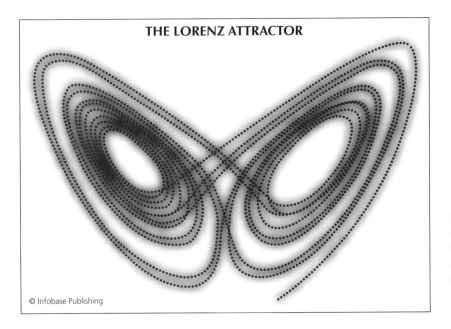

THE LORENZ ATTRACTOR

© Infobase Publishing

The Lorenz attractor, seen here, represents a stable system. Coincidentally, it looks like a butterfly flexing its wings—the symbol representing how small-scale effects may lead to chaos.

small differences in beginning conditions would not make a difference in model output.

Intrigued, Lorenz continued to study how model output was affected by the minutest changes in model input. He concluded that the smallest differences could lead to radically different forecasts and that the differences became greater as the forecast period lengthened. His discovery meant that modelers would find it more difficult to produce long-range (months and years) forecasts than they had previously thought.

Lorenz's discovery that infinitesimal changes in the atmosphere can lead to profound differences in atmospheric behavior became known as the "butterfly effect," from the title of his 1972 talk "Does the Flap of a Butterfly's Wings in Brazil Set Off a Tornado in Texas?" given at the 139th meeting of the American Association for the Advancement of Science. In fact, Lorenz had originally used flapping seagulls as a metaphor for the idea that the very slightest movement somewhere on Earth could change the weather thousands of miles away. The point remained the same: The atmosphere is inherently unstable with respect to small physical changes—it is chaotic. Climate change is just as likely to be a rapid event as a slow one—and the probability that a long-range forecast will ever be perfect is extremely small.

Still Warming Up

Increasing levels of atmospheric CO_2 gave credence to the idea that people were the primary cause of warming surface temperatures. While the popular media published articles about "weird weather," scientists continued to argue about temperature trends and just what they meant for the future.

The geophysicists W. Maurice Ewing (1906–74) and William Donn (1918–87) had proposed that warming would cause the Arctic ice sheet to break up. This event would, they thought, lead to increased precipitation in higher latitudes, triggering a new ice age. Although Ewing and Donn's ideas tended to stay within scientific circles, the idea of a new ice age was picked up by the journalist Betty Friedan (1921–2006) (later known for her work in feminist causes) writing for a popular audience in *Harper's Magazine* in 1958. Just as most people were coming to grips with Earth's surface temperature's warming up, it appeared that the warming might be short-lived. Just what was happening with the temperature pattern?

Guy Stewart Callendar, who had continued his work analyzing the effects of CO_2 emissions on atmospheric warming, published his last paper in 1961. He concluded that there had been a significant increase in the temperature north of 45° latitude, CO_2 levels had increased by 7 percent since 1920, and the increasing back radiation due to CO_2 was responsible for the temperature increases. Since the data clearly showed that CO_2 levels were continuing to rise, it was to be expected that surface temperatures would increase.

Temperatures were "above average" when compared to temperatures over the previous 100 years. The question as the decade opened: Was the

Climate Models Take the Stage

While weather forecasting models were still in their primitive operational stage in the late 1950s, meteorologists moved on to modeling the general circulation of the atmosphere. Although the original intent was to continue the development of atmospheric theory, it soon became evident to those involved that modeling the general circulation would lead to models of climate—the long-term manifestation of the weather that depends upon geographical location and local topography.

General circulation modeling was the mission of the Geophysical Fluid Dynamics Laboratory (GFDL), which was part of the U.S. Weather Bureau. Under the direction of Joseph Smagorinsky (1924–2005), an increasingly mathematically and physics-savvy group of young meteorologists sought to uncover the effects of changes in atmospheric chemistry, radiative transfer, and moisture content (humidity) on atmospheric behavior by running experiments on the computer. Unlike laboratory sciences such as physics, chemistry, and biology, meteorology has as its "laboratory" the atmosphere. Because it is impossible to recreate the entire global atmosphere indoors, meteorologists needed to find another way to see what happened when atmospheric variables such as temperature, pressure, and humidity were modified. They did it by "tweaking" these same variables in their computer programs, running them out over a predetermined number of computer "weeks," and analyzing the results.

The early general circulation–turned–climate models were not very good. Computers were not powerful enough to allow modelers to include more than two layers of the atmosphere in their calculations. Neither could they include the presence of the oceans—a major force in changing the composition of the atmosphere—and mountains. In those very early models, the Earth was flat and all land.

By the early 1960s, models included many atmospheric layers and meteorologists started to introduce a number of thermal (heat-related) processes such as changes in radiation, condensation, and heat transfer. Gradually they included the effects of CO_2, water vapor, and ozone on the absorption of solar radiation. In so doing, modelers tried to examine how air of different temperatures became distributed throughout Earth's atmosphere—an important step in determining what factors most affect climate.

In 1967, Syukuro Manabe (1931–) and Richard T. Wetherald (1936–), both of the GFDL, published their paper "Thermal Equilibrium of the Atmosphere with a Given Distribution of Relative Humidity," which included the combined effects of radiation transfer and the *hydrologic cycle*. They considered the effect of changing amounts of solar radiation, the influence of cloudiness on radiative transfer, the extent to which Earth's albedo changed the energy budget, and ways that chemical constituents in the atmosphere acted as absorbers of radiation and affected surface temperatures. To include these factors, Manabe and Wetherald could only look at one small column of the atmosphere and redo the computations many times.

Since the time of Arrhenius at the end of the 19th century, questions about the effect of anthropogenic warming had come down to this one: What would the temperature be if the CO_2 level doubled? Since the extrapolation of Keeling's curve showed this would probably happen in the 21st century, there was considerable interest in seeing just what a climate model would predict. In 1963, the German meteorologist Fritz Müller's (1906–83) climate model had predicted that doubling the CO_2 level would raise the surface temperature a whopping 18°F (10°C). The new Manabe-Wetherald model predicted a still-substantial 4°F (2.3°C) increase. Because their model included enough of the atmospheric variables meteorologists thought necessary to give an accurate representation of climate, scientists took the predicted greenhouse warming effect seriously. (The term *Greenhouse warming* refers to the heat trapped by the glass of a greenhouse. In the atmosphere, gases such as CO_2, water vapor, and methane do the trapping.) From this point on, climate models would take the lead as atmospheric scientists tried to determine Earth's future climate.

temperature trend up or down? Callendar said it was up. According to the U.S. Weather Bureau, it was down. Having worked through a massive amount of data, the bureau climatologist J. Murray Mitchell, Jr. (1928–), concluded that global temperatures had risen through 1940 but had been falling since. Mitchell had apparently been prompted to undertake the temperature calculation because of preliminary work in Scandinavia showing that Arctic temperatures were leveling off. Because temperature change tends to be most obvious at higher latitudes, atmospheric scientists looked for slight variations there first. Given the concern over warming, Mitchell had decided that it was time for the bureau to make a detailed analysis of all the data. He did not have a reason to account for a cooling trend. The extra CO_2 should be causing warming, and it certainly would not lead to cooling. Perhaps, Mitchell thought, the cooling was due to changes in the solar constant or to greater than average amounts of volcanic ash being carried in the upper atmosphere. Neither of these explanations seemed plausible. In his article "Recent Secular Changes of Global Temperature," Mitchell declared the situation "an enigma."

There is a fundamental difficulty with determining temperature trends. The calculations must be made for the entire Earth, not for just one location, nor even for several locations scattered around the world. This is not a trivial undertaking now, and it was even more difficult in the 1960s before the introduction of the World Weather Watch and other programs that ensured the systematic sharing, gathering, and processing of tens of thousands of observations made every day. It took scientists several years after the data were collected to determine what had happened. That is why the "warming" trend that everyone thought had occurred during the 1940s was actually a cooling trend, and why the "cooling" trend that Mitchell thought had occurred in the 1950s was actually a warming trend. The global temperature continued to rise in the last half of the 1950s and remained high, although cooling, during the 1960s. It would not be until the 1970s that questions—and concerns—about atmospheric cooling would push into the forefront of public awareness. In the 1960s, CO_2 levels and warming were still a concern only in scientific circles. In those circles, climate change had become an issue that was not going away.

Looking at El Niño

Examinations of climate, as well as of weather, were a common feature of this decade. Meteorologists began looking for connections between atmospheric and oceanographic phenomena that might seem unrelated at first glance. One meteorological event that drew increased interest was known as El Niño.

El Niño is the term used to describe the change in the oceanic current along the coasts of Ecuador and Peru from cold to warm. Translated "the Christ Child," El Niño typically appears around Christmas (hence the name) and lasts for several months. Some years, the water becomes espe-

cially warm and remains warm into the early summer, the fishing industry collapses because the fish move to colder waters, and rains become
abnormally heavy. It is for this extended change in ocean currents and
the subsequent weather patterns that atmospheric scientists now reserve
the term *El Niño*. During particularly severe El Niño events, such as the
one that took place in 1982–83, the weather pattern becomes radically
different all around the world. The illustration below depicts ocean temperature and wind pattern changes accompanying El Niño.

In the early 20th century, few, if any, meteorologists outside South
America had been trying to determine what happened during an El Niño
event. During the 1920s, the British meteorologist Sir Gilbert Walker
had gone to India to examine weather records related to the onset of the
Indian *monsoons*. He was startled to find that when the barometric pressure readings were highest on the western side of the Pacific Ocean, they
were lowest on the eastern side, and vice versa. Walker named this seesaw

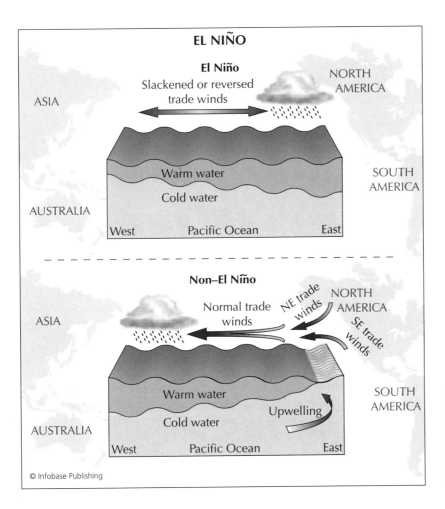

During El Niño years, the atmospheric and oceanic circulation patterns change from their normal configurations and carry unusual weather to people around the world.

Scientist of the Decade: Edward N. Lorenz (1917–   )

Often referred to as the father of chaos theory, the meteorologist Edward N. Lorenz was born and raised in West Hartford, Connecticut. Fascinated by numbers at a young age, Lorenz experienced his first spark of scientific interest during an encounter with an astronomical atlas when he was seven years old. When a total eclipse of the Sun occurred the next summer, he was hooked. As are most people interested in astronomy, Lorenz was interested in the weather, since the condition of the night sky determined what could be seen during a night of telescopic observations. He also enjoyed stamp collecting and playing chess—a game he had learned from his mother.

Entering Dartmouth College in 1934, Lorenz pursued a bachelor's degree in mathematics and then entered Harvard University as a doctoral student in mathematics in 1938. World War II brought change: Offered a choice between being drafted into the army or signing up for a special course being offered at MIT to train weather forecasters for the military, Lorenz decided to seek weather training. An outstanding student, he remained at MIT as an instructor after he completed the course and was later assigned to Saipan and Okinawa as an Army Air Corps forecaster.

With his military service ending, Lorenz had to decide whether to return to graduate school in mathematics or turn his attention to meteorology. Deciding that meteorology was a better option, he completed his doctorate in meteorology at MIT in 1948 with research related to numerical weather prediction. Remaining at MIT, Lorenz began working as a research scientist on a project dealing with the general circulation of the atmosphere. He would have been happy to remain in his research position at MIT, but after a visit to UCLA in 1953, Jacob Bjerknes encouraged him to spend the next year in Los Angeles as a visiting professor. As that year at UCLA ended, MIT invited Lorenz to become a faculty member. Clearly it would be a better career decision to accept a faculty position than to remain a research

pattern of barometric pressures across the Pacific the *Southern Oscillation*. He called the pattern with high pressure in the east coupled with low pressure in the west a "high-index" state; the reverse was the "low-index" state. During the high-index period, the pressure difference drove the normally easterly trade wind flow from the Galapagos Islands off South America to just east of Indonesia. Those strong easterly winds weakened during the low-index period. West of the international dateline, the easterlies would sometimes completely disappear.

As the easterlies slackened, Walker noted that Australia, Indonesia, India, and some parts of Africa tended to be affected by drought. And considering regions outside the immediate vicinity of his study, he noted that western Canada seemed to experience a much milder winter during the low-index periods. Roundly criticized by other meteorologists at the time—how could the weather in Canada be in any way connected to what was going on in the western Pacific and the Indian Ocean?—Walker insisted that there was a connection, even if he could not explain it.

scientist, so Lorenz agreed and joined the faculty in 1955. He never left MIT.

Although his immediate task was to take over the statistical forecasting project, he remained attached to the general circulation research project, which was heavily involved with numerical weather prediction. At the time, many people thought that the two fields had nothing in common. It was because Lorenz was working in both simultaneously that he was able to convince others that statistical methods and numerical weather forecasting were complementary. After finally obtaining a small computer for his office, he turned increasingly to computer modeling.

Lorenz's interest in computer modeling combined with statistical methods eventually led to what became known as chaos theory. Proponents of statistical forecasting argued that their methods would produce a forecast at least as good as any other method, including numerical forecasting, would. Lorenz was doubtful. He thought he could strengthen the statistical argument by showing that the atmosphere was periodic—that is, it would regularly return to a similar pattern. If not, then the statistical meth-ods would not be as promising as some maintained. Running his model, he discovered that the atmosphere was not periodic. Starting one of these models from the middle instead of the beginning, Lorenz discovered that even small changes in initial conditions would lead to large differences in the final atmospheric outcome. The atmosphere was chaotic. The atmospheric system appeared to be random, but it was not. Lorenz's discovery was not only a major breakthrough in meteorology—various other scientific and management disciplines adopted it for their own use.

Lorenz retired as a full-time faculty member in 1981. He continues to work on problems related to chaos theory and the predictability of the atmosphere. Lorenz has been honored with many awards, including the 1983 Crafoord Prize, the 1991 Kyoto Prize, the 1992 Roger Revelle Medal from the American Geophysical Union, the 1995 Louis J. Battan Author's Award from the American Meteorological Society, and the 2000 International Meteorological Organization Prize, the top international prize in meteorology and related geophysical sciences.

With time, more clues appeared. During World War II, data started arriving from Pacific islands that had never had a rain gauge before the start of military action. They showed that the islands received torrential rainfall some years, and in other years they got very little, if any, rain. That explained why they had so little vegetation—during the high-index years there was not enough moisture to support plant life. It was only during the low-index years of the weakened easterlies that moisture was plentiful.

During the 1960s, Jacob Bjerknes turned his attention toward climatic change and decided to take another look at El Niño. While analyzing the presence of the unusually warm sea surface temperatures off South America, he noticed that it occurred at the same time as the slackened easterlies and the heavy tropical rainfall. El Niño was another manifestation of the low-index state of the Southern Oscillation. (The term *La Niña* [the girl child] was used to describe the high-index state.) This *teleconnection* showed that climate changes in one part of the world definitely affected the climate thousands of miles away.

Now that they recognize the meteorological signs pointing to an ENSO—El Niño–Southern Oscillation—event, scientists have incorporated them into numerical models to help predict the onset and severity of El Niño. These models are not a "sure thing" because scientists are still trying to determine the ENSO triggers. Using past data, they have tried to "predict" previous El Niños so they can modify their models to predict future ones better. Although it might seem that a change in water temperature or wind velocity might not be worth worrying about, a severe El Niño year can be highly disruptive to the world's economy. In addition to the problems caused in the Tropics, El Niño may change rainfall patterns across the United States, leaving some areas (Texas to Florida) with much greater rainfall rates and flooding, while others experience significantly less rainfall and endure crop losses. Temperatures may be milder in western Canada and the northern parts of the United States (not usually viewed as a bad thing by residents).

Climate scientists are continuing their exploration of the connections among global temperature, local climate changes, and possible changes in ENSO frequency. As Jacob Bjerknes's work makes clear, it is no longer wise to consider "local" weather pattern changes to be truly local.

Further Reading

Books and Articles

Bluestein, Howard B. *Tornado Alley: Monster Storms of the Great Plains.* Oxford: Oxford University Press, 1999. The tornado expert and chaser Bluestein shares his love of tornadoes and the science behind them.

Heavy rains triggered by an El Niño event led to flooding in Rillito Creek, Tucson, Arizona, that caused substantial damage in October 1983. (USGS)

Budyko, Mikhail I., O. A. Drozcov, and M. I. Yudin. "The Impact of Economic Activity on Climate." *Soviet Geography: Review and Translation* 12 (December 1971): 666–679. Translated from *Sovremennyye problemy klimatologii*, M. I. Budyko, editor. Leningrad: Gidrometeoizdat, 1966. Budyko and his colleagues point out how humans are modifying climate through the burning of fossil fuels and industrialization.

Ewing, Maurice, and William L. Donn. "A Theory of Ice Ages." *Science* 123 (1956): 1061–1066. Ewing and Donn argue that the melting of the Arctic ice sheet due to global warming will ultimately trigger a new ice age as precipitation increases in the high latitudes.

Fagan, Brian. *Floods, Famines, and Emperors: El Niño and the Fate of Civilizations.* New York: Basic Books, 2000. The author discusses the impact of El Niño around the world.

Friedan, Betty. "The Coming Ice Age." *Harper's Magazine* 217 (September 1958): 39–45. Friedan discusses the possibility that global climate is heading for a much colder phase.

Gleick, James. *Chaos: Making a New Science.* New York: Viking, 1987. This delightful, nontechnical book explains the role of chaos throughout the natural world.

Lorenz, Edward N. "Deterministic Nonperiodic Flow." *Journal of Atmospheric Sciences* 20 (1963): 130–141. Lorenz introduces the concept of chaos theory.

———. "The Problem of Deducing the Climate from the Governing Equations." *Tellus* 16 (1964): 1–11. Lorenz examines why climate modeling may be more difficult than weather modeling.

Manabe, Syukuro, and Richard T. Wetherald. "Thermal Equilibrium of the Atmosphere with a Given Distribution of Relative Humidity." *Journal of the Atmospheric Sciences* 24 (1967): 241–259. This article discusses their climate model, which included the combined effects of radiation transfer and the hydrologic cycle.

Mitchell, J. M. "Recent Secular Changes of Global Temperature." *Annals of the New York Academy of Sciences* 95 (1961): 235–250. Mitchell discusses global temperature trends as of the early 1960s.

Philander, S. George. *Our Affair with El Niño: How We Transformed an Enchanting Peruvian Current into a Global Climate Hazard.* Princeton, N.J.: Princeton University Press, 2004. Philander describes how El Niño and La Niña are part of an atmospheric oscillation that has been taking place for many years.

Purdom, James F. W., and W. Paul Menzel. "Evolution of Satellite Observations in the United States and Their Use in Meteorology." In James Rodger Fleming, editor, *Historical Essays on Meteorology 1919–1995: The Diamond Anniversary History Volume of the American Meteorological Society.* Boston: American Meteorological Society, 1996. The authors provide a brief discussion of the early development of weather satellites.

Weart, Spencer R. *The Discovery of Global Warming.* Cambridge, Mass.: Harvard University Press, 2003. This excellent book gives the background and current status of the global warming debate; the companion Web site contains more information. Available online. URL: http://www. aip.org/history/climate. Accessed March 14, 2006.

Web Sites

Ping Chang. "The Physics of El Niño." Physicsweb. Available online. URL: http://physicsweb.org/articles/world/11/8/8/1. Accessed March 15, 2006. Physicsweb is the Web version of the magazine *Physics World,* which includes articles of interest by, and about, the world physics community.

8

1971–1980:
Climate Change—Heating Up or Cooling Down?

Meteorological developments in the 1970s—both practical and theoretical—were primarily due to improvements in computer capacity, which allowed modelers to include more atmospheric variables. Improvements in remote sensing devices, especially satellites and weather radar, improved meteorologists' ability to track storm systems and to collect more data in smaller time increments over wider geographic areas. As a result, routine and tropical predictions continued to improve and cover longer forecast periods.

In climatology, the Earth was either heating up or cooling down, depending on one's point of view. Drought and crop failures in Africa in the early 1970s focused public attention on climate change. Almost no one still thought of climate as static. Desertification was rapidly stripping away vegetation and a food crisis seemed likely. While the anecdotal evidence pointed to a warming Earth, further analysis of global temperature data showed a cooling trend from the 1940s. Concerns about warming gave way to concerns about cooling due to natural or human-produced particles and aerosols thrown up into the atmosphere. These events opened up the possibility that the Sun's energy might be significantly blocked by particles, thus leading to rapid cooling and a return of ice age conditions. Scientists pointed out that rising atmospheric carbon dioxide levels would offset cooling with greenhouse warming. Any consensus about cooling that may have existed in scientific circles at the beginning of the decade evaporated when two New Zealand scientists reported that temperatures were definitely warming in the Southern Hemisphere. Scientists might not have agreed about whether global temperatures were rising or falling, but they did agree that the scientific and public debate about climate change was heating up.

Crunching the Numbers

By the early 1970s, numerical weather prediction (NWP) had become more sophisticated. Weather services around the world were using

In 1973, 13 European nations joined to create the European Centre for Mid-Range Weather Forecasting (ECMWF), one of the world's major weather prediction centers, in Reading, England. (ECMWF)

improved short-range forecasting models, while researchers were testing long-range forecasting and climate models. These improvements would remain limited until meteorologists had a better theoretical understand-

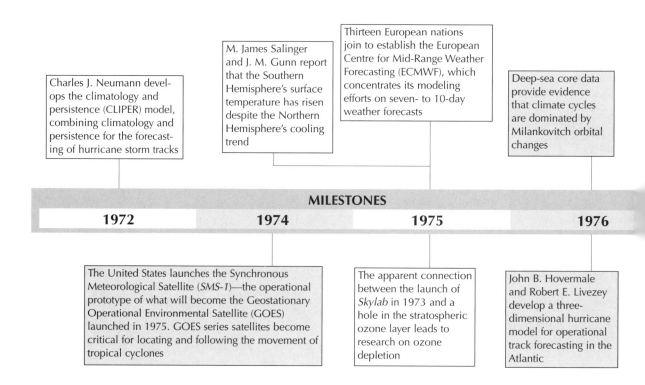

Charles J. Neumann develops the climatology and persistence (CLIPER) model, combining climatology and persistence for the forecasting of hurricane storm tracks

M. James Salinger and J. M. Gunn report that the Southern Hemisphere's surface temperature has risen despite the Northern Hemisphere's cooling trend

Thirteen European nations join to establish the European Centre for Mid-Range Weather Forecasting (ECMWF), which concentrates its modeling efforts on seven- to 10-day weather forecasts

Deep-sea core data provide evidence that climate cycles are dominated by Milankovitch orbital changes

MILESTONES

1972 **1974** **1975** **1976**

The United States launches the Synchronous Meteorological Satellite (*SMS-1*)—the operational prototype of what will become the Geostationary Operational Environmental Satellite (GOES) launched in 1975. GOES series satellites become critical for locating and following the movement of tropical cyclones

The apparent connection between the launch of *Skylab* in 1973 and a hole in the stratospheric ozone layer leads to research on ozone depletion

John B. Hovermale and Robert E. Livezey develop a three-dimensional hurricane model for operational track forecasting in the Atlantic

ing of atmospheric processes, more detailed and widely distributed observational data, and faster computers.

The National Meteorological Center (National Weather Service) was producing wind and temperature forecasts at six levels in the atmosphere with a horizontal resolution of 186 miles (300 km) (the distance between data grid points), as were the U.S. Navy and Air Force. Research models, being run by the Geophysical Fluid Dynamics Laboratory (GFDL) in Princeton, New Jersey, and by the National Center for Atmospheric Research (NCAR) in Boulder, Colorado, made calculations for up to 18 vertical levels with a grid spacing as fine as 112 miles (180 km). Research groups in the United Kingdom, France, and the USSR ran similar models. These extremely sophisticated models took almost 24 hours to compute a 24-hour forecast and were used only to study the atmosphere, not to make operational predictions. Modelers discovered they would need many more observations to define initial atmospheric conditions and to verify their predictions. None of these models could effectively forecast local phenomena such as thunderstorms and tornadoes, which were so "small" that they disappeared between model grid points.

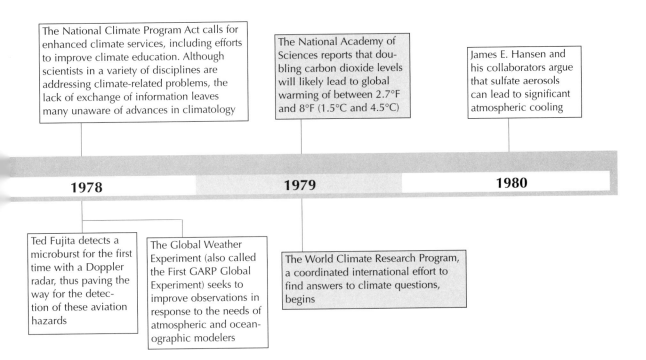

The National Climate Program Act calls for enhanced climate services, including efforts to improve climate education. Although scientists in a variety of disciplines are addressing climate-related problems, the lack of exchange of information leaves many unaware of advances in climatology

The National Academy of Sciences reports that doubling carbon dioxide levels will likely lead to global warming of between 2.7°F and 8°F (1.5°C and 4.5°C)

James E. Hansen and his collaborators argue that sulfate aerosols can lead to significant atmospheric cooling

1978   1979   1980

Ted Fujita detects a microburst for the first time with a Doppler radar, thus paving the way for the detection of these aviation hazards

The Global Weather Experiment (also called the First GARP Global Experiment) seeks to improve observations in response to the needs of atmospheric and oceanographic modelers

The World Climate Research Program, a coordinated international effort to find answers to climate questions, begins

Meteorologists also used research models to determine factors limiting their forecasting abilities. Did a lack of observations, incorrect grid size, or model representations of physical processes hamper their ability to forecast more than 72 hours ahead accurately? To address data issues, meteorologists working with the World Meteorological Organization (WMO) planned a massive experiment for the end of the decade. The Global Atmospheric Research Program (GARP) would be critical to the future of atmospheric modeling.

Unlike forecasting models, climate models were not affected by observed data. Modelers used averaged climatological values, modified the amount of received solar radiation and the average sea surface temperature, and then let the model run until it reached equilibrium—a new climate. Meteorologists examined how the atmosphere and the oceans interacted with each other or were coupled. They focused climate modeling efforts to determine the physical processes controlling the addition of energy to the atmosphere, specifically the transport of heat and moisture at the interface of the atmosphere and oceans, and the influence of polar ice. Meteorologists also wanted to find out how human activities influenced climate. The question in the early 1970s: Are natural variations in climate so large that they will mask changes due to rapid industrialization?

Despite the introduction of new and faster computers, the 1970s did not see uniform advances in model output. There had been significant improvements in forecasting temperature and pressure, but very little in predicting precipitation, the weather element of interest for the public. Meteorologists did see some improvement in forecasting precipitation when they reduced grid spacing. Many difficulties remained for operational NWP, including the poor handling of severe weather phenomena such as thunderstorms and tornadoes. Forecasting small-scale features would remain a challenge for atmospheric modelers.

Meteorologists making weather forecasts for geographic areas that bordered the world's oceans enthusiastically welcomed the availability of satellite pictures—even grainy ones. In the Northern Hemisphere, satellite images were especially critical for meteorologists working on the western sides of continents because weather systems arrived from over the oceans—areas that provided only a handful of observations from ships and transiting aircraft. Tropical meteorologists whose job it was to forecast for tropical storms, hurricanes, and typhoons were also excited about the possibilities presented by satellite images. Because tropical storms are born and live over tropical ocean waters far from observation stations, satellite images provided meteorologists with a way to see them form from small patches of billowy clouds—often just off of West Africa for Atlantic hurricanes—and strengthen into organized systems with powerful winds and unique cloud patterns. Meteorologists used these new images to forecast where these large storms would arrive onshore and to gain new understanding of their

GOES-1 *Goes Up*

The United States launched *ATS-1*, the first geostationary satellite, in 1966. Although it had a television camera suitable for sending back grainy black-and-white photographs of Earth's cloud systems, its primary mission had been to test out communications systems. Because of the success of its meteorological application, the National Aeronautics and Space Administration (NASA) began work on a dedicated geostationary weather satellite. NASA launched the first prototype, the Synchronous Meteorological Satellite (*SMS-1*), from Cape Canaveral, Florida, on May 17, 1974, and placed it into orbit directly above the equator at 45°W longitude (the central Atlantic Ocean). It was followed by a second prototype, *SMS-2*, in February 1975 (above 135°W longitude—Pacific Ocean), and then by *GOES-1* on October 16, 1975.

GOES-1 was the first operational meteorological satellite in the National Oceanic and

(continues)

A "full-disk" satellite image from GOES-1. (© EUMETSAT/ NERC/Dundee University)

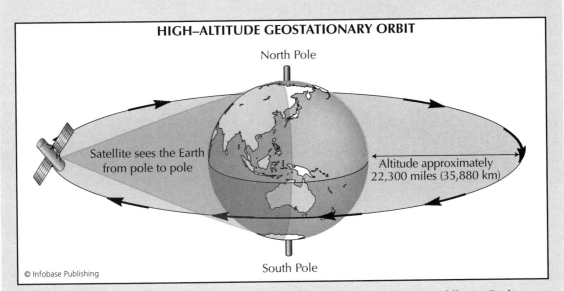

Geostationary satellites such as GOES remain in a high-altitude orbit over the same location, following Earth as it moves.

(continued)

Atmospheric Administration's (NOAA's) geosynchronous weather satellite system. Over 15,000 solar cells powered the 650-pound (295-kg) cylinder, which was 75 inches (190 cm) in diameter and 106 inches (270 cm) high. The satellite carried a visible and infrared spin scan radiometer that allowed it to provide full-disk photographs of the Earth 24 hours a day. (The visible channel used the same technology as a regular camera; the infrared channel measured temperatures, with colder temperature clouds appearing bright white and warmer clouds appearing in shades of gray.) Placed into orbit over the Indian Ocean, when combined with the two SMS satellites, *GOES-1* allowed meteorologists to track large weather

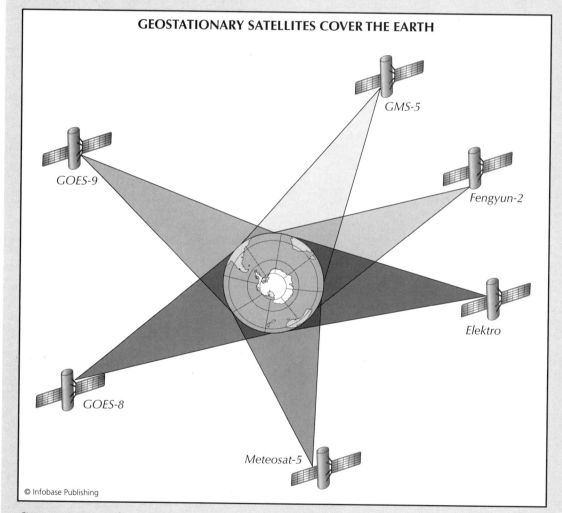

GEOSTATIONARY SATELLITES COVER THE EARTH

GMS-5

GOES-9

Fengyun-2

Elektro

GOES-8

Meteosat-5

Six geostationary weather satellites in stationary orbit above Earth's equator transmit photos continuously, providing full coverage of Earth's surface and atmosphere.

events, including hurricanes and major frontal systems across 60 percent of Earth's surface. This was a huge boon for meteorologists. Although they had been able to "see" large tropical and frontal systems with polar orbiting satellites, the 12-hour delay between images of the same area made it difficult to track these systems. With *GOES-1* and its cousins, they were able to get an updated picture every 30 minutes.

GOES-1 also allowed weather centers to transmit processed satellite images (including latitude/longitude grids) as well as weather maps all over the world. Weather centers would send signals carrying the maps to the satellite, which would bounce them down to receiving stations. GOES's Data Collection System enabled over 10,000 surface stations to transmit their observations to central processing centers for use in NWP models.

GOES-1 also provided finer-resolution images. With a one-kilometer visible resolution, meteorologists used these new images to advance their understanding of *mesoscale* features, including thunderstorms. With GOES, meteorologists effectively had an observation station every one kilometer across the satellite's "footprint" on Earth's surface—far closer together than surface observation stations. As a result, meteorologists used the presence of organized cumulus clouds in images to issue severe weather watches and warnings.

NASA launched three additional GOES satellites during this decade, replacing the earlier SMS and *GOES-1* satellites and providing additional remote sensing capability to meteorologists. Continued advances throughout the century would provide increasing amounts of information to atmospheric scientists, enhancing their ability to create increasingly complex numerical models of the atmosphere.

underlying physics. Satellites were to become an important tool in cracking the secrets of tropical storms.

Climate Fears: Drought and Desertification

As scientists mulled over whether the global climate was warming or cooling, one climatic impact was making headlines all over the world: the devastating drought and accompanying expansion of deserts in the African Sahel. The Sahel, a region extending in an east-west band (4,000 miles wide by 1,000 miles [6,400 km by 1,600 km] long) just south of the massive Sahara and home during this period to between 40 and 60 million people, depends on the summer monsoons for most of its yearly rainfall. If the monsoons fail, as they had since 1969, crops wither and die, livestock perish through lack of food and water, and people either die with them or migrate to find water. By late 1972, it appeared that a major famine threatened the Sahel. Although most nations in the region were unable to keep track of their populations over vast rural areas with limited communications, the western Sahel nation of Mauritania estimated that 80 percent of the cattle, 30 percent of the camels, and over 50 percent of the sheep and goats within its borders had died. Government officials

Cracking Hurricane Secrets

Improved satellite images, advanced computer design, and increasingly sophisticated models all helped atmospheric scientists learn how hurricanes came to be born, live, track across the oceans, and die—either a natural death at sea or a violent one when they went ashore. An early hurricane model (HURRAN) predicted a hurricane's potential track by comparing its current atmospheric situation with those of previous hurricanes. The model assumed that if the existing weather pattern had occurred before, the current hurricane would repeat the previous hurricane's path. HURRAN did not always provide useful information, but it was better than no guidance at all.

Similar hurricane patterns were not always available, so the meteorologist Charles J. Neumann developed the climatology and persistence (CLIPER) model in 1972. A climatological forecast bases its decision on averages, while a persistence model extends a storm's path along its existing route. This model combined the two to derive prediction information from both past and current situations. CLIPER was not perfect, but meteorologists tested new hurricane models against CLIPER. If model forecasts were more accurate than CLIPER, then they were "skilled." If not, they were modified until they became skilled.

Meteorologists also developed theoretical models to gain knowledge of hurricane struc-ture. They abandoned 1960s era models because computers were not large enough to allow the hurricane to "interact" with its environment—an absolute necessity for scientists to determine the factors influencing hurricane intensification, dissipation, and movement. John B. Hovermale (1938–94) and Robert E. Livezey's (1920–) 1976 Movable Fine Mesh (MFM) model had dif-ficulties with short-range forecasts (12–24 hours) because of problems inputting the initial atmo-spheric state. The longer-range forecasts were more accurate. The MFM eventually transitioned from research to operational model. By 1980, the National Hurricane Center was using seven different models to predict the most likely hur-ricane track.

Other advances in hurricane understanding resulted from the hurricane modification project STORMFURY. The special aircraft purchased to probe hurricanes for STORMFURY were outfit-ted with special communications equipment that allowed technicians to send data directly to the National Hurricane Center. The real-time availability of this detailed information greatly assisted meteorologists in the forecast center to make sense of hurricane behavior. Since the late 1970s, hurricane forecasting has continued to improve, allowing ample warning time so people can escape from approaching tropical storm systems.

estimated that between 5 million and 10 million people were in danger of starving. In an area already known for political instability, the mass migration of millions of people looking for water and food to survive would further destabilize the region.

Early in the decade, some atmospheric scientists were convinced that a basic shift in weather patterns was the root cause of the drought and the resulting southward migration of the Sahara. In the more typical pattern, cold polar air receded northward during the spring and sum-mer, allowing warmer—and moister—air masses to fill the void. The summer monsoons would produce large cumulus clouds that provided showery rains to the area. In the autumn, the cooler, dry air masses

Climate change can worsen the effects of desertification, as seen in this photograph taken in central Negev. (Photo by Annette Wefer-Roehl, Pedro Berliner, and Yoav Avni. Initiative for Collaboration to Control Natural Resource Degradation [Desertification] of Arid Lands in the Middle East)

would return and the skies would clear until the next spring and summer. Over the previous two decades, a cooler air pattern had begun to predominate. It appeared that the larger, cooler air mass to the north could no longer recede far enough to allow the monsoon rains into the region. If this were true, there would be no way to stop the desert's advance. The possibility of permanently reduced global grain harvests loomed when the same pattern occurred in South Asia and the U.S. Great Plains.

By 1977, the Sahel drought had ended, but the world's deserts were still growing by 14 million acres per year; 43 percent of Earth's surface was already desert or semidesert. Scientists estimated that if desertification were not slowed, by the end of the century at least one-third of the world's arable land would be lost as the population and demand for food grew. It was time to look at the causes of desertification.

The U.S. meteorologist Jule Charney thought scientists needed to consider the possibility that a biogeophysical *feedback mechanism* might be at work in desertification. In desert regions, the light-colored, sandy soil reflects back solar radiation, a process that leads to overall cooling of the upper atmosphere. Colder air sinks back to the surface, and as it does, it warms and dries. This sinking air reduces the possibility of precipitation and dries out what little moisture is available. Reduced moisture in turn leads to dying vegetation that generates exposed dry soil, higher albedo, and even less precipitation. This feedback pattern, Charney thought, would lead to recurrent drought in areas bordering deserts, which would slowly creep into neighboring semiarid regions.

As the soil dried, there would also be less *evapotranspiration*—the release of moisture into the air from both soil and plants. Charney surmised that only a shift in atmospheric circulations would break the pattern. If no shift occurred, the area's new climate would be drier. Numerical models were not producing conclusive results. Other options needed to be considered.

By the end of the decade, many scientists had abandoned climate-based drought ideas in favor of human-induced desertification concepts. As previously nomadic peoples settled in one place, overgrazing became a serious problem. Once the meager vegetation was gone and the moisture left with it, they were forced to migrate. Others had to migrate too and soon people and animals outstripped water and vegetation. Some areas had been forested, but the cutting of trees for shelter and fuel left the ground susceptible to erosion as the soil dried and the winds picked up the topsoil and blew it away. As the dust was blown into the upper atmosphere, it further blocked the incoming solar radiation, leading to more cooling, sinking air, and drying. Although all of these human impacts had been occurring over thousands of years, it was not until the late 1970s that the populations had exceeded the *carrying capacity* of the land.

The thought of mass starvation caused by a combination of climate change and human-induced desertification was frightening. As images of small children with swollen bellies standing in sparse landscapes littered with the desiccated bodies of livestock flickered across the world's television screens, people became increasingly concerned that their planet was in trouble.

On the Other Hand: A New Ice Age?

"Colder Winters Held Dawn of New Ice Age" screamed a front page *Washington Post* headline on January 11, 1970. The *Post* writer David R. Boldt reported that some climatologists were arguing that Earth had entered a cold period in 1950 and it could last for hundreds of years. In support of this argument, the climatologists noted that the global temperature had dropped 0.6°F (0.33°C) since 1950. If the current rate of decline continued, in 240 years Earth's temperature would be 7.2°F (4°C) lower and gripped by an ice age climate—more snow in winter, less snow melting in summer. As far as the University of Wisconsin meteorologist Reid A. Bryson (1920–   ) was concerned, "There's no relief in sight."

Not everyone in the scientific community agreed. Bryson contended that human-created pollution was cutting off solar radiation and causing the cooling. The National Weather Service's J. Murray Mitchell strongly disagreed. He maintained that volcanoes produced more dust than people. Volcanic activity had increased significantly since 1940, about the time the global temperature started dropping. Mitchell also argued that any possible ice age might be postponed by thermal pollution from factories and home heating. Another prominent meteorologist, MIT's Hurd

C. Willett, presented evidence that the cooling trend was due to changes in solar radiation. In terms of past solar behavior the Sun was emitting less radiation, but it would be back to full strength before the occurrence of an ice age. Willett thought that after a short period of cooling, Earth would heat up even more than it had 6,000 years before.

Some scholars disputed the cooling trend. Britain's Lord Peter Ritchie-Calder (1906–82) pointed to increases of greenhouse gases in the atmosphere and argued that global temperatures might increase 6.5°F (3.6°C) by 2020. Comparing the claims of scientists supporting global cooling with those supporting global warming, an editorial in the April 7, 1970, *Christian Science Monitor* pleaded, "Physicists, please coordinate!"

The arguments in favor of cooling were mainly based on the amount of atmospheric dust. A Smithsonian study had shown a 16 percent decrease in sunlight in the Washington, D.C., area over the previous 50 years. Other scientific groups had reported that the amount of dust in the air over the North Atlantic and Indian Oceans was twice as great as 1900s levels and was due entirely to human-made pollutants. Using computer models to project the impact of increasing atmospheric dust on future climate, the NASA atmospheric scientists S. Ichtiaque Rasool (1933–) and Stephen Schneider (1945–) concluded that dust created by burning fossil fuels could screen out enough sunlight to drop the global temperature by 10.8°F (6°C). If this temperature decrease continued over five to 10 years, it could trigger a new ice age. Rasool recommended that people stop burning fossil fuels and use nuclear energy instead. Other scientists were less concerned about the *aerosols* from burning fossil fuels than they were about the release of sulfates, nitrates, and hydrocarbons. They were convinced that those combustion by-products were more likely to alter the global climate by raising temperatures than the aerosols were to cool it.

In the summer of 1971, MIT sponsored a conference called Study of Man's Impact on Climate. Hosted by the Royal Swedish Academy of Sciences in Stockholm, the participants tried to reach a consensus on how human actions were currently changing or could in the future change Earth's climate. Briefing the press, the scientists acknowledged that atmospheric dust could lead to cooling, but they could find no evidence of the global effects of dust. The participants thought that naturally occurring events such as volcanic eruptions influenced atmospheric behavior more than human activity. They were concerned that jet contrails in the stratosphere could upset climatic conditions and recommended more study.

Despite the apparent disagreements, the global cooling argument was more prominent in the first half of the decade. Reid Bryson, in particular, pressed his theory of global cooling. He pointed to declining temperatures, the southward shift of the Gulf Stream, worsening Arctic conditions, and the failure of the summer monsoons as evidence for a profound shift in the climate. Early 20th-century weather, Bryson said, had been extremely abnormal. Between 1918 and 1960, the Indian subcontinent had experienced many fewer droughts than would have been expected on the basis of past records. This period, with its excellent growing conditions, had lulled people into thinking that the climate was always hospitable. Now that it was changing, people were getting worried.

Concerns over climate change led the National Science Foundation to establish its Office of Climate Dynamics, and extensive climate research began at NOAA and the National Center for Atmospheric Research in Boulder, Colorado. Scientists tried to determine the lengths of past warm and cold climates. Some meteorologists, most notably B. J. Mason, director of the British Meteorological Office, argued that Earth's climate was "robust" and "inherently stable," and not likely to change any time soon. There was plenty of time to determine what could be done about problems related to climate change. Other scientists were not so sure.

One scientist who doubted that Earth was cooling was Wallace S. Broecker (1931–) of the Lamont-Doherty Geological Observatory—part of Columbia University. Broeker had been examining past weather records and concluded that Earth naturally warmed approximately every 80 years. He predicted that it would warm again in the 1990s, only this time there would be much more carbon dioxide in the atmosphere. The excess carbon dioxide would enhance the warming effect and lead to warmer global temperatures than in the previous 1,000 years. With 10 times more carbon dioxide being spewed into the atmosphere in 1970 than in 1900, Broeker was convinced that the warming effect of the carbon dioxide had been masked by the periodic cooling trend. NOAA's J. Murray Mitchell, Jr., concurred. He pointed out that there could be some serious consequences of global warming: the melting of Arctic ice, the melting of ice caps on Greenland and Antarctica, and changing storm tracks and rainfall patterns.

Additional evidence disputing the cooling trend appeared in 1975. A team of British scientists reported that between 1970 and 1974, sea ice—which had been advancing—had begun retreating, cold northerly winds had weakened, and temperatures in the North Atlantic were warmer. At about the same time, two scientists from New Zealand, M. James Salinger and J. M. Gunn, reported that while the Northern Hemisphere may have been cooling, the Southern Hemisphere had actually been warming. This finding was backed up two years later when the National Academy of Sciences (NAS) concluded a 30-month study of climate change. In the first major federally funded report that provided specific figures and a position on greenhouse gases, the 23-member scientific team concluded that the continued burning of fossil fuels could lead to a 10.8°F (6°C) temperature increase in 200 years.

Peering into the Past

As climatologists puzzled over current warming or cooling trends, some of their colleagues attempted to reconstruct the record of past climate. This was a difficult task because scientifically accurate meteorological observations taken with high-quality, calibrated instruments had only become available during the previous century. Although scientists are usually uneasy about using proxies, that is, records from which scientific information may be inferred, in this case there were very few options.

Tree rings provided one *proxy* for climate. The University of Arizona's Laboratory for Tree Ring Research concentrated on reconstructing meteorological data on wet and dry years back to 1600 by looking at trees in the desert Southwest. Trees that live in marginal growing zones are more sensitive than those living in optimal climates. Any climatic changes show up more distinctly in tree ring width—wider in wetter years, narrower in drier years. The use of tree rings to determine past climate, called *dendroclimatology,* provides information back several hundred years. Another use of tree ring data, which uses radioactive carbon 14, matches tree age with high and low concentration of carbon 14. Carbon 14, an isotope of naturally occurring carbon, increases in concentration when sunspot activity is low and decreases when it is high. Using information from tree cores gathered from Douglas fir trees on Vancouver Island, Canada, and in Oregon and Washington, the University of Washington researchers Minze Stuiver (1929–) and Paul D. Quay (1949–) correlated periods of relative cold in Europe with the occurrence of low sunspot activity.

Another proxy, the examination of fossilized pollen found in ancient lakebeds, allowed researchers to track changes in vegetation. Since known plant species tend to grow in warm, temperate, or cold climates, the change in pollen types found in cores taken from lakebeds

Tree rings can be dated and used as a proxy for past climate conditions. (Photo by Gary Braasch)

provided clues to climate change and the speed with which it took place. Similarly, scientists examine deep-sea cores looking for fossilized shells of sea creatures and for changes in the amount of volcanic ash as a way of determining changes in sea surface temperature and the level of volcanic activity through hundreds of thousands of years.

Other proxies are drawn from human records. Managers of medieval manors and their surrounding farmlands kept meticulous records of harvest yields and notes on the appearance of

(continues)

(continued)

spring blooms and the time of vine harvests. These records were then used to create a description of the weather for a given year. Scholars also examined paintings for images of cloud types, snow levels on mountains, and positions of glaciers. When dating the image, they had to consider that artists often produce field sketches years before they create the final painting. Scientists also used old almanacs, ships' logs, personal diaries, and newspaper accounts to get a sense of what the weather was like. Balancing this information against scientific data, they could fill in gaps in the record.

In the next decade, scientists would continue to research past climate. Peering back into the climatic past was becoming just as important as trying to see into the climatic future.

Coral cores, like these being taken from the Florida Garden Banks National Marine Sanctuary, provide information about paleoclimate. (USGS)

And yet, at the end of the decade there was still no firm conclusion about whether the climate was warming or cooling. Less than six months after the NAS released its report that concluded that warming was a problem, another scientific team drawn from the United States, Japan, and West Germany announced that there was still solid evidence of a cooling trend. Despite this team's results, the number of scientists making the claim for cooling was starting to shrink. In the next decade the data would cause most scientists to reconsider whether the climate was cooling down or warming up.

Ozone Dangers

The potential dangers of uncontrolled climate change were joined by yet another possible human-induced problem, high surface ozone concentrations in urban areas and the reduction of stratospheric ozone concentrations. Ozone is a naturally occurring unstable gas that makes up 0.000007 percent of the lower atmosphere (or 0.07 part per million [ppm]). It is also created by photochemical reactions when nitrogen oxides produced by motor vehicle exhaust and a variety of hydrocarbons from both human and natural sources react in the presence of sunlight. Combined with other photochemical compounds, ozone composes the hazy, eye-stinging, breathing-impairing air known as *smog*. In thick smog, ozone concentrations may be 10 times normal levels, causing a variety of respiratory problems.

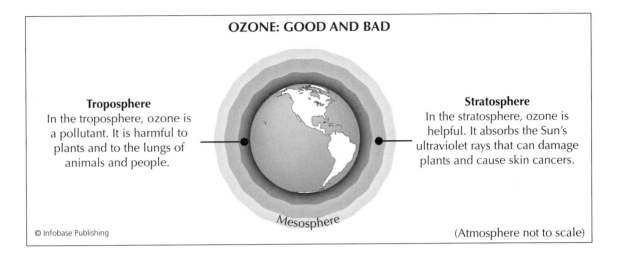

OZONE: GOOD AND BAD

Troposphere
In the troposphere, ozone is a pollutant. It is harmful to plants and to the lungs of animals and people.

Stratosphere
In the stratosphere, ozone is helpful. It absorbs the Sun's ultraviolet rays that can damage plants and cause skin cancers.

Mesosphere

© Infobase Publishing

(Atmosphere not to scale)

Surface ozone became the lesser of the two ozone problems. Early in the decade, the discussion around ozone depletion centered on the effect of supersonic transports (SSTs) on the stratosphere. At the time, SSTs were thought to be the transportation mode of the immediate future. Flying higher and faster than normal jet aircraft, they would whisk people across continents and oceans in just a few hours. The U.S. Federal Aviation Administration estimated that by 1985 there would be 500 SSTs, each spending seven hours per day cruising through the stratosphere. The problem: Scientists estimated that the water vapor in the SSTs' contrails would reduce stratospheric ozone by 3.8 percent. Although this estimate was too high, further research showed that other exhaust chemicals would halve stratospheric ozone—ozone that screened out cancer-causing ultraviolet radiation. When the SST proved to be uneconomical and only a few were built, the concern over ozone depletion temporarily faded away.

In the early 1970s, the University of California, Irvine, scientists F. Sherwood Rowland (1927–) and Mario Molina (1943–) became intrigued by the behavior of chlorofluorocarbon (CFC) gases. These human-made *inert* (that is, nonreactive) gases were used as propellants in spray cans and as coolants in air-conditioning systems and refrigerators. Using laboratory experiments, Rowland and Molina showed that when CFCs combined with solar radiation and decomposed, they released chlorine atoms and chlorine monoxide, which destroyed large numbers of ozone molecules. In their 1974 scientific article in *Nature*, they hypothesized that CFCs released from millions of spray cans eventually found their way to the stratosphere and started destroying the ozone.

As more scientists studied ozone depletion, they determined that even if CFC emissions remained constant starting in 1974, ozone destruc-

Atmospheric ozone may be good or bad, depending on where it is found.

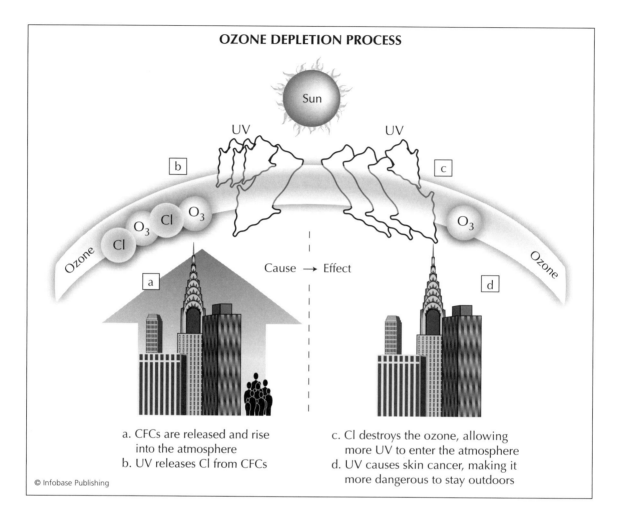

OZONE DEPLETION PROCESS

Sun

UV   UV

b   c

Cl   O₃
Ozone   Cl   O₃   O₃   Ozone

a   Cause → Effect   d

a. CFCs are released and rise   c. Cl destroys the ozone, allowing
   into the atmosphere   more UV to enter the atmosphere
b. UV releases Cl from CFCs   d. UV causes skin cancer, making it
                                        more dangerous to stay outdoors

© Infobase Publishing

*Chlorofluorocarbons (CFCs)
released on Earth's surface
enter the stratosphere, where
they attack ozone.*

tion would reach a maximum in 1990 and remain high for decades. Additional studies indicated that a 10 percent annual increase in the refrigerant Freon could lead to a 16 percent reduction in stratospheric ozone by 2000. As research continued, additional ozone-destroying chemicals were added to the list. Alarmist warnings that people were in imminent danger from spray cans led some to doubt that there was any problem at all.

The debate was settled, at least in scientific circles, with the publication of the National Research Council's (NRC's) report on stratospheric ozone. The NRC reported that continued release of CFCs into the atmosphere could lead to drastic climate changes (by enhancing the role of carbon dioxide in the greenhouse effect) as well as the previously discussed problem of allowing too much ultraviolet radiation to reach Earth's surface. The report recommended banning

CFCs from spray cans after January 1, 1978, and restricting their use in automobile air conditioners and industrial refrigerating units a few years later.

The United States did ban CFC propellants in 1978, but production increased outside the United States and threatened to cut the amount of stratospheric ozone in half by 2000. Convincing other nations to reduce CFC use was difficult. Scientists had no direct measurements of

The ozone hole over Antarctica grew significantly between 1980 and 1991.

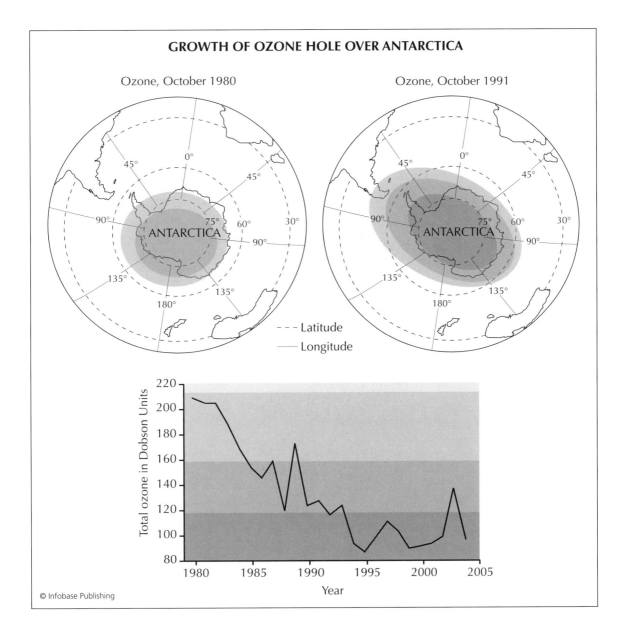

GROWTH OF OZONE HOLE OVER ANTARCTICA

Ozone, October 1980

Ozone, October 1991

- - - Latitude
—— Longitude

© Infobase Publishing

stratospheric ozone—they were using laboratory results and computer models—and industries dependent upon CFCs resisted a change that could potentially cost them hundreds of millions of dollars. In the next decade, observations of ozone depletion would exert pressure on the international community to curb CFC use.

Joining Forces to Solve Atmospheric Problems

The need for additional detailed meteorological observations, particularly in the Tropics, spurred the international community to propose a massive multinational effort to gather and evaluate weather data. Organized by the World Meteorological Organization (WMO) and the International Council of Scientific Unions (ICSU), planning began in the 1960s with a target year of 1974 for the Global Atmospheric Research Project (GARP). According to the GARP proposal, "The entire atmosphere of the Earth and the sea surface will be observed in detail for the first time."

The plan included monitoring the weather with ships, planes, automated buoys, weather balloons, and satellites, and then using computers

The First Global Atmospheric Research Program (GARP) Global Experiment (FGGE), some of the planning for which is depicted here, studied the global atmospheric circulation and related weather systems. (© University Corporation for Atmospheric Research)

100 times more powerful than those that were then in use to process the data. Meteorologists focused their research on the Tropics. Not only was the area poorly understood, it also received the greatest percentage of solar radiation, which was then transported throughout the atmosphere. Meteorologists wanted to understand this energy transport mechanism so their computer models could produce accurate forecasts two weeks in advance.

The first set of tropical experiments was the GARP Atlantic Tropical Experiment (GATE). Concentrating their efforts on tropical thunderstorms found in a band extending from Brazil to Africa and covering 20 million square miles (51.8 km^2), 70 nations deployed 40 ships and 12 specially instrumented aircraft to examine how these large thunderstorms were related to the origin and development of hurricanes. In addition to the tropical storm studies, the GATE scientists examined the weather mechanisms that seemed to be playing a role in the Sahel drought.

The First Global Atmospheric Research Program (GARP) Global Experiment (FGGE) in 1978–1979 gathered atmospheric information from a variety of sensors. (NOAA Central Library)

FIRST GARP GLOBAL EXPERIMENT CONCEPT

TIROS-N

GOES

CONSTANT
LEVEL
BALLOON

DROPSONDE
AIRCRAFT

COMMERCIAL
AIRCRAFT

DROPSONDE

RADIOSONDE

NIMBUS

RADIOSONDE
RELEASE

DRIFTING BUOYS

OMEGA STATION

MERCHANT VESSEL

LAND STATION

MOORED BUOY

SATELLITE
GROUND
STATION

AUTOMATIC STATION

RESEARCH
VESSEL

Scientists of the Decade: Participants in International Projects

Unlike many other disciplines, the atmospheric sciences thrive on the international exchange of tens of thousands of observations daily. These observations originate from land stations, drifting buoys, military and merchant ships transiting the oceans, radiosondes, airplane pilots, radar, and satellites. Analyzing all of these observations is a massive undertaking and requires the cooperation of scientists all over the world whether their national governments are allies or not. In the mid-1960s, leading meteorologists from around the world agreed that if they were to advance numerical weather prediction to the point where two-week-long forecasts were accurate enough to be useful to the many consumers of weather information, a multinational undertaking was required.

This decision led to the successful multinational meteorological and oceanographic field experiments of the 1970s that were carried out under GARP. Given that more than 4,000 participants in the First GARP Global Experiment in 1978, and lesser numbers of participants in the smaller field experiments with the alphabet-soup titles of GATE, ALPEX, MONEX, and CEPEX, it is apparent that it would be inappropriate to single out one scientist as having had the greatest influence during this decade. The top atmospheric scientists from 147 nations participated in these data-gathering experiments, which led to revolutionary improvements in the international sharing and use of meteorological data. Participating scientists and their colleagues have produced over 1,000 scholarly papers, and new papers based on these data are still being published today.

In smaller experiments, scientists gathered and analyzed polar observations, conducted experiments in the Sea of Japan, and studied the Asian monsoon as it related to global atmospheric circulation. Meanwhile, participants from 147 nations were preparing for the main yearlong experiment: the First GARP Global Experiment (FGGE—pronounced "fig-ee"). FGGE, sometimes called the Global Weather Experiment, started in December 1978. The $500 million project involved four polar orbiting and five geosynchronous satellites, over 300 buoys launched between 20°S and 65°S latitude, and over 300 constant level balloons drifting along on air currents some 47,000 feet (14.2 km) above Earth's surface as they measured temperature and upper-level winds. All of the data were sent to "world data centers" in Moscow; Washington, D.C.; and Melbourne, Australia. After additional processing, the data were sent to research laboratories for study.

GARP was a huge success. Not only were the data critical to meteorological research, they were almost immediately used to improve operational forecasting. GARP showed that all nations could work together successfully on a scientific project of mutual interest even during the politically tense years of the cold war. Such a global data collection effort had not been seen since the International Geophysical Year in the late 1950s.

Further Reading

Books and Articles

Bryson, Reid A., and Thomas J. Murray. *Climates of Hunger.* Madison: University of Wisconsin Press, 1977. Bryson and Murray provide a fascinating, nontechnical review of how climate has changed over time, and how climate change affects civilizations.

Charney, J. G., P. H. Stone, and W. J. Quirk. "Drought in the Sahara: A Biogeophysical Feedback Mechanism." *Science* 187 (1975): 435–436. This article discusses the factors that contribute to desertification.

Emanuel, Kerry A. "The Dependence of Hurricane Intensity on Climate." *Nature* 326 (1987): 483–485. The atmospheric scientist Emanuel addresses how climate change may lead to changes in the strength of hurricanes.

———. *Divine Wind: The History and Science of Hurricanes.* Oxford: Oxford University Press, 2005. This well-illustrated book explains hurricane processes and the histories of several of these major tropical storms.

Fagan, Brian. *The Little Ice Age: How Climate Made History, 1300–1850.* New York: Basic Books, 2000. Fagan, an archaeologist, discusses the impact of these extremely cold years on European history.

Ladurie, Emmanuel Le Roy. *Times of Feast, Times of Famine: A History of Climate since the Year 1000.* New York: Doubleday, 1971. This fascinating description of past climate is based mostly on historical documents.

Ponte, Lowell. *The Cooling.* Englewood Cliffs, N.J.: Prentice-Hall, 1976. Written by a science journalist, this book raises the possibility that another ice age is imminent.

Rosenfeld, Jeff. "Satellites in the Sky." *Weatherwise* 33(1) (2000): 24–29. Rosenfeld gives a nontechnical account of the role of weather satellites in prediction.

Salinger, M. J., and J. M. Gunn. "Recent Climatic Warming around New Zealand." *Nature* 256 (July 31, 1975): 396–398. Salinger and Gunn examine warming near New Zealand at a time when the Northern Hemisphere was showing a cooling trend.

Schneider, Stephen H., with Lynne E. Mesirow. *The Genesis Strategy: Climate and Global Survival.* New York: Plenum, 1976. Addressing a general audience, the atmospheric scientist Schneider wrote this book to draw the public's attention to the possible impact of climate change on the global food supply.

Williams, Jack, and Bob Sheets. *Hurricane Watch: Forecasting the Deadliest Storms on Earth.* New York: Vintage, 2001. Bob Sheets, former director of the National Hurricane Center in Miami, Florida, and Jack Williams, formerly of *USA Today*, describe what it is like to predict the path and strength of these killer storms.

Winkless, Nels III, and Iben Browning. *Climate and the Affairs of Men.* New York: Harper's Magazine Press, 1975. This book explains the impact of climate changes on people around the world.

Web Sites

Hurricane Research Division. "Frequently Asked Questions." Atlantic Oceanographic and Meteorological Laboratory. Available online. URL: http://www.aoml.noaa.gov/hrd/tcfaq/tcfaqHED.html. Accessed March 14, 2006. AOML is part of the National Oceanic and Atmospheric Administration. This Web site offers many interesting details about hurricanes and typhoons.

Laboratory of Tree-Ring Research. "The Study of Tree Rings." The Laboratory of Tree-Ring Research, University of Arizona. Available online. URL: http://www.ltrr.arizona.edu/treerings.html. Accessed March 14, 2006. This Web site offers information on basic tree-ring analysis and the opportunity to practice gathering information from tree rings.

Office of Satellite Operations. "Geostationary Satellites." NOAA Satellite and Information Service. Available online. URL: http://www.oso.noaa.gov/goes/. Accessed March 14, 2006. A short discussion on geostationary satellites, with links to additional information about GOES and real-time images.

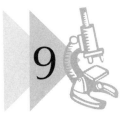

9

1981–1990:
Climate Change Takes Center Stage

While meteorological advances were incremental—primarily dependent upon the availability of new and better hardware (computers, radar, and satellites) for obtaining and processing data—climate change drew the most attention at the end of the century. Scientists were trying to determine whether global temperatures were warming or cooling, and if they were, what could (or should) be done about it.

Initial concerns about global warming due to an increase in greenhouse gases gave way to concern that the increasing quantity of atmospheric aerosols would reduce the amount of solar energy reaching Earth. "Nuclear winter"—rapid cooling hypothesized to result from a nuclear exchange between the United States and the Soviet Union—dominated climate change discussions (both political and scientific) in the early 1980s. By the end of the decade, increasing evidence of rising global temperatures and their connection to rising carbon dioxide (CO_2) levels focused attention on the greenhouse effect and global warming.

In addition to global warming concerns, the thinning of the stratospheric ozone layer, and the resulting "ozone hole" over Antarctica discovered in the late 1980s, led to calls for a reduction in ozone-depleting substances. Within a year, an international treaty restricting the use of chlorofluorocarbons (CFCs) was in place.

No Consensus on Warming—or Cooling

In its 1981 report "Global Energy Futures and the Carbon Dioxide Problem," the U.S. Council of Environmental Quality commented that the impact of increasing levels of atmospheric CO_2 was "the ultimate environmental dilemma." They were already 17 percent higher than in the pre–Industrial Revolution (late 18th century) period and 7 percent higher than in 1958, when Keeling started his famous curve. Scientists had reached no consensus on what the impact would be.

Some scientists strongly argued that increased CO_2 levels equaled warming; other scientists were not convinced. Some thought the

Large volcanic eruptions, like Mount Pinatubo's on June 12, 1991, throw so much particulate matter into the air that global temperatures may drop temporarily. (USGS/ Cascades Volcano Observatory, Vancouver, Washington)

Ronald L. Gilliland and others conclude that a greenhouse warming "signal" should be apparent by the end of the 20th century

Richard D. Turco, Owen B. Toon, Thomas P. Ackerman, James B. Pollack, and Carl Sagan present their "TTAPS" study "Global Atmospheric Consequences of Nuclear War" at an international scientific meeting. They argue that an exchange of nuclear weapons would produce atmospheric debris reducing sunlight by 5 percent and dropping coastal temperatures to −13°F (−25°C)—a "nuclear winter"

The NOAA scientist Susan Solomon, leader of an 18-member team, reports on the annual depletion of the ozone layer over Antarctica. Later measurements show highly elevated levels of chlorine dioxide, a gas resulting from ozone breakdown. A smaller ozone hole appears over the Arctic

MILESTONES

| 1981 | 1982 | 1983 | 1985 | 1986 |

Willi Dansgaard and his team obtain and analyze data from 67,000 ice core samples and find evidence of rapid climate change. When Hans Oeschger and his team confirm these results, rapid climate changes are dubbed Dansgaard-Oeschger events

Analysis of Antarctic ice cores provides evidence that atmospheric carbon dioxide level and global temperature increases have occurred simultaneously in the past

Wallace S. Broecker, writing in *Nature,* proposes that changes in North Atlantic Ocean circulation patterns can contribute to radical climate changes

A British team confirms a 1°F (0.6°C) global temperature increase between 1861 and 1974. The temperature increase accelerated between 1969 and 1974

atmosphere would warm, but by a much smaller amount—fractions of a degree instead of several degrees Celsius. Others maintained that global temperatures would rise several degrees, but CO_2 levels were not the sole cause. These scientists argued that other greenhouse gases, such as methane, would enhance the effects of CO_2 to produce global warming. The problem was that while scientists were pointing to numerical computer models that indicated that warming was a natural consequence of atmospheric greenhouse gases, a measurable temperature increase had not yet appeared. The geophysicist Wallace Broecker claimed that the temperature increase was being masked by a naturally occurring cooling cycle in the atmosphere. Once that cooling cycle ended, Broecker argued, the temperature would rapidly increase.

With CO_2 levels clearly rising and no consensus on the impact, policy makers were perplexed. Some scientists, including David M. Burns of the American Association for the Advancement of Science, argued that by the time science determined that global warming was taking place, the impacts on physical, biological, and social systems might have already reached an irreversible point. He urged nations to assume that global warming was happening, and to slow the process by conserving energy

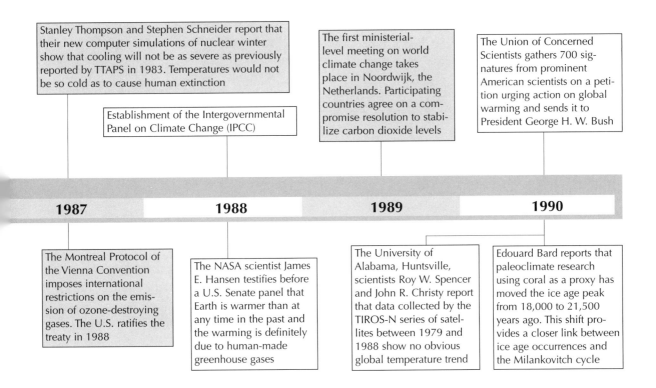

Stanley Thompson and Stephen Schneider report that their new computer simulations of nuclear winter show that cooling will not be as severe as previously reported by TTAPS in 1983. Temperatures would not be so cold as to cause human extinction

Establishment of the Intergovernmental Panel on Climate Change (IPCC)

The first ministerial-level meeting on world climate change takes place in Noordwijk, the Netherlands. Participating countries agree on a compromise resolution to stabilize carbon dioxide levels

The Union of Concerned Scientists gathers 700 signatures from prominent American scientists on a petition urging action on global warming and sends it to President George H. W. Bush

1987   **1988**   **1989**   **1990**

The Montreal Protocol of the Vienna Convention imposes international restrictions on the emission of ozone-destroying gases. The U.S. ratifies the treaty in 1988

The NASA scientist James E. Hansen testifies before a U.S. Senate panel that Earth is warmer than at any time in the past and the warming is definitely due to human-made greenhouse gases

The University of Alabama, Huntsville, scientists Roy W. Spencer and John R. Christy report that data collected by the TIROS-N series of satellites between 1979 and 1988 show no obvious global temperature trend

Edouard Bard reports that paleoclimate research using coral as a proxy has moved the ice age peak from 18,000 to 21,500 years ago. This shift provides a closer link between ice age occurrences and the Milankovitch cycle

The atmospheric scientist Wallace Broecker, seen here visiting the Moreno Glacier— an outlet glacier of the South Patagonian Ice Cap in the southern Argentine Andes. (Photo by Steve Porter)

and developing renewable energy sources such as solar power. Burns also urged more research to determine the interdependencies of the physical and biological world—knowledge that would be useful whether global warming occurred or not.

Evidence of regional warming appeared in fall 1981. George J. Kukla (1930–   ) of the Lamont-Doherty Geological Observatory concentrated his work on high-latitude regions most likely to warm first. Analyzing Arctic summer temperature records, he discovered that average temperatures remained constant, but average summer temperatures had increased by almost 1.8°F (1°C) since the mid-1930s. Although Kukla found no evidence of a shrinking Arctic ice pack, using satellite images, he did find significant summer ice pack shrinkage in Antarctica. Kukla did not conclude that CO_2 was the cause, but his discovery did provide one more piece of circumstantial evidence.

A team from NASA's Goddard Institute for Space Studies reported that the average global temperature had risen by 0.9°F (0.5°C) since 1880 and would increase another 10.8°–16.2°F (6°–9°C) by 2080. Team members had drawn this conclusion after the comparison of current and past weather observations from hundreds of weather stations, the first study that directly measured the world temperature. Scientists disputing the NASA report reacted quickly. The National Center for Atmospheric Research's (NCAR's) William Kellogg (1917–) agreed that warming would take place but disagreed that temperatures would rapidly rise in a short time. Sherwood Idso (1942–), a U.S. Department of Agriculture climate specialist, thought temperature increases would be only one-tenth that suggested by the NASA team and that CO_2 level increases would be so conducive to agricultural output that there was no problem. Still others, such as MIT's Reginald Newell (1931–2003), thought that temperature increases would be moderated as the oceans dispersed additional heat.

In mid-1982, the National Academy of Sciences (NAS) reassessed its 1979 study and concluded, once again, that doubling CO_2 levels would lead to a global temperature increase of 2.7°–8°F (1.5°–4.5°C). Dissenters, including Newell and Idso, claimed the NAS report relied on numerical models that did not include all the factors that determined global climate. The NAS committee found Newell's and Idso's studies to be "flawed and incomplete." As the report chairman Joseph Smagorinsky pointed out, "Ultimately, of course, nature will reveal to us all the truth."

A year later, in fall 1983, the Environmental Protection Agency (EPA) became the first government agency to predict greenhouse warming would begin by 1990 and continue into the 21st century. Only the extent and speed of temperature change were uncertain. Using computer simulations, the EPA predicted a global increase of 3.6°F (2°C) by the year 2040, with increases up to three times as large in sensitive polar regions. The EPA called for a "soberness and sense of urgency" when responding to the global warming threat and advised that only a ban on the burning of coal, shale oil, and synthetic fuels could delay the temperature increase.

Three days later, the National Research Council (NRC) issued its report, "Changing Climate." Writing that the CO_2 "problem appears intractable," the report did not recommend changes in fuel consumption; it did recommend additional research into the causes of greenhouse warming. Although there was "cause for concern" in the long term, the NRC thought there was enough time to deal with the problem. People had adapted to changing atmospheric conditions over the years, the NRC wrote; they lived successfully in vastly different climates around the world; and they would learn to adapt to a warmer world.

The EPA and NRC reports illustrate the lack of consensus on the severity of global warming. By the mid-1980s, more scientists agreed that

Relying on Remote Sensors

The increasing complexity of remote sensors became very important to scientists researching climate change because they provided data that would otherwise have been impossible to obtain. The global warming debate was fueled in large part by the apparent discrepancy between model predictions and observed temperatures. Surface temperature observations were widely scattered. Industrialized nations had the densest data networks. They also had large urban areas covered with heat-absorbing concrete and asphalt. Observing stations that had been in the country were now in the city and hence reported warmer temperatures. Some global warming critics used this fact to dispute that there was any warming at all. Satellites then became an important tool in determining the average global temperature. Using passive microwave radiometers, polar orbiting satellites could obtain temperatures from the entire Earth surface—and at various levels in the atmosphere—in 24 hours. The radiometers obtained temperature information by measuring the thermal emissions of radiation by atmospheric oxygen (O_2). Scientists could obtain measurements accurate to 0.02°F (0.01°C), sufficient for climate monitoring. With these data, scientists would be able to compare model output with observations and thus determine the usefulness of model predictions.

In addition to direct temperature measurements, scientists used satellite photographs to look for changes in the Antarctic ice pack. Comparing recent photographs with older photographs as well as with whaling records from the 1930s, they discovered a 35 percent decrease in the ice pack between 1973 and 1980 and a significant decrease in the total ice pack since the early 20th century. These data comparisons provided indirect evidence that summer temperatures were increasing in high southern latitudes.

Satellites equipped with laser altimeters provided data on ice thickness and movement. Radio-observing stations on ice sheets allowed scientists to determine ground locations to within a fraction of an inch. Repeated measurements of the distance between the satellite and the surface provided clues about climate change—the faster the movement and thinning, the warmer the temperature.

Meteorologists also used new satellite sensors to understand the role of clouds in controlling Earth's temperature. They discovered that the billowing cumulonimbus clouds of the Tropics, which can extend up to 9.9 miles (16 km) into the atmosphere, trapped three times more heat than the "average" cloud, but their bright, white tops reflected so much incoming light that the heat loss matched the heat trapping. Twenty percent of Earth's surface lies in the Tropics, and because tropical clouds have a proportionally greater effect than clouds outside the Tropics, this was a major finding for the scientists. To unravel cloud complexity, scientists added aircraft measurements and balloon soundings to the satellite data. Without these remote sensing techniques, the critical role of clouds in climate change would have remained uncertain.

warming was imminent. Just how much of a problem it would be, and what actions were advisable, were still being debated.

The Specter of Nuclear Winter

Given the thousands of nuclear warheads that were stockpiled in the United States and the Soviet Union, the threat of nuclear war, inadver-

The astrophysicist Carl Sagan codeveloped the ideas behind nuclear winter. (NASA)

tent or not, was real in the early 1980s. At the same time, climate models that included volcanic dust indicated that an eruption would lead to temporary cooling. From this starting point, the Cornell astrophysicist Carl Sagan (1934–96) and his colleagues used the same models to determine the climatic effects of a nuclear exchange between the United States and the USSR.

In their December 1983 *Science* article, the "TTAPS" (for the authors' initials) report argued that fine dust due to surface nuclear bursts combined with the soot created by structural and forest fires created by airbursts (explosions in the atmosphere) would encircle Earth in one to two weeks. This airborne debris would leave Earth in the dark and cause surface temperatures to plummet to between 5°F and -13°F (-15°C and -25°C). Furthermore, the outcome did not require a large exchange of weapons—100-megaton bombs detonated over major urban centers would be a sufficient trigger.

The airborne soot would absorb solar radiation, leading to large temperature differences between regions, enhancing winds, and transporting particles and radioactive fallout from the Northern Hemisphere (the war site) to the Southern Hemisphere. Ozone-depleting chemicals would quickly reach the stratosphere, allowing more cancer-causing ultraviolet

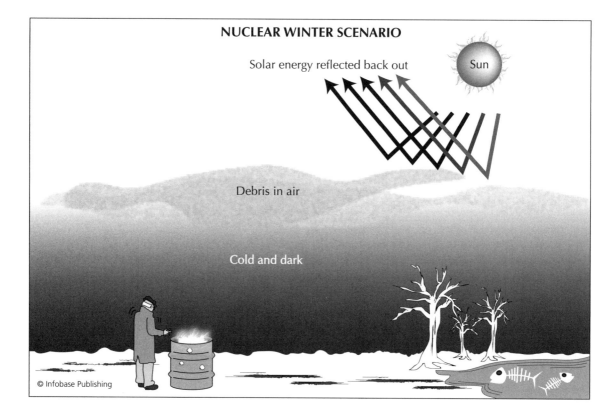

NUCLEAR WINTER SCENARIO

Solar energy reflected back out

Sun

Debris in air

Cold and dark

© Infobase Publishing

The nuclear winter scenario suggests that multiple nuclear explosions would lead to rapid cooling of Earth's surface.

rays to reach Earth's surface. The resulting "nuclear winter" could potentially take more lives than the initial blasts. Dissenting scientists disagreed with Sagan's and the media's portrayal of nuclear winter. The University of Miami's Curtis C. Covey (1951–   ) pointed out that the model did not include the release of heat from warmer ocean waters into the newly chilled atmosphere. The "TAPPS" group had acknowledged this model flaw and had explained that their land cooling values were exaggerated, but the media had pounced on the large temperature drop. Most people equated "nuclear winter" with a "global deep freeze." Furthermore, Covey noted that climatic outcomes were of little importance compared to the direct effects of nuclear explosions. He argued that people needed to be focused on the unfortunate outcome of any nuclear exchange and act on that knowledge. The debates over the reality of nuclear winter were about politics and the antiwar movement as well as about science.

As scientific studies on nuclear winter continued, the world's political situation took a radical and unexpected turn. In early 1989, the Hungarian parliament challenged the Soviet Union's leadership, and within months the iron curtain began to weaken. By the end of the year, the Berlin Wall, which had separated Communist East Germany from West Germany since 1961, had collapsed. As the Soviet Union disintegrated, it was no longer viewed as a threat. Nuclear warfare appeared less likely, and nuclear winter fell from the atmospheric science agenda.

Mud, Ice, and Sunspots

As the global warming controversy continued, scientists were eager to examine past climates. Paleoclimatologists sought to connect past climate changes to solar and terrestrial events. They focused their attention on proxies derived from mud, ice, and sunspots.

Columbia University's Lamont-Doherty Geological Observatory had been collecting deep-sea cores for several decades when the university announced the establishment of its Center for Climate Research in June 1984. Lamont's 18,000 cores, from all the world's oceans, held information about Earth and its climate extending back 140 million years. University of Michigan researchers also gathered core samples from the East Pacific Rise—which runs southeastward from the Gulf of California into the Pacific Ocean—while taking part in the internationally sponsored Deep Sea Drilling Program. They were looking for evidence of previous periods of high CO_2 levels.

Lamont scientists also drilled cores in ancient lakebeds. Drilling at the site, located on the campus of New Jersey's Rutgers University and dating back 230 million years, researchers analyzed cores for minerals, fossils, and pollen samples to determine the exact age of the sample and discern possible clues about the climate over 30 million years. The team leader, Paul E. Olsen (1953–   ), reported that they had found three basic climatic cycles, 20,000 years, 100,000 years, and 400,000 years—cycles that correspond to Earth's orbital patterns.

Drilling for ice cores in southern Greenland, a joint American-Swiss-Danish effort examined core samples in ice cave laboratories they had carved out below the surface. Using the relative concentrations of two oxygen isotopes, oxygen 16 and oxygen 18, the scientists could determine when the snow in the ice cores had fallen. Oxygen 18, the heavier of the two isotopes, is more prevalent in warmer temperatures (summer snow), while oxygen 16 is more prevalent in colder temperatures (winter snow). By analyzing the relative abundance of the isotopes, the scientists could count back the number of years on the basis of the layers, starting at the present. For the immediate past 900 years, the scientists could place geologic and atmospheric events within one year of their occurrence; between 900 and 1,400 years back, they could date the event to within three years of its occurrence.

On the basis of the condition of the ice cores, scientists determined that the atmosphere had been extremely dusty during the final one-third of the last ice age—perhaps from a volcanic eruption or from large plains that had been exposed when the sea level dropped as water became locked in the ice. The dust disappeared from the ice core samples formed by snows that had fallen about 20 years after the ice age had ended. In addi-

A scientist removes an ice core from a drill. (NOAA)

tion to evidence of volcanic eruptions around the globe, by analyzing the percentage of the annual snow layer that had melted, the scientists could determine climate signals extending back a little over 2,000 years. On the basis of their assessments of these data, the scientists determined that Greenland experienced significantly warmer temperatures between

950 and 1400—a time when the Vikings established settlements on Greenland's coastline.

Scientists found a greater challenge in attempting to date the ice as they approached solid earth. The layers, crushed by the weight of the ice above, became very thin and were too old to be dated by carbon-14 techniques, accurate back to 50,000 years. They analyzed water drawn from ice samples for acidity—another indicator of volcanic activity. During the melting process, they captured ancient air trapped in the ice and looked for evidence of CO_2 and other compounds. They found very little CO_2. Ice formed during the ice age had only 200 ppm of carbon dioxide. This increased to 275 ppm just before the beginning of the Industrial Revolution, and in the early 1980s it was 331 ppm. (It reached 381 ppm in 2005.) Similar projects in Antarctica extended paleoclimate knowledge back to 160,000 years.

Information drawn from ice cores pulled from deep within ice caps yields valuable information about Earth's temperature history. (Drawing based on Figure 6.2 from Richard B. Alley, The Two-Mile Time Machine)

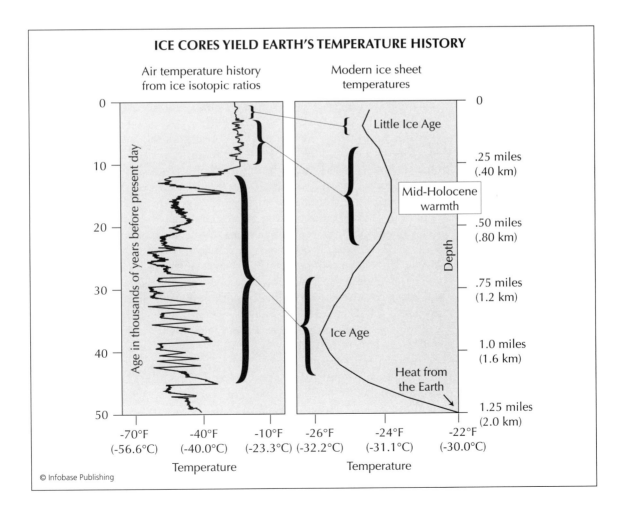

ICE CORES YIELD EARTH'S TEMPERATURE HISTORY

© Infobase Publishing

Scientists also looked for climate change clues in the relationship between sunspot activity and drought. The Sun has an 11-year sunspot cycle (the Hale cycle) between minimum and maximum—or 22 years between maximums. The magnetic polarity of the spots reverses during this same 22-year period. The NOAA climate expert J. Murray Mitchell, Jr., compared the sunspot cycles with the global occurrence of drought and found that while the droughts did not occur exactly at the same time as the sunspot maxima, they had followed a roughly 22-year pattern over the previous 400 years. Mitchell noted that droughts also occur at other times, and so the sunspots could not be used as accurate predictors. During extremely active solar periods, the droughts were significantly more severe. A possible mechanism is still under investigation.

Ancient mud and ice served as naturally occurring climate recording devices as layer after layer accumulated. Working backward in time, scientists would continue to test their climate models against these data to see how effective they would be in predicting the future.

Closing the Ozone Hole

Concerns about the effects of supersonic transport (SST) contrails on stratospheric ozone had given way to concerns about CFCs, which the United States, Canada, Sweden, and Norway took steps to reduce in the late 1970s. Then in early 1982, the World Meteorological Organization (WMO) warned that the existing fleet of subsonic aircraft could also lead to ozone depletion. The WMO reiterated that if the global community continued to release CFCs into the atmosphere at the 1977 rate, a significant reduction of stratospheric ozone would most certainly result.

The scientific community did not yet agree on the extent of ozone depletion. Three months later, in March 1982, the NRC downgraded its 1980 prediction of a 15–18 percent reduction in ozone to 5–9 percent if the 1977 CFC rate continued. The NRC further decreased the ozone loss prediction to 2–4 percent by the end of the 21st century in a third study completed in 1983 and concluded that human activity was not depleting ozone as much as had been thought. Chemical companies that produced CFCs greeted this finding favorably, especially DuPont, which had long maintained that there was no immediate ozone crisis.

Ozone depletion faded from the public agenda until fall 1985, when an analysis of *Nimbus*-7 images showed a stratospheric ozone "hole" over Antarctica. Scientists at the Goddard Space Flight Center had been monitoring ozone over Antarctica for several years, and the ozone hole appeared every October—springtime in the Southern Hemisphere—as sunlight returned to the region. The hole was getting bigger, the rate of depletion was increasing, and the amount of depletion was much larger than expected. NASA scientists had not been previously alerted because their computer model had tossed out the "invalid" information indicating the ozone loss. British and Swiss teams provided data that supported the hole's presence. The 1983 ozone levels were the lowest in 60 years, and scientists had blamed the reduction on the 1982 eruption of Mexico's El Chichon. The effects of the volcano should only have lasted for a year, according to the ozone researcher F. Sherwood Rowland; three years later, there was clearly something else at work.

A collaborative effort of 150 scientists from 11 countries culminated in a 1986 NASA report that assigned humans the blame for the 40 percent loss of stratospheric ozone. In a *New York Times* article published on January 13, 1986, Rowland agreed with the report that by continuing the release of gases into the atmosphere humans were conducting "a totally uncontrolled experiment with no kind of knowledge of where we are going in the end." Ozone depletion was again a major environmental problem.

To determine the extent of the problem, NOAA's Susan Solomon (1956–) and her team of researchers flew to Antarctica in August 1986—the middle of the Southern Hemisphere winter—to release 33 high-altitude balloons carrying advanced instruments to measure ozone in situ. Solomon found "strong evidence" that chemical processes were causing the ozone hole. Furthermore, the 40 percent reduction in ozone took place in 20 to 30 days. Still not ready to blame ozone destruction on CFCs, the expedition members called for more research to unravel the complicated process.

Within a few months, the EPA released a report warning that ozone depletion could double the number of skin cancers and cancer deaths in the

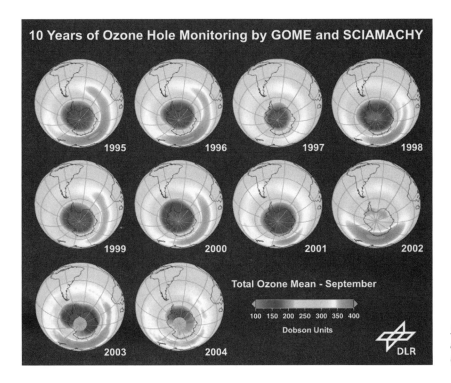

Satellites monitor the presence of ozone over the Antarctic. (NASA)

United States in 88 years. Acknowledging the estimates included a "wide margin of error," the administration of President Ronald Reagan (1911–2004) proposed a "near-term freeze" on manufacturing ozone-destroying chemicals. The United States would not be able to solve the ozone depletion problem on its own—other nations would have to be involved.

The United Nations Environment Programme held a meeting in Geneva December 1–5, 1986, where members of industrialized nations discussed ways to limit the growing use of CFCs. Reaching no final agreement, they did reach a consensus: The world's nations needed to curb the use of CFCs and the starting point was a freeze on their production. Meetings in Vienna and Montreal followed. At the September 1987 Montreal meeting, industrial and developing nations agreed to control the use and manufacture of CFCs and halons—both ozone depleting chemicals. The United States was the first country to ratify the treaty, known as the Montreal Protocol.

The atmosphere would not be easily purged of CFCs and the destruction of ozone would continue for years. By 1989 nations returned to the bargaining table to consider complete bans on CFCs and related substances. While scientists and policy makers alike considered their next step, new research showed that the ozone layer was also thinning in the Northern Hemisphere. Considering the much larger population in the Northern Hemisphere, this new discovery was viewed with alarm. By the summer of 1990, the amount of stratospheric ozone had declined by 10 percent since 1967 over the middle latitudes of Europe and North America, and 3 percent over the equator since 1980. The continent-sized ozone hole in 1990 was almost as large as in 1987, the year of greatest depletion. The years of delay in taking action on CFCs were catching up. More work remained to be done on the ozone depletion problem.

Warming—Real or Imaginary?

The controversy surrounding the greenhouse effect and global warming was not about the nature of the greenhouse effect—the mechanism was an established scientific fact. The controversy continued over the extent of the warming. As the decade continued, the evidence for human and natural causes continued to mount.

More evidence supporting global warming due to increasing CO_2 levels started to appear middecade. Deep-sea cores from the Pacific indicated that Eocene epoch (50 million years ago) crustal movement released heat and minerals from the mantle into the ocean, which caused the ocean to double its production of CO_2 and produce warming. The role of trace gases in enhancing the greenhouse effect also gained new attention. Scientists were mostly concerned about increasing quantities of methane (which is produced by the decay of organic material), nitrous oxide, and CFCs. Some scientists disputed that the trace gases could have a significant effect, but NCAR researchers, and scientists who had confirmed their study of 30 trace gases, argued that the effects were sufficient to demand more study.

When the Senate Environmental Pollution subcommittee held hearings in June 1986, witnesses testified that the outlook for Earth's climate over the next 100 years had worsened. NASA's James E. Hansen (1941–   ) told senators that global temperatures would rise to a 100,000-year high by early in the 21st century. In addition to the indirect effects often discussed in relation to global warming—rising sea level, increasing storm frequency and violence, and widespread drought conditions—the rising temperatures themselves could pose a problem for the world's inhabitants. Hansen thought it likely that by the 1990s the global temperature would be outside its natural variability. Only then, he mused, would global warming garner needed attention from governments. But Alvin W. Trivilpiece of the Office of Energy Research disputed a cause-and-effect relationship between CO_2 levels and warming. It was inappropriate, he said, to modify energy policy to reduce CO_2 emissions until the link had been proven.

Not everyone was thinking of climate change as taking place over a 100-year period. One of those looking at rapid change was Lamont's Wallace S. Broecker. According to Broecker, the climate models being used by decision makers did not include the ocean's role. Climate records drawn from deep-sea and ice cores had both provided evidence that the climate had changed very quickly in the past—so quickly some species did not survive the change. Broecker argued that a warming atmosphere could trigger a change in the ocean circulation that could send temperatures plunging in Europe and the British Isles, areas that were usually warmed by the shallow, warm Gulf Stream.

On June 23, 1988, NASA's James E. Hansen testified again before a Senate committee. He told them that global temperatures had been higher during the first five months of 1988 than at any time since systematic measurements had begun 130 years before. Hansen told senators that he was "99 percent certain" that this measurable warming was due to CO_2 and other human-produced gases—not a result of natural climatic variations. Warming, Hansen testified, "is already happening now."

Hansen may have galvanized Washington politicians with his words, but many scientists had been saying privately what he had just said publicly for a number of years. Other scientists, including the statistician Andrew R. Solow of the Woods Hole Oceanographic Institution in Massachusetts, were not impressed. Writing in the *New York Times* on December 28, 1988, Solow disputed the accuracy of climate models. The climate was too complex, and our understanding too limited, even to create good models, Solow argued. There were no solid data to support greenhouse warming, and there was no reason to "overreact" to non-peer-reviewed statements made to the press or congressional committees.

Was Solow's charge on the efficacy of models correct? Models did not include every possible factor that could affect temperature change. Of critical importance was the lack of *feedback mechanisms*, which had the potential both to enhance and to reduce the effects of greenhouse warming. But most feedback mechanisms would enhance warming. For

Scientists Take a Stand on Warming

Disturbed by the George H. W. Bush administration's go-slow attitude toward issues surrounding global warming, the Union of Concerned Scientists (UCS)—formed in 1969 by a group of MIT students and faculty members—petitioned the president to develop a "new National Energy Policy" in February 1990. Signed by 700 members of the National Academy of Sciences (including 49 Nobel Prize winners), the UCS petition reached President Bush just before he was scheduled to address an Intergovernmental Panel on Climate Change (IPCC) meeting in Washington, D.C.

The UCS members argued in their letter and petition that global warming was emerging as the "most serious environmental threat of the 21st century." They pointed to wide agreement in the scientific community that human activity was introducing greenhouse gases into the environment. While acknowledging that no one yet knew how quickly the climate would change or what the ultimate impacts of climate change would be, the scientists urged President Bush to support steps that would lead to viable renewable energy sources as an alternative to CO_2 producing fossil fuels. They also encouraged the president to support improved fuel efficiency standards for automobiles and trucks, as well as increased reforestation (because plants absorb CO_2).

Realizing that the administration's position on global warming was influenced by its concern for the nation's economic health, the scientists argued that efforts in fuel efficiency and the development of alternate fuel sources would make the United States less dependent upon imported oil and natural gas—an important political consideration because of the relative instability of oil producing countries in the Middle East and South America. New energy technologies developed in the United States could be marketed overseas and thus provide another source of economic gain for the nation.

The "Appeal by American Scientists, to Prevent Global Warming" was not the first, nor the last, open letter to the U.S. government. Concerned about the proliferation of nuclear weapons and a variety of environmental issues, the Union of Concerned Scientists continues to draw issues of a broad scientific nature to the attention of national leaders.

example, warming could destabilize the oceans and release methane gas that was stored in the sediment resting on the ocean shelves. If more methane were added to the atmosphere, that would increase the rate of warming. One possibility for a cooling effect was additional clouds: The warmer temperatures would increase the evaporation of water from Earth's surface and create a denser cloud cover. Those clouds would serve to trap heat at the surface, but they would also reflect the Sun's radiation away, thereby providing a cooling effect. As the University of Chicago's Veerabhadran Ramanathan (1944–   ) pointed out to the *New York Times* writer Philip Shabecoff, "It would be a dangerous mistake to assume . . . that clouds will take care of the greenhouse effect."

After Hansen's testimony in 1988, international political interest in global warming accelerated. The U.S. response was not as aggressive as that of European nations; American scientists thought it should be. Within a few months, the World Meteorological Organization and the United Nations (UN) Environment Programme established the Intergovernmental

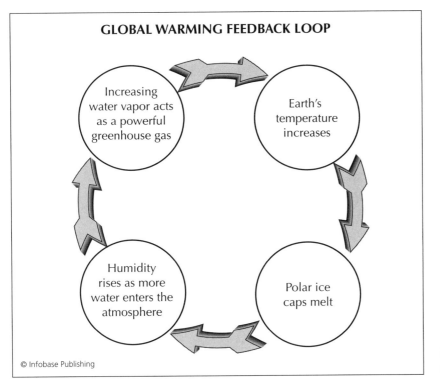

GLOBAL WARMING FEEDBACK LOOP

Increasing water vapor acts as a powerful greenhouse gas

Earth's temperature increases

Humidity rises as more water enters the atmosphere

Polar ice caps melt

© Infobase Publishing

Feedback loops like this one can lead to a warmer Earth.

Panel on Climate Change (IPCC) to analyze published research related to global warming and provide technical reports to international decision makers. And by early 1990, prominent American scientists were putting pressure on President George H. W. Bush (1924–   ) to take action on global warming—immediately.

International Commissions Address Warming

In 1985, WMO, ICSU, and the UN Environment Programme sponsored a conference on CO_2 and climate change in Villach, Austria. Those who attended the Villach Conference concluded that the first half of the 21st century could see the largest increase in global temperatures in human history. After the conference, the three sponsors established the Advisory Group on Greenhouse Gases (AGGG) to provide "periodic assessments of the state of scientific knowledge on climate change and its implications." Composed of an elite group of climate experts, these scientists arranged international workshops and advocated additional research. Without official funding and with only seven scientists, the AGGG was not very effective. An organization that drew from a broader, interdisciplinary base from more countries was needed.

Scientists of the Decade: Intergovernmental Panel on Climate Change (IPCC)

The governments of 120 nations nominated their leading scientists to take part in the IPCC. They had a wide variety of backgrounds: academics, research facilities, industry, government, and non-government organizations. While they represented their governments, the nominating government did not necessarily agree with the scientific viewpoints expressed by their scientific teams; nor did the scientists necessarily represent their governments' viewpoints. By nominating scientists, governments were making a commitment to provide financial support for the work of their scientists with IPCC, but even a financial commitment was not a requirement. Many developing countries had no funds to send their scientists to Geneva. In that case, the IPCC itself provided the funds that enabled scientists from poorer countries to partici-pate actively in this ground-breaking panel, which fulfilled both a political and a scientific role.

More than 170 scientists were assigned to one of the three working groups on the basis of their specific areas of expertise. Gathering together for workshops, they reviewed and studied the latest scientific findings—some of which had not yet been formally published—to draft statements that could not be disputed on scientific grounds. Once they all agreed on a draft statement, it was sent to scientific experts around the world. When their comments had been returned and been incorporated into the draft, it was sent out a second time—this time to experts and governmental officials. Once again, the comments were analyzed by the working group members and incorporated as needed. In the final draft, the working

In 1988, the AGGG was superseded by the IPCC, which was charged with assessing "the scientific, technical, and socioeconomic information relevant for the understanding of the risk of human-induced climate change." Unlike GARP, which had produced many new data on the atmosphere and oceans in the previous decade, the IPCC was not to conduct new research or monitor the production of new data. Instead, the IPCC was to analyze published, peer-reviewed scientific articles and issue comprehensive assessments on the state of the atmosphere for the use of international policy makers without making policy recommendations itself. The panel provided objective scientific information and independent scientific advice for international leaders struggling with policies related to global warming.

The IPCC formed three distinct working groups. Working Group I was assigned the task of assessing greenhouse gases and aerosols, the role of radiative forcing, variations found in observational data, and the possible influence of the greenhouse effect in observations. Working Group II was charged with assessing how science understood the impact of climate change on agriculture and forestry, existing ecosystems, freshwaters and ocean waters, human settlements, and snow- and ice-covered areas. Working Group III was to examine possible strategies that could "delay, limit, or mitigate" the impacts of climate change.

groups submitted their reports to the entire IPCC for acceptance. The IPCC then reviewed and approved the "Summaries for Policymakers" line by line. By the time the final report had been produced, more than 1,000 scientists from around the world had been involved in the process to create an objective report based on the best available scientific knowledge.

The IPCC's work does not rely on any one scientist, but a scientist who has been important to its success is the Swedish meteorologist Bert Bolin (1925–). Bolin was a student of Carl-Gustav Rossby and took over leadership of Rossby's International Meteorological Institute at the University of Stockholm after Rossby's untimely death in 1957. Because of Sweden's political neutrality, the institute was always a place where scientists from both the Soviet Union and the eastern bloc countries could work cooperatively with scientists from the West. As a result of these early international contacts, Bolin became increasingly active in large-scale international atmospheric projects of the latter half of the 20th century. He was the first chairman of the GARP Organizing Committee and remained an active member of the committee for another 10 years. He was also instrumental in establishing the World Climate Research Program, an outgrowth of GARP that considered climate issues. When the IPCC was established in 1988, Bolin was once more asked to take the lead. Because of his outstanding leadership, the IPCC became and has remained an important entity representing both scientific thought and political concerns in the climate change debate. Although he is no longer the chairman, Bolin remains active in atmospheric policy circles.

Issuing its first report in 1990, the IPCC concluded that Earth was warming, and that the warming might be due to naturally occurring processes. The panel further concluded that it would take another 10 years before scientists could determine conclusively that warming was due to human activity. It firmly rejected the idea, which had been put forth by scientists who objected to the focus on CO_2 levels, that observed climate changes were due to slight variations in the Sun's radiative output.

On the basis of the panel's first report, in November 1990 the Second World Climate Conference strongly recommended that action be taken to curb global warming. The United Nations General Assembly followed up by urging that an international conference be held to negotiate an agreement that would curb the rise of global warming. As a result, the First Earth Summit was held in Rio de Janeiro, Brazil, in 1992. Although no agreement was reached on limiting greenhouse gas emissions at the Rio conference, primarily because of U.S. government refusal to accept mandatory limits, it did provide a beginning point for future negotiations. The IPCC has continued to play a critical role in international decision making related to combating global warming, and its assessments published in the early 1990s played an important role during the 1997 UN Conference on Climate Change in Kyoto, Japan.

Further Reading

Books and Articles

Alley, Richard B. *The Two-Mile Time Machine: Ice Cores, Abrupt Climate Change, and Our Future*. Princeton, N.J., and Oxford: Princeton University Press, 2000. The geoscientist Alley has written a fascinating book about the drilling of ice cores in Greenland and the ways the information they provided changed scientific ideas about the nature of climate change.

Bard, Edouard, Bruno Hamelin, Richard G. Fairbanks, and Alan Zindler. "Calibration of the ^{14}C timescale over the past 30,000 years using mass spectrometric U-Th ages from Barbados corals." *Nature* 345 (May 31, 1990): 405–410. Bard and his team report on the use of corals as proxies for paleoclimate.

Broecker, Wallace S., Dorothy M. Peteet, and David Rind. "Does the Ocean-Atmosphere system have more than one stable mode of operation?" *Nature* 315 (May 2, 1985): 21–26. Broecker and his team examine the possible influence of North Atlantic Ocean circulation patterns on climate change.

Christie, Maureen. *The Ozone Layer: A Philosophy of Science Perspective*. Cambridge: Cambridge University Press, 2000. The historian Maureen Christie discusses how scientists used data pointing to the development of an ozone hole in the late 20th century.

Firor, John. *The Changing Atmosphere: A Global Challenge*. New Haven, Conn.: Yale University Press, 1990. The meteorologist Firor discusses 100 years of changes in the atmosphere, including global warming, ozone depletion, and acid rain.

Herman, John R., and Richard A. Goldberg. *Sun, Weather and Climate*. New York: Dover, 1985. In a reprint of NASA report SP-426 (1978), Herman and Goldberg provide evidence linking solar activity with weather and climate.

National Research Council. *Changing Climate*. Washington, D.C.: National Academy Press, 1983. In this report, the NRC argues that the CO_2 and climate change problem is a serious one, but that there is still enough to time to address it.

Revkin, Andrew. *Global Warming: Understanding the Forecast*. New York: Abbeville Press, 1992. The science journalist Revkin's book for general audiences about the history of the atmosphere and climate discusses the effect of greenhouse gases on global warming.

Schneider, Stephen H. *Global Warming: Are We Entering the Greenhouse Century?* San Francisco: Sierra Club Books, 1989. Informative and non-technical, this book is accessible to a general audience and explains the global warming controversy.

Schneider, Stephen H., and Stanley L. Thompson. "Simulating the climatic effects of nuclear war." *Nature* 333 (May 19, 1988): 221–227. Schneider and Thompson argue that the climatic effects of a nuclear conflict would be less severe than those claimed by Carl Sagan and the TTAPS group.

Solomon, S., R. R. Garcia, F. S. Rowland, and D. J. Wuebbles. "On the depletion of Antarctic ozone." *Nature* 321 (1986): 755–758. Solomon and her team describe a large ozone hole over the South Pole.

Spencer, Roy W., and John R. Christy. "Precise Monitoring of Global Temperature Trends from Satellites." *Science* 247 (1990): 1558–1562. Spencer and Christy report that satellite data show no obvious global temperature trend.

Stevens, William K. *The Change in the Weather: People, Weather, and the Secret of Climate.* New York: Delacorte Press, 1999. Stevens, a science writer for the *New York Times*, discusses the effects of weather on people, the disciplinary development of meteorology, and the effects of humans on global climate.

Turco, R. P. et al. "Nuclear Winter: Global Consequences of Multiple Nuclear Explosions." *Science* 222 (1983): 1283–1292. The "TTAPS" team discusses the rapid global cooling that might result from the detonation of several nuclear warheads.

Web Sites

IPCC. "About IPCC." The IPCC Web Site. Available online. URL: http://www.ipcc.ch/about/about.htm. Accessed February 7, 2006. This article explains the purpose of the Intergovernmental Panel on Climate Change. The Web site includes links to a history of the panel, organizational charts, copies of reports, lists of authors, and contact information.

NOAA. "Science: Ozone Basics." Stratospheric Ozone Monitoring and Research in NOAA Web site. Available online. URL: http://www.ozonelayer.noaa.gov/science/basics.htm. This site explains where ozone is found in the atmosphere, how human activity affects its concentration, and the kinds of issues presented by the presence or absence of ozone.

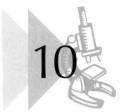

10

1991–2000:
Global Warming

The last decade of the 20th century was dominated by the threat—real, some said; imagined, others said—of global warming. Pressure was building to do something about global warming. Although most scientists were increasingly convinced that global warming was both real and caused by anthropogenic carbon dioxide (CO_2), a few continued to argue that current warming was due to a naturally occurring cycle. Lawmakers, eager to appease business interests, questioned whether reducing greenhouse emissions was the answer—or would cripple the economies of developed nations, while developing nations continued to pump massive amounts of CO_2 into the air. The 1997 Kyoto Protocol, which would have reduced the rate of increase, but not the total amount of carbon dioxide in the atmosphere, became a flash point in the global warming controversy. The U.S. Senate refused to ratify the treaty, jeopardizing its implementation.

Throughout the decade, increased computer capacity and advanced modeling techniques allowed climate scientists to refine their predictions about future global temperatures, while more sophisticated satellite sensors permitted global data collection. Although a handful of scientists attempted to discredit the accuracy of satellite data, by decade's end there was virtually no doubt that warming since the 1940s was primarily due to human activity.

The Evidence Stacks Up

As the global temperature (average temperature for the entire planet) hit almost 60°F (15.6°C) in 1990—the warmest since systematic weather record taking had begun—scientists continued to look for evidence that would distinguish natural warming from greenhouse gas–induced warming. They found it difficult to isolate these "fingerprints." Some were not as clear as scientists had hoped. A definitive connection between greenhouse gases and global warming remained elusive.

Surface temperatures continued to rise during the decade, although this determination was not without controversy. In 1991, a scientific team conducted a detailed statistical analysis of several independent temperature data sets. Although each set gave the same result—global warming over the past century—the timing of the increases differed from set to set. This discovery compromised their scientific reliability. However, the next record year was not far away. Global highs occurred in 1995, 1997, and again in 1998. The entire decade, according to the climatologist Michael E. Mann (1965–   ) and his associates, was the warmest in 10,000 years and 1998 was the warmest year of all.

As temperatures increased, scientists from a variety of disciplines gathered indirect evidence of climate change to augment surface station observations. Paleoclimatologists continued to drill deeper into sediments and ice sheets as they tried to identify earlier instances of warm and cold climates and the transitions between them.

Glaciologists examined the behavior of small glaciers in the Alps, large ice sheets in Greenland and Antarctica, and ice floes in the Arctic,

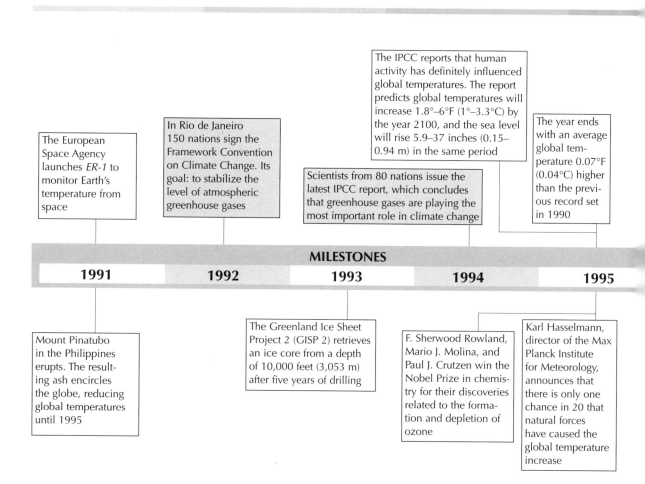

The IPCC reports that human activity has definitely influenced global temperatures. The report predicts global temperatures will increase 1.8°–6°F (1°–3.3°C) by the year 2100, and the sea level will rise 5.9–37 inches (0.15–0.94 m) in the same period

The year ends with an average global temperature 0.07°F (0.04°C) higher than the previous record set in 1990

In Rio de Janeiro 150 nations sign the Framework Convention on Climate Change. Its goal: to stabilize the level of atmospheric greenhouse gases

The European Space Agency launches *ER-1* to monitor Earth's temperature from space

Scientists from 80 nations issue the latest IPCC report, which concludes that greenhouse gases are playing the most important role in climate change

MILESTONES

| 1991 | 1992 | 1993 | 1994 | 1995 |

Mount Pinatubo in the Philippines erupts. The resulting ash encircles the globe, reducing global temperatures until 1995

The Greenland Ice Sheet Project 2 (GISP 2) retrieves an ice core from a depth of 10,000 feet (3,053 m) after five years of drilling

F. Sherwood Rowland, Mario J. Molina, and Paul J. Crutzen win the Nobel Prize in chemistry for their discoveries related to the formation and depletion of ozone

Karl Hasselmann, director of the Max Planck Institute for Meteorology, announces that there is only one chance in 20 that natural forces have caused the global temperature increase

looking for evidence of retreat or thinning from a warming Earth. A team from the University of Grenoble, France, found glacial volume in the Alps had declined by one-third to one-half in the previous 100 years, and the melting rate had increased since 1980. Researchers studying similar small glaciers in the Russian Caucasus and Urals, and in the South American Andes, reported similar losses. Studies of glaciers in Scandinavia, Greenland, Iceland, and New Zealand showed they were *growing*. Both findings supported a warming Earth: At lower latitudes, smaller glaciers would shrink as the temperature rose; at higher latitudes, warming would lead to greater precipitation rates while temperatures would still support the formation of snow or ice.

Early in the decade, the Arctic did not exhibit climate model–predicted warming. Some scientists wondered whether there were problems with the models. Other scientists attributed the lack of warming to natural polar region variability. Arctic ice showed no evidence of thinning,

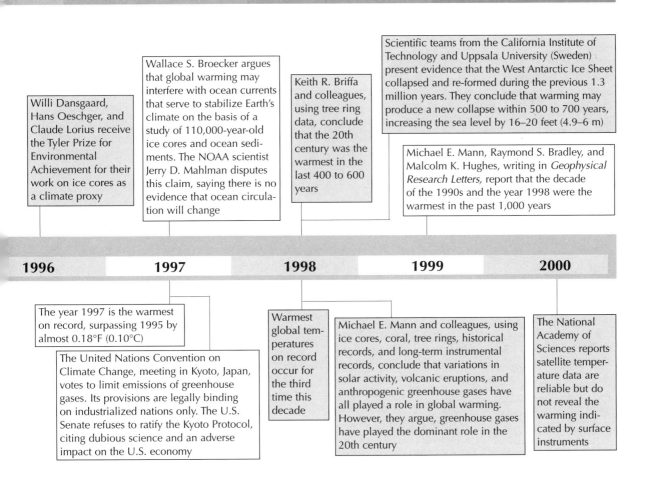

Willi Dansgaard, Hans Oeschger, and Claude Lorius receive the Tyler Prize for Environmental Achievement for their work on ice cores as a climate proxy

Wallace S. Broecker argues that global warming may interfere with ocean currents that serve to stabilize Earth's climate on the basis of a study of 110,000-year-old ice cores and ocean sediments. The NOAA scientist Jerry D. Mahlman disputes this claim, saying there is no evidence that ocean circulation will change

Keith R. Briffa and colleagues, using tree ring data, conclude that the 20th century was the warmest in the last 400 to 600 years

Scientific teams from the California Institute of Technology and Uppsala University (Sweden) present evidence that the West Antarctic Ice Sheet collapsed and re-formed during the previous 1.3 million years. They conclude that warming may produce a new collapse within 500 to 700 years, increasing the sea level by 16–20 feet (4.9–6 m)

Michael E. Mann, Raymond S. Bradley, and Malcolm K. Hughes, writing in *Geophysical Research Letters,* report that the decade of the 1990s and the year 1998 were the warmest in the past 1,000 years

1996   **1997**   **1998**   **1999**   **2000**

The year 1997 is the warmest on record, surpassing 1995 by almost 0.18°F (0.10°C)

The United Nations Convention on Climate Change, meeting in Kyoto, Japan, votes to limit emissions of greenhouse gases. Its provisions are legally binding on industrialized nations only. The U.S. Senate refuses to ratify the Kyoto Protocol, citing dubious science and an adverse impact on the U.S. economy

Warmest global temperatures on record occur for the third time this decade

Michael E. Mann and colleagues, using ice cores, coral, tree rings, historical records, and long-term instrumental records, conclude that variations in solar activity, volcanic eruptions, and anthropogenic greenhouse gases have all played a role in global warming. However, they argue, greenhouse gases have played the dominant role in the 20th century

The National Academy of Sciences reports satellite temperature data are reliable but do not reveal the warming indicated by surface instruments probably because wind, not temperature, is a more critical factor in Arctic ice development. By the decade's end, satellite measurements showed declining sea ice coverage and increased melting after 1979, with 5.3 more melting days per year. Until more data were available, scientists could not declare this melting to be a trend.

Biological studies also provided indirect evidence of a warming Earth. Using Arctic pond core samples, researchers found plant life had already started to include warmer-region genuses by the 19th century. An analysis of satellite photographs showed that plant growth had increased 12 percent in northern latitudes between 45°N and 70°N between 1981 and 1991. Signs of plant life were appearing eight days earlier in spring and lasting four days longer in autumn. Plants were also migrating up the Alps's mountainsides 3.3–13 feet (1–4 m) per decade. Similarly, a study of coastal creatures along Monterey Bay, California, showed that populations of species more common to southern areas were increasing while those of species more common to northern areas were declining. The former were moving into the area, while the latter were moving out of the area and migrating to the north as water and air temperatures increased.

Paleoclimatologists, working with a variety of proxies, continued their work to identify warmer and colder periods. They found periods that had been significantly warmer 5,000–6,000 years ago, 125,000 years ago, and between 3.3 and 4.3 million years ago. Clearly, people were not the cause of these warming periods. Exploring the possible causes, scientists considered the roles of changes in solar radiation, Earth's orbit, outgassing during volcanic eruptions, and changes in the relationship between land and water as Earth's plates shifted on its surface over millions of years. Were any of these natural causes of global warming still at work? Eigil Friis-Christensen and Knud Lassen of the Danish Meteorological Institute in Copenhagen, Denmark, claimed to have correlated sunspots with temperature change over 130 years. When sunspot cycles, which average 11 years, were shorter than usual, then solar activity was more intense and temperatures went up. If the cycles were longer, solar activity lessened and temperatures dropped. If that were the case, then the influence of CO_2 would need to be downgraded. The problem was that this was not a predictive method and CO_2 levels continued to rise. In order to offset the warming trend, the Sun would need to emit 2 percent less energy, and that was unlikely. So while there was still no proof that human-created greenhouse gases were causing global warming, neither was there proof that natural cycles were causing global warming.

Martin I. Hoffert (1938–) and Curt Covey, writing in *Nature*, discussed their examination of climate data from 20,000 and 100,000 years ago. The first, an ice age climate, and the second, which was 18°F (10°C) warmer, both changed. By including solar radiation and greenhouse gases in their models, they were able to determine that in both cases doubling CO_2 levels would have led to an increase of 4°F (2.2°C). They concluded that Earth's atmosphere possessed a basic sensitivity to CO_2 levels that did not depend on the current climatic state.

As the decade closed, no one could say with absolute certainty that greenhouse gases were the direct cause of the observed warming, but circumstantial evidence that supported climate model predictions was stacking up. Scientists were close to reaching a consensus that would connect anthropogenic CO_2 and a warming Earth.

The Skeptical Few

By the 1990s, skepticism over the connection between greenhouse gases and warming was gradually giving way to acceptance by most atmospheric scientists. The majority of journal articles no longer disputed that warming was real, and the arguments for exclusively natural causes had become a minority viewpoint. Newspapers, magazines, and television programs—in the interest of presenting all sides of the controversy—continued to give "equal time" to skeptics. This left some members of the public thinking that global warming was an excuse by environmentalists to impose controls on automobile exhaust and business practices.

Some skeptics operated on the margins of science, but others were prominent scientists who could not accept the evidence offered by their colleagues in support of warming. One of those was the MIT atmospheric scientist Richard Lindzen (1940–). Lindzen, a fellow of the National Academy of Sciences, told the *New York Times* science writer William K. Stevens, "We don't have any evidence that this [warming due to greenhouse gases] is a serious problem." In particular, Lindzen charged that computer models, upon which most conclusions about CO_2 levels and global warming were based, were flawed and meaningless, and hence did not provide valid scientific evidence. Furthermore, Lindzen charged that scientists were pursuing global warming research because of abundant funding available for those looking for a connection between CO_2 and warming. Many other scientists were serious about climate change, Lindzen claimed, but they thought the claims were exaggerated. The main player in warming was water vapor, not CO_2 and other "waste gases." Because water vapor would amplify warming, determining its upper-level limit was important. Lindzen argued that if Earth's atmosphere were as sensitive to climate change as many scientists claimed, then the effects of volcanic eruptions on climate should linger longer than they had in the past. (The illustration on page 194 shows the effect of Mt. Pinatubo's eruption on temperature.) Given all these factors, global warming claims were overblown and not being seen within the context of natural variability.

The physicist S. Fred Singer (1924–) was another prominent skeptic. In his book *Hot Talk, Cold Science*, Singer laid out his objections to the possibility of imminent, disastrous global warming. Acknowledging that the global temperature had risen 1.0°F (0.6°C) in the past century, he argued that there was no evidence that humans had caused

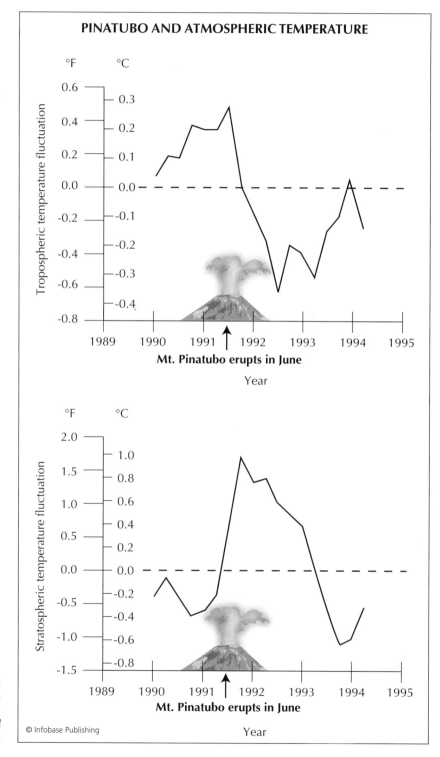

PINATUBO AND ATMOSPHERIC TEMPERATURE

As these two graphs show, debris from volcanic eruptions, like that of Mount Pinatubo, may cool the troposphere and warm the stratosphere.

© Infobase Publishing

that warming. According to Singer, most of the temperature increase took place *before* 1940, whereas CO_2 levels increased *after* 1940. Until scientists could rule out the influence of air-sea interaction, variations in solar radiation, dust from volcanic eruptions, and sulfate aerosols on climate, then global warming and climate change could not be connected to human activity. Furthermore, none of these factors had been adequately included in the general circulation models used for climate prediction. Until they were, scientists could not use climate models as "proof" of warming.

Looking at observational data, Singer pointed out surface temperatures had been lower than model predictions. Most of this heating appeared to be due to the effect of "urban heat islands"—those small, warm domes of air-hugging asphalt- and concrete-cloaked cities that had overrun rural weather stations. He also argued that satellite data do not show the temperature increases that should be present if global warming were taking place as the IPCC and others had claimed.

Singer also attacked the idea that global warming was a threat to life on Earth. He claimed that plant life would benefit from increased CO_2 levels, longer frost-free growing seasons, more water due to increased precipitation, and the increasing availability of viable farmland in northern latitudes. Singer also contested that warming would lead to diminished polar ice and rising sea levels. He declared that falling sea levels were more likely because increased precipitation in polar regions would lead to greater ice accumulation, not less.

Skeptical viewpoints were reinforced through advertising campaigns run by industries opposing controls on fossil fuel consumption, particularly oil companies and utilities that used coal as fuel for electricity generation. The advertisements tended to point to isolated observations—perhaps colder temperatures in one area of the country—as "proof" that global warming did not exist. In fact, global warming in no way implies that individual locations will not experience colder temperatures, only that the average temperature of the entire global system will experience an increase. Although a false argument, it made sense to many people, especially those who had just endured record cold temperatures and the accompanying high heating bills. If government-mandated emission controls meant they would be spending more on heating the next year, most people wanted to be sure there was a valid reason for doing so. Cartoons that showed people mired in snow on their way to global warming conferences reinforced the idea that there was really no problem.

Skeptics are quick to point out that the fact that many scientists have reached a consensus on a scientific issue does not mean they are correct. As the skeptics await new data to back up their arguments, so too do their opponents, convinced that warming is real and greenhouse gases are the cause.

Collapsing Ice Sheets—Rising Water

In terms of information gathered from tide gauges all over the world and measurements from radar altimeter–carrying satellites, sea level has risen 0.08 inch (2 mm) annually for several decades. Scientists studying the behavior of global ice were concerned that as warming continued, additional ice melting would lead to significant sea level increases.

To raise sea level, the melting would need to affect land-based ice, not floating sea ice—although the melting of sea ice could lead to other problems, such as changes in ocean currents. Just as ice floating in a glass of water does not raise the water level when it melts, floating sea ice that melts has no impact on sea levels. The Antarctic ice cap, which holds 90 percent of Earth's ice, rests on land. If it were to melt completely, sea level is projected to rise 197 feet (60 m). The resulting coastal flooding would drive many millions of people from their homes.

Paleoclimatic data had shown Earth to be significantly warmer in the past. Had the Antarctic ice cap remained stable during these warm periods, or had it melted? The University of Nebraska's David M. Harwood, among others, presented evidence to support his contention that the Antarctic ice sheet completely melted during the Pliocene epoch about 3 million years ago. His result implied that increasing global temperatures could lead to a repeat occurrence. Harwood's conclusion, based on fossilized beach diatoms found at the top of the Transantarctic Mountains, was challenged in 1995 by David E. Sugden of the University of Edinburgh, Scotland. Sugden and his team claimed to find evidence of ice that was 8 million years old in an area that Harwood reported had been devoid of ice 3 million years ago. They concluded that the Antarctic ice cap is an extremely stable feature and will not be susceptible to catastrophic melting. Sugden's dating of the ice by a layer of volcanic ash was subsequently challenged by other scientists, who argued the ash may have been pushed onto much younger ice, thus leading to the false dating of the layers beneath it. Scientists continue to explore ice cap behavior.

Even if the ice cap did not melt completely, ice was moving from the center of the continent toward the ocean. "Ice streams"—relatively fast moving (3,000 feet [914 m]/year) rivers of ice embedded within the cap—were annually transporting 19 cubic miles (79 km^3) of ice from the West Antarctic Ice Sheet into the ocean. Previously unknown ice streams in East Antarctica were capable of moving ice almost 500 miles (800 km) from the ice cap's center to the ocean. Since this ice originated on land, it was adding water to the ocean.

On the edges of Antarctica, several ice shelves (floating glaciers) collapsed (fell apart and melted) in the last half of the 20th century. This raised concerns that two very large ice shelves the size of Texas—Filchner-Ronne and Ross—could also collapse, but a 1997 study by the British Antarctic Survey indicated that warming would actually lead to a thickening of the larger ice sheets. Warming temperatures cause the weakening of

NOT QUITE THAT DEEP

© Infobase Publishing

Even if all of the ice caps and glaciers melted, Hollywood's version of a global warming disaster would not occur.

warm, highly saline currents that melt ice sheets from below. If the warm currents weakened, there would be less melting and the ice shelves could be expected to thicken. If air temperatures increased, surface melting could send water flowing into *crevasses* and weaken the entire ice structure. The behavior of ice in ice shelves is very complex and needs much more study.

In spring 2000, an iceberg slightly smaller than the state of Connecticut broke off the Ross Ice Shelf from Antarctica's west side. Within a couple of weeks, another large iceberg—about one-third the size of the first—broke off and subsequently disintegrated. The first berg was the largest since 1956. Dubbed B-15, it was about 1,300 feet (396 m) thick, and only 100 feet (30.5 m) of that was above the waterline.

Greenland experienced significant ice losses by the end of the decade. Between 1993 and 1998, the Greenland ice sheet lost two cubic miles (8.3 km^3) of ice, or enough to cover the state of Maryland with one foot (0.3 m) of ice. Thinning was greater than thickening on the east coast of the country—in some cases, three feet (0.9 m) per year. Scientists were not sure whether the thinning was due to melting, glacier movement, or a combination of the two.

Using satellite sensors as well as on-site field surveys by glaciologists, scientists are continuing to document the thinning and thickening of polar ice sheets as they work to unravel the complexities of ice behavior. The potential inundation of the world's islands and heavily populated coastal regions makes ice monitoring of the utmost importance.

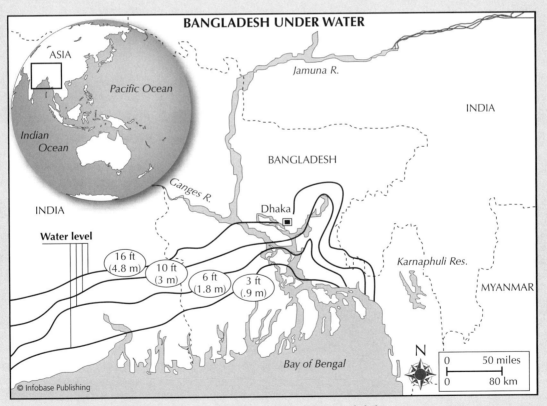

This map shows the impact of rising sea level on low-lying countries such as Bangladesh.

> ## The Proliferation of Atmospheric Models

As the fourth decade of numerical weather prediction began, the number and complexity of weather and climate models exploded along with data availability and computing power. As cold war threats declined, supercomputers previously used for defense purposes took on the task of evaluating climate models. Since no two models ever provided exactly the same answer, arguments about long-range weather forecasting and climate predictions were often fought over the appropriateness of data, the combination of variables considered, and the presence or absence of feedback mechanisms.

Scientists expanded their use of climate models to run atmospheric experiments. They ran the general circulation models on a variety of virtual atmospheres modified to represent different levels of greenhouse gases, areas of snow and ice cover, and warmer or colder sea surface temperatures, to investigate how Earth's climate might change. Assuming a fourfold increase in CO_2 levels over preindustrial levels, the climate modelers Syukuro Manabe and Ronald Stouffer (1954–　) found the resultant warming increased the amount of precipitation and river runoff in high latitudes. This "freshening" of the North Atlantic caused the North

Oceanic circulation models, including Wallace S. Broecker's controversial "conveyor belt," give scientists a way to think about what could happen to Earth's climate if ocean currents changed.

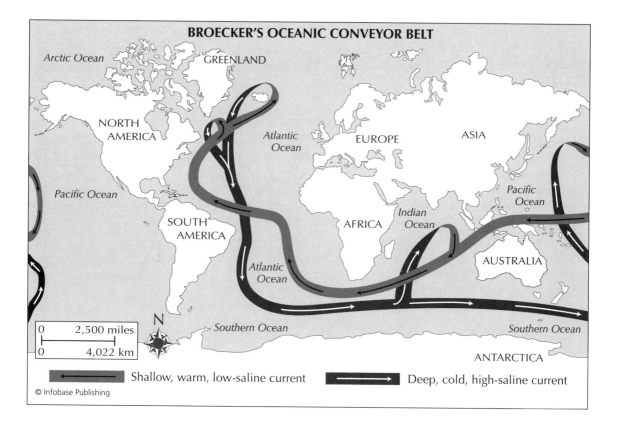

BROECKER'S OCEANIC CONVEYOR BELT

Arctic Ocean　GREENLAND

NORTH AMERICA　Atlantic Ocean　EUROPE　ASIA

Pacific Ocean　Pacific Ocean

SOUTH AMERICA　AFRICA　Indian Ocean

Atlantic Ocean　AUSTRALIA

N

0　2,500 miles
0　4,022 km

Southern Ocean　Southern Ocean

ANTARCTICA

← Shallow, warm, low-saline current　→ Deep, cold, high-saline current

© Infobase Publishing

Atlantic conveyor belt to stop almost 60 years after reaching heightened CO_2 levels—a result that would lead to cold temperatures in Europe. Letting the model continue to run, they found that the conveyor then started again after about 2,000 years, although a mechanism for causing such a reaction was not apparent.

Another team, this one led by Robert D. Cess (1933–   ) of State University of New York, Stonybrook, investigated the influence of reduced snow cover on future climate. Leading a team of 33 scientists from eight countries, Cess tested 17 climate models to see whether reduced snow cover—an assumed outcome of warming—and its corresponding reduced albedo would spur a positive feedback mechanism and accelerate warming. Twelve of the models provided the expected result: enhanced warming due to positive feedback. Five of the models produced very different results. Some of them led to cooling because the melting snow was tied to increased cloud cover. In others, the reduced snow cover led to increased energy emissions from Earth.

A follow-up study showed that the world's 19 best climate models had difficulty simulating atmospheric moisture processes. Researchers found that a 3.6°F (2°C) change in the virtual Earth's sea surface temperature led to significant differences in incoming and outgoing radiation, all related to the models' handling of moisture processes. Previous discussions on model improvements had centered on the need for more powerful computers; however, project leaders pointed out that increased computer power would not have improved model outcome in this case. The focus needed to be on understanding atmospheric processes and applying new knowledge to models.

Additional modeling of North Atlantic currents by researchers from the University of Victoria, British Columbia, Canada, provided information on conveyor belt behavior. Instead of operating at one speed, the conveyor belt operated at one of three possible speeds: very slow, a midrange speed (current situation), and fast. The midrange speed is extremely stable under present conditions, but when the researchers warmed up the virtual climate and subsequently increased evaporation and precipitation rates, the conveyor responded by switching erratically among slow, medium, and fast speeds. This important result provided evidence of a possible reason behind rapid climate change in the past.

By the end of the decade, the number of ocean-atmosphere climate models had quadrupled from five to 20. All of them reached the same conclusion: Doubling CO_2 levels causes the global temperature to rise 3°–8°F (1.7°–4.4°C), with the range of values stemming from model differences. While the models provided a consistent global solution, they still failed to provide good regional solutions. The grid spacing was too large, and topography and vegetation were not part of the virtual Earth. To solve this problem, some modelers took the global model output and then used a second model with a finer grid spacing to look for regional changes, a process called *nesting*. Regional models will become increasingly important since global warming's effects will depend on location. Newer models also include deep-ocean processes and the effects of aerosols. Running these models, scientists have been able to replicate climate change in the 20th century—the approximately 1.8°F (1°C) increase in global temperature, and the horizontal and vertical changes in temperature distribution. They have also come close to replicating the climate situation during the last ice age. The models remain unable to predict accurately the temperature changes inherent during an El Niño event and fail completely to predict regional changes. Until they can do so, skeptics will continue to challenge model output as representing scientific evidence of warming.

This diagram from the Intergovernmental Panel on Climate Change (IPCC) 2001 report shows the range of temperature increases predicted by a variety of climate models.

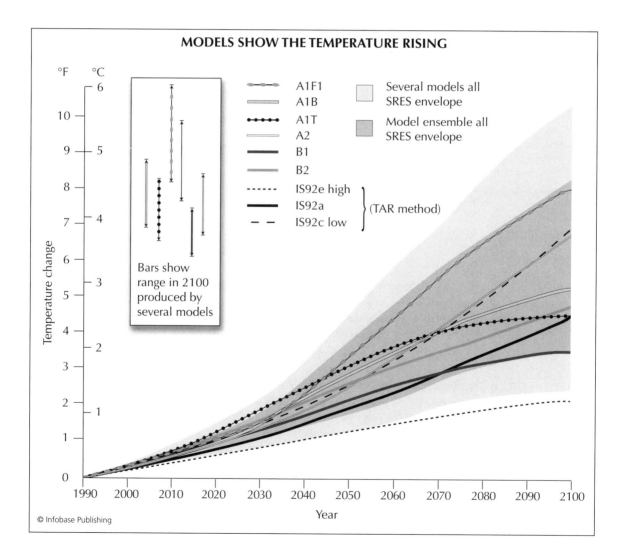

A Technological Fix?

Since the end of World War II, the *technological fix* has been applied to numerous naturally occurring and human-made problems. Dams provide water to arid and semiarid regions to support agriculture, industry, and large populations in areas with insufficient water. Levees hold back the waters of the Mississippi and other large rivers. Tunnels punch through mountains to create an easier route for motor vehicles and rail traffic. As global warming and ozone depletion appeared to be worsening problems, scientists and engineers once again started proposing solutions to "fix" them.

Some of the proposals bordered on the realm of science fiction. They included using lasers to break down CFCs in the lower atmosphere before they could drift to the stratosphere and destroy the ozone layer. Alternatively, ozone could be replenished through regular deliveries of ozone to the stratosphere by rockets, balloons, or aircraft.

Some of the ideas provided a direct attack on the warming problem by reflecting solar energy back into space. Proposals included covering the oceans with white styrofoam disks, painting all roofs white, or placing large reflectors (mirrors, thin sheets of reflective film) into orbit. Other reflection-related projects included shooting sulfur dioxide droplets into the stratosphere or putting fleets of ships or power plants in the middle of oceans so their sulfur-laden exhaust would generate clouds.

A third type of technological fix focused on absorbing excess CO_2 from the atmosphere and storing it in plants. The more practical of these schemes included planting large tracts of fast-growing trees or adopting minimal-tillage agricultural practices that would draw CO_2 out of the atmosphere and store it in biomass. A less practical idea involved fertilizing the ocean with iron to promote the growth of phytoplankton, an experiment that was tried in the waters south of the Galápagos. In late 1994, a team of researchers dumped 1,000 pounds (480 kg) of iron into an 18-square-mile (46.6-km^2) region 310 miles (500 km) south of the Galápagos Islands to test a hypothesis that phytoplankton growth rates were limited by low iron concentrations. Watching the test site for nine days,

the researchers found a surge of phytoplankton growth in response to the iron. The amount of CO_2 absorbed by the phytoplankton, however, was only one-tenth as much as had been expected. Plant-eating plankton in the area feasted on the rapidly growing phytoplankton, thus keeping the population in check. To keep growth rates up, almost constant fertilization would be required, an unfeasible idea. When scientists repeated the experiment two years later, they introduced the iron gradually. The phytoplankton growth was so explosive that it absorbed 386 tons (350,000 kg) of CO_2 from the surrounding ocean. The experimental outcome gave more credence to the idea that airborne iron-laden dust may have boosted phytoplankton growth during past transitions from glacial to interglacial climates. Researchers did not wish, however, to encourage those who were suggesting that seeding the oceans with iron to boost phytoplankton growth and remove CO_2 from the atmosphere would be a way to slow down the advance of global warming. The "cure" would profoundly alter the ocean ecosystem and possibly lead to large releases of methane—a greenhouse gas that traps more heat than CO_2.

The final set of proposals also focused on carbon sequestration, but instead of tying up carbon in plants, these proposals involved liquefying CO_2 and pumping it either into the ground or deep into the ocean. Both of these suggestions had potential problems. Because CO_2 is heavier than air, if it escaped from an underground storage location and into an inhabited area, it could suffocate the inhabitants. In the ocean, CO_2 could acidify the water and harm sea life.

The world's nations are trying to work together to reduce the accumulation of greenhouse gases through the Kyoto Protocol. Part of that agreement focuses on reducing the consumption of fossil fuels, but part of it focuses on reducing greenhouse gas levels through fixes. Technological fixes always have the potential to create more problems than they solve, but if global warming starts to create serious problems, there will be public pressure to "do something," and the ideas for technological fixes will continue to grow.

Scientific Event of the Decade: The Kyoto Protocol

After two years of preliminary negotiations on issues surrounding greenhouse gases and global warming, more than 5,000 delegates from 160 nations met December 1–10, 1997, for the Third Conference of Parties to the Framework Convention on Climate Change in Kyoto, Japan. They were joined by thousands of lobbyists representing a wide spectrum of environmental viewpoints, and journalists covering the proceedings for their countries' media. The negotiators were trying to agree on the extent to which greenhouse emissions need to be reduced, a time frame for implementing those reductions, ways nations would share the burden, and which gases would be included on the reduction list.

Using IPCC reports as scientific background, the Kyoto meeting focused on the political and technical issues surrounding the goal of achieving "stabilization of greenhouse concentrations in the atmosphere at the level that would prevent dangerous anthropogenic interference with the climate system." Even if all nations complied with the target reductions, CO_2 levels would still increase to 382 ppm (parts per million) by 2010. The purpose was to reduce the rate of increase, not the amount of CO_2 in the atmosphere.

A major source of disagreement between nations focused on which nations would be subject to emissions controls and which gases would be included. European members wanted to limit coverage to CO_2, methane, and nitrous oxide, while the United States added hydrofluorocarbons, perfluorocarbons, and sulfur hexafluoride—gases that had not been included in the Montreal Protocol. Negotiators agreed to reduce the emissions of CO_2, methane, and nitrous oxide to 5.2 percent below 1990 levels by 2012. The other gases would be included but would meet different level requirements. The levels would also vary by nations. Europe, the United States, and Japan were expected to reduce emissions. Russia, Ukraine, and New Zealand were to return to 1990 levels. Australia and Iceland were to stabilize emissions to 8–10 percent above 1990 levels.

Industrial countries were divided into two groups. Within a group, if one country reduced its emissions below the target level, it could sell "pollution rights" to another country. Nations could also earn emission credits by planting new forests or preserving existing ones; however, the details would not be worked out until negotiators met again a year later in Buenos Aires, Argentina. Thirty-nine of the nations would face binding emission controls, but 121 nations that were less economically developed would not have to meet emission requirements even though they were already emitting large amounts of greenhouse gases. This was a major problem for U.S. negotiators, who announced the United States would not ratify the treaty unless it required all nations to reduce emissions.

A variety of options are being explored to reduce CO_2 levels, maintain them at current levels, or reduce the rate at which the CO_2 level is increasing. The question of how best to gain control over greenhouse gas emissions and subsequent atmospheric warming is difficult to answer. Economic, political, and cultural values all play a role in national decisions. Engineering solutions, such as those discussed earlier, are a possibility, but every technological fix is accompanied by a consequence, often one that is unintentional. For example, when automobiles first became inexpensive enough for the average person to

One year later, the United States signed the Kyoto Protocol but still refused to ratify it. Only three countries—Fiji, Antigua, and Barbuda—had ratified the treaty. The protocol was in trouble and national representatives reached no agreement during the Buenos Aires meeting. The conflict still focused on emission credits and the ruling that developing countries did not have to reduce emissions.

Two years after the Kyoto meeting, negotiators met once again in Bonn, Germany, to discuss reporting and technical requirements for carrying out the protocol, but the emissions issues remained. They were addressed yet again in November 2000, during negotiations held at The Hague, Netherlands. Among the points being worked on during the meeting were ways that wealthy, industrialized countries could gain emission credits by aiding developing countries with projects that would curtail greenhouse gas emissions as their economies grew, and whether those projects should include nuclear power and "clean coal" plants. By November 2000, more than 150 countries (including the United States) had signed the protocol, but it had not been ratified by any industrialized nations. The United States was holding out for promises that large developing nations such as China and India would also be required to limit greenhouse emissions. Meeting leaders removed those items from the agenda to prevent the United States from scuttling the talks. Demonstrators representing a variety of environmental organizations protested the lack of agreement on details that had slowed action to reduce greenhouse gas emissions. There were major disagreements between these groups over whether credits should be given for existing forest. Some said yes, thinking that such a decision would prevent the destruction of forests. Others said no, because they thought countries with large forests would use them as an excuse not to reduce greenhouse gas emissions.

After two weeks of tense negotiations, including a final all-night session, talks collapsed when the United States and the European Union failed to reach agreement on the use of forests and properly managed farmland as CO_2 *sinks* (absorbers of the gas from the atmosphere). Because the United States has many more acres of forests than does Europe, and the open space to plant even more, the Europeans objected that such a provision would be too favorable to the United States. Representatives from poorer developing countries were irritated that the negotiations failed because of what they perceived as a lack of flexibility on the part of the wealthiest participants. All parties then agreed that they would continue the negotiations set for the next year in Marrakech, Morocco.

The Kyoto Protocol was an unprecedented attempt to coordinate a global effort on the Earth's environment. Concerns in developed countries about possible damage to their economic situation threatened to stop the entire process. Negotiators would continue to struggle with the details into the next century.

buy one, people were delighted to have the freedom to travel when and where they wanted to go. They did not anticipate the traffic jams and polluted air that were unintended consequences of this new technology. The same is true of the possible technological fixes for reducing the effects of greenhouse gases. Therefore, such fixes must be approached with caution.

An alternative to engineering a solution is to reduce the amount of greenhouse gas emissions at their source. That too is a solution fraught with potential problems—many of them political. All nations have their self-interest in mind when governing bodies make decisions on international issues, even ones that affect every human on the planet. Such was the case during the conferences that led to the Kyoto Protocol—an effort to reduce the rate at which CO_2 is accumulating in the atmosphere—which was the most significant event concerning weather and climate in the last decade of the 20th century.

Further Reading

Books and Articles

Broecker, Wallace S. "Thermohaline Circulation, the Achilles Heel of Our Climate System: Will Man-Made CO_2 Upset the Current Balance?" *Science* 278 (1997): 1582–1588. Broecker argues that global warming may upset ocean currents and upset global climate stability.

Cess, R. D., et al. "Intercomparison and Interpretation of Climate Feedback Processes in 19 Atmospheric General Circulation Models." *Journal of Geophysical Research* 95 (1990): 16,601–16,615. Cess and an international team of researchers analyzed 19 climate models and found problems with the way they simulated atmospheric moisture.

Christianson, Gale E. *Greenhouse: The 200-Year History of Global Warming.* New York: Walker, 1999. Starting with Fourier's early 19th-century hypothesis that Earth's atmosphere acted as a "bell jar" and continuing through the Kyoto conference, the historian Christianson discusses the recent history of global warming.

Cox, John D. *Climate Crash: Abrupt Climate Change and What It Means for Our Future.* Washington, D.C.: Joseph Henry Press, 2005. Cox reviews the preceding eight years of climate science.

Hoffert, Martin I., and Curt Covey. "Deriving Global Climate Sensitivity from Paleoclimate Reconstructions." *Nature* 360 (December 10, 1992): 573–576. Hoffert and Covey argue that Earth's atmosphere possessed a basic sensitivity to CO_2 levels that was independent of the current climate state during two climatic periods: one 20,000 and the other 100,000 years ago.

Houghton, John. *Global Warming: The Complete Briefing.* Cambridge: Cambridge University Press, 2004. This is an excellent nontechnical guide to the science behind global warming.

LeMasurier, Wesley E., David M. Harwood, and David C. Rex. "Geology of Mount Murphy Volcano; An 8-m.y. History of the Interaction between a Rift Volcano and the West Antarctica Ice Sheet." *GSA Bulletin* 106 (1994): 265–280. The authors contend that the Antarctic ice sheet completely melted three million years ago and could completely melt again as a result of global warming.

Lindzen, Richard S. "Some Coolness Concerning Global Warming." *Bulletin of the American Meteorological Society* 71 (1990): 288–299. The atmospheric scientist Richard Lindzen argues that dire warnings on global warning are overblown.

Manabe, S., and R. J. Stouffer. "The Role of Thermohaline Circulation in Climate." *Tellus* 51 A–B(1) (1999): 91–109. The authors discuss the impact of freshwater runoff on ocean currents in the North Atlantic and how it could lead to significantly colder temperatures in Europe.

Pearce, R. P., editor. *Meteorology at the Millennium.* San Diego: Academic Press, 2002. This book presents an overview of the atmospheric science disciplines at the end of the 20th century.

Philander, S. George. *Is the Temperature Rising? The Uncertain Science of Global Warming.* Princeton, N.J.: Princeton University Press, 1998. The author, a geoscientist, explains the dynamics of the oceans and atmosphere as they are related to global warming and climate change.

Ruddiman, William F. *Plows, Plagues, and Petroleum: How Humans Took Control of Climate.* Princeton, N.J.: Princeton University Press, 2005. Ruddiman argues that humans have been changing their climate for the past 8,000 years—ever since they started farming large amounts of land.

Singer, S. Fred. *Hot Air, Cold Science: Global Warming's Unfinished Debate.* Oakland, Calif.: Independent Institute, 1997. A global warming skeptic, the meteorologist S. Fred Singer argues in his book that not all scientists are in agreement on global warming or its causes.

Sugden, David E. et al. "Preservation of Miocene Glacier Ice in East Antarctica." *Nature* 376 (1995): 412–414. The authors present evidence to support the existence of a stable Antarctic ice cap.

Web Sites

National Climatic and Data Center. "A Paleo Perspective on Abrupt Climate Change." NOAA Satellites and Information. Available online. URL: http://www.ncdc.noaa.gov/paleo/abrupt/index/html. Accessed March 15, 2006. A discussion of what is known and not known about abrupt climate change.

Office of Fossil Energy. "Carbon Sequestration R&D Overview." U.S. Department of Energy. Available online. URL: http://www.fe.doe.gov/programs/sequestration/overview.html. Accessed March 15, 2006. Explains the reasoning behind carbon sequestration and provides links to additional information.

Office of News Services. "Antarctic Ice Sheet Losing Mass, According to CU-Boulder Study." University of Colorado, Boulder. Available online. URL: http://www.colorado.edu/news/releases/2006/86.html. Posted March 2, 2006. Accessed March 15, 2006. Information on the loss of Antarctic ice based on satellite data is presented.

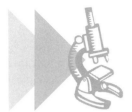

Conclusion:
Into the Twenty-first Century

In the early years of the 21st century, climate change—global warming, in particular—remains at the forefront of weather and climate research as 2005 set another record for the amount of carbon dioxide in the atmosphere. It also remains at the forefront of national and international politics. Worldwide, the public wants and depends on accurate weather forecasts from a variety of governmental and private sources. However, the long-term trend in global temperatures, and what it portends for our futures, dominates the media.

The Kyoto Protocol, ratified in November 2004, took effect over seven years after its initial signing in 1997. The United States declined to take part because of concerns over possible adverse economic outcomes, points government negotiators continued to press during the United Nations Climate Change Conference held in Montréal, Canada, from November 28 through December 9, 2005. Almost 10,000 delegates and observers from 189 countries attended this meeting to discuss how to implement the Kyoto Protocol and address emerging climate change problems. By the close of the conference, delegates had adopted more than 40 decisions designed to strengthen efforts to reduce greenhouse emissions. As the demand for energy increases, particularly as India and China rapidly industrialize, the world's nations will look for technological solutions. With the only real answer to greenhouse gas production resting on nonpolluting energy sources, scientists and engineers will be challenged throughout the 21st century to create new ways to heat and light homes, power factories, and transport people across the globe.

Scientific studies of rising global temperatures are no longer limited to meteorologists and climatologists, and research is not limited to determining the *whys* of global warming. Meteorologists are increasingly focused on weather pattern changes that could be triggered by global warming, which will not necessarily produce a warmer climate for everyone. The possibility that the El Niño phenomenon causes drought in large expanses of Africa already experiencing the problems of desertification is cause for continued concern. Life scientists are investigating the long-term effects of climate change on the ecosystem. Medical researchers are examining the geographical expansion of diseases. Glaciologists are probing shrinking glaciers and melting ice sheets, which were showing accelerated melting in 2006. Agriculturalists are studying the effect of temperature change on crops. Oceanographers are measuring the relationship between higher atmospheric temperatures and changes in sea surface temperature, and potential changes in the general oceanic circulation. Hydrologists are examining changing patterns of precipitation and their relationship to the availability of freshwater to a steadily increasing world population.

Robert Watson, chairman of the Intergovernmental Panel on Climate Change (IPCC), warned of serious drought and other severe weather due to air pollution. (International Institute for Sustainable Development)

Climate change will be a concern for nations, individuals, and the scientific community for the foreseeable future.

All of these scientists will be aided by advances in remote sensors and supercomputers. NASA's *Aura* and *ICESat* satellites will be measuring ozone concentrations and ice, cloud, and landforms, respectively, providing real-time information about changes in atmospheric chemistry and Earth's atmospheric, oceanic, and geologic features. Supercomputers will be helping scientists to analyze these data, and they will be running increasingly complex weather and climate models that will aid researchers in determining future climate change. Advanced computing power will also assist in evaluating the connection, if any, between changing climate and weather disasters—an issue that began to take on some urgency after weather caused over $90 billion damage around the world in 2004 and Hurricane Katrina inundated the city of New Orleans, Louisiana, and surrounding areas in 2005.

When dealing with the atmosphere, it is unlikely that there will be a definitive answer to any scientific question. The atmosphere incorporates too many variables that cannot be adequately measured and too many physical processes that are still little understood. The past century has seen meteorology and climatology move from the fringes of science to become the most dynamic sciences of today. Throughout the 21st century, atmospheric scientists will continue their work on remote sensing, numerical modeling, and data analysis to gain further understanding of the complex nature of the air-ocean-land system that creates Earth's weather and climate. The results of their research will have a profound impact on other scientific disciplines, and ultimately on Earth's future.

Awards of Merit

in Weather and Climate

The Crafoord Prize

The Crafoord Prize is awarded by the Royal Swedish Academy of Sciences to recognize contributions in geosciences, biosciences, mathematics, and astronomy. The Crafoord Foundation maintains a Web site (http://www.crafoord.se/eng/) that provides information on the prize, links to lists of winners, and the description of their awards. The academy awards the geoscience award once every three years. The following scientists received the Crafoord Prize for contributions made to meteorological and climatological research.

1983

Edward N. Lorenz and Henry Stommel, United States. For fundamental contributions to the field of geophysical hydrodynamics, which in unique ways have contributed to a deeper understanding of the large-scale of the atmosphere and the sea.

1995

Willi Dansgaard, Denmark, and Nicholas Shackleton, Great Britain. For fundamental work on developing and applying isotope geological analysis methods for the study of climatic variations during the Quaternary period.

The International Meteorological Organization (IMO) Prize

The IMO Prize for "outstanding work in meteorology and international collaboration in this field" is awarded by the World Meteorological Organization (WMO). It is the highest honor bestowed upon atmospheric scientists and (since 1971) hydrologists. Award criteria may be found on the WMO Web site (http://www.wmo.ch/web-en/awards_imo.html), but there is no list of those who have received awards. The *World Meteorological Organization Bulletin* usually includes information about this annual award in one of their issues.

1956

Theodor Hesselberg, Norway. "In recognition of his unique record of service to the International Meteorological Organization and to the WMO, and in recognition for his valuable contribution to the science of meteorology."

1957

Carl-Gustav Rossby, Sweden and United States. For his lifetime of achievement in meteorological theory development and disciplinary advancement.

1958

Ernest Gold, United Kingdom. For distinguished contributions to meteorology. (Gold was a Fellow of the Royal Society and a leader of the British Meteorological Office).

1959

Jacob A. Bjerknes, Norway and United States. For original research leading to the development of the polar front theory and for his work on general atmospheric circulation.

1960

Professor Jacques M. Van Mieghem, Belgium. For distinguished contributions to meteorology.

1961

Kalapathi Ramakrishana Ramanathan, India. For noteworthy contributions on atmospheric and solar radiation, upper atmosphere structure, and general circulation over India.

1962

Anders Knutsson Ångström, Sweden. For his work in theoretical and applied meteorology concerned with radiation and climatology, including energy changes in the atmosphere.

1963

Reginald Cockcroft Sutcliffe, United Kingdom. For achievement in dynamical meteorology.

1964

Francis W. Reichelderfer, United States. For his service as the first president of the World Meteorological Organization (1951–1955) and his 25-year leadership of the U.S. Weather Bureau.

1965

Sverre Petterssen, Norway and United States. For his important role in facilitating development of meteorological activity on a world scale.

1966

Tor Bergeron, Sweden. For his work at the Bergen School and in spreading its methods around the world; for his work in cloud physics and precipitation theory development.

1967

Kirill Yakovlevi Kondratyev, USSR. For theoretical and experimental studies of radiative energy transfer in the atmosphere, problems of satellite meteorology, and meteorology in the upper atmosphere.

1968

Sir Graham Sutton, United Kingdom. For fundamental research into the theory of atmospheric diffusion.

1969

Erik H. Palmén, Finland. For contributions on large-scale atmospheric circulation in extratropical and tropical regions, and for introducing the concept of the atmospheric jet stream.

1970

Richard Th. A. Scherhag, Federal Republic of Germany. For achievements in synoptic meteorology, including his discovery of sudden warming in the stratosphere.

1971

Jule G. Charney, United States. For outstanding contributions to dynamical meteorology and numerical weather prediction research.

1972

Victor Antonovich Bugaev, USSR. For his leadership of Soviet geophysical institutions and several aerological expeditions.

1973

Charles Henry B. Priestley, Australia, and John S. Sawyer, United Kingdom. Priestley: for his work on turbulent processes as well as his leadership of the Environmental Physics Laboratory of the Commonwealth Scientific and Industrial Research Organization (CSIRO). Sawyer: for his outstanding work in dynamical meteorology and as director of research for the United Kingdom Meteorological Office.

1974

Joseph Smagorinsky, United States. For his work with the U.S. Weather Bureau and as head of the Geophysical Fluid Dynamics Laboratory, as well as his role as a leader in GARP.

1975

Warren L. Godson, Canada. For research on atmospheric ozone, atmospheric thermodynamics, and numerical weather prediction.

1976

E. K. Federov, USSR. For his pioneering work on the Soviet drifting station in the Arctic (1937–38) and for his work as the vice president of the WMO.

1977

George P. Cressman, United States. For his pioneering work in numerical weather prediction.

1978

Alf E. G. E. Nyberg, Sweden. For his valuable contributions as head of the Swedish Meteorological and Hydrological Institute for 22 years and for his work with the WMO.

1979

Helmut E. Landsberg, United States. For his efforts as the president of the WMO Commission on Climatology and his significant contributions to climatological research.

1980

Robert M. White, United States. For his leadership of the National Oceanic and Atmospheric Administration (NOAA) and his role as the Permanent Representative (1963–78) from the United States to the WMO.

1981

Bert Bolin, Sweden. For his work on the chemistry of the atmosphere and the dispersion of atmospheric pollutants, as well as his role in investigating the effect of carbon dioxide on climate change.

1982

William J. Gibbs, Australia. For significant work on synoptic and satellite meteorology, hydrometeorology, and climate.

1983

Muhamed F. Taha, Egypt, and Juan J. Burgos, Argentina. Taha: for his work in the establishment of the Egyptian National Meteorological Service and his many activities in international cooperation. Burgos: for his outstanding work in agricultural meteorology and climate studies related to agriculture.

1984

Thomas F. Malone, United States. For his lifelong dedication to global environmental issues.

1985

Sir Arthur Davies, United Kingdom. For his leadership in international meteorology and his assistance to nations establishing their own meteorological services.

1986

Hermann Flohn, Federal Republic of Germany. For his outstanding work in atmospheric circulation and climatology, especially in Asia and Africa.

1987

Mikhail Ivanovich Budyko, USSR. For his outstanding work in climate change and his leadership of the World Climate Program.

1988

F. Kenneth Hare, Canada. For his significant contributions to climate change research.

1989

P. R. Pisharoty, India. For his contributions to the calculations of water vapor fluxes across the Indian Ocean.

1990

Richard E. Hallgren, United States. For his outstanding leadership in meteorology, both nationally and internationally; he served as Permanent Representative to the WMO from the United States.

1991

Ragnar Fjørtoft, Norway. For his outstanding work in dynamical meteorology and numerical weather prediction.

1992

Yuri A. Izrael, USSR. For his leadership of the Hydrometeorological Service, his service as the Permanent Representative to the WMO, and his climate research.

1993

Verner E. Suomi, United States. For his outstanding work in satellite meteorology.

1994

James P. Bruce, Canada. For his role in educating the public about meteorology and climate change; he was also a founding member of the WMO Commission on Hydrology.

1995

Roman L. Kintanar, Philippines. For his service as WMO President and Permanent Representative to WMO from the Philippines.

1996

Tiruvalam N. Krishnamurti, United States. For his outstanding work in tropical meteorology and numerical weather prediction; he was also a leader in GARP.

1997

Mariano A. Estoque, Philippines. For his outstanding work in the climatology of rainfall, mesoscale meteorology, and air pollution meteorology.

1998

Sir John Houghton, United Kingdom. For his pioneering work in the development of remote sensing equipment that could take Earth observations from spacecraft.

1999

James C. I. Dooge, Ireland. For his pioneering work in applying mathematical and scientific techniques to the study of hydrology, in particular the application of linear systems theory to hydrological problems and the study of open channel flow.

2000

Edward N. Lorenz, United States. For his work on available potential energy, and his identification of the sensitivity of models to initial conditions that led to chaos theory and the introduction of ensemble forecasting.

2001

Mahammed Hassan Ganji, Iran. For his extensive publications in both English and Persian on the subjects of human geography, meteorology, and climatology; he created the first climatic atlas of Iran in 1965.

2002

Joanne Simpson, United States. For her pioneering work on cloud modeling, observational experiments on convective cloud systems, and hurricane research.

2003

Ye Duzheng, China. For over six decades of meteorological investigation, research, training and service in China, Asia, and internationally;

Ye Duzheng was the first meteorologist to stress the importance of the Tibetan Plateau as a heat source in summer and a cold source in winter, which affects atmospheric circulation patterns.

2004

Bennert Mauchenhauer, Denmark. For his work in the development of spectral modes (a leading model in weather and climate forecasting) and advanced research in numerical weather prediction.

2005

John Zillman, Australia. For his visionary leadership in international meteorology.

2006

Lennart Bengtsson, Sweden and Germany. For his outstanding contribution to international scientific collaboration in meteorology.

The Tyler Prize

The Tyler Prize for Environmental Achievement, established in 1973 by the late John and Alice Tyler, honors exceptional work in environmental science, policy, energy, and health that is of worldwide importance and is of great benefit to humanity. The Tyler Prize Web site (http://www.usc.edu/dept/LAS/tylerprize/) lists the names of laureates and a short description of their awards. The following scientists have won the prize for their work in meteorology or climatology:

1983

Harold S. Johnston, Mario J. Molina, and F. Sherwood Rowland, United States. Johnston: for calling attention to the possibility that stratospheric contamination by nitrogen oxides might threaten the Earth's ozone layer. Molina: as the codeveloper of the Rowland-Molina hypothesis on ozone depletion by chlorofluorocarbons. Rowland: for his policy initiatives that led to regulations that controlled the use of chlorofluorocarbons as aerosol propellants in the Western world.

1988

Bert Bolin, Sweden. For helping focus international attention on the potential dangers to the world's climate posed by greenhouse gases and acid rain.

1989

Paul J. Crutzen, United States. For making landmark discoveries on stratospheric and tropospheric ozone, nuclear winter, and humanity's capacity to upset the global atmosphere.

1992

Robert M. White, United States. For his work as a world leader in designing cooperative networks and building institutions and for initiating international efforts to understand global climate change and the effects of greenhouse gases.

1996

Willi Dansgaard, Denmark; Hans Oeschger, Switzerland; and Claude Lorius, France. Dansgaard: for his work as the first paleoclimatologist to demonstrate that measurements of the trace isotopes oxygen-18 and deuterium (heavy hydrogen) in accumulated glacier ice could be used as an indicator of climate change over time. Oeschger: for his work as a pioneer of gas composition and radiocarbon measurements on polar ice. His measurement of carbon dioxide concentrations from air bubbles trapped in ice revealed for the first time the important role that the world's oceans play in influencing global climate. Lorius: for his promotion of international cooperation as he led a Russian, American, and French scientific team in the recovery and analysis of the longest ice core drilled to date (the Vostok Core).

2002

Wallace S. Broecker, United States, and Liu Tungsheng, China. Broecker: for his work as a pioneer in the development of geochemical tracers to describe basic biological, chemical, and physical processes that govern the behavior of carbon dioxide in the oceans and the interactions of oceanic carbon dioxide with the atmosphere. Liu: for his work as a pioneer in developing ways to measure paleoclimate change over the last 2.5 million years through studies of loess, a windblown dust, that forms thick deposits over much of central China.

2005

Charles David Keeling and Lonnie G. Thompson, United States. Keeling: for his rigorous time series measurements of atmospheric carbon dioxide and their interpretation. Thompson: for his pioneering work in the collection and analysis of valuable climatic information contained in tropical glacier ice cores from all over the world.

Glossary

aerosol a tiny (about 4 x 10⁻⁵ inch [1 micrometer]) liquid droplet or dust particle uniformly suspended in a gas

albedo the ratio of reflected light to incident light such that a higher value indicates a more reflective surface

anemometer instrument for measuring wind speed

anthropogenic caused by human activity, often applied to global warming

anticyclone a high-air-pressure center accompanied by clockwise, outward airflow in the Northern Hemisphere

applied science scientific research focused on solving a defined problem

atmosphere the gaseous envelope surrounding Earth and other planets that is held in place by gravity

aurora light occasionally seen in the high-latitude night sky that is produced by electrical activity in the ionosphere and may be related to magnetic storms on the Sun

barometer instrument used to measure air pressure

basic science scientific research focused on developing knowledge in a scientific discipline for its own sake

carrying capacity the maximum amount of life supportable in a given geographic area before it begins to deteriorate

ceiling the height of the lowest level of clouds that covers six-tenths or more of the sky

climate the average (over 30 years) observed weather at a given location plus weather extremes observed during the same period that change slowly over time

climatology the scientific study of climate and its underlying processes

cloud condensation nucleus small hygroscopic particles on which water vapor condenses to form clouds

condensation the process whereby water changes phase from a gas to a liquid

crevasse a deep, narrow fissure in a glacier

cyclone a low air pressure center accompanied by counterclockwise, inward-flowing air in the Northern Hemisphere

dendroclimatology the determination of climate by the analysis of annual tree ring growth

desertification the process of becoming a desert, usually due to climate change or mismanagement of land

diurnal cycles that occur within 24 hours, for example, the change of temperature from cool to warm and back

dynamic meteorology the branch of meteorology dealing with atmospheric motion

eccentricity the deviation of a planetary orbit away from being circular toward being elliptical

empirical based on observation

evapotranspiration the evaporation of moisture directly from Earth's surface combined with the release of water vapor from plants

feedback mechanism in a process, when the change in one variable reinforces the original process

geophysics the physics of Earth, its atmosphere, and space

glacial period a geologic period when glaciers cover a significant amount of Earth's surface and temperatures are cold

glaze a transparent layer of ice that develops as a result of slowly cooling supercooled water

hoarfrost ice crystals, often fernlike, that form when water vapor is deposited (frozen) directly onto exposed surfaces

hurricane a uniquely structured cyclone that develops over tropical oceans and has sustained winds in excess of 74 miles (119 km) per hour

hydrologic cycle the movement of water from Earth's surface to the atmosphere and back through evaporation, condensation, and precipitation

hygrometer instrument for measuring water vapor in the atmosphere

hygroscopic nuclei tiny water-attracting particles that permit condensation when the atmosphere is not saturated with water vapor, that is, when the relative humidity is less than 100 percent

initial conditions in numerical weather prediction, the values of temperature, pressure, moisture, and other atmospheric variables at a given point in time before the model is started to predict a future condition

insolation incoming solar radiation

interglacial period a geologic period when warmer temperatures exist and glaciers retreat to mountains

isothermal having a constant temperature

latent heat heat released when water changes phase from gas to liquid, or from liquid to solid. During the phase change, the water itself does not change temperature

line of convergence a line along which air is converging horizontally

mesoscale meteorology phenomena that cover from a few to tens of miles (kilometers) horizontally and up to 0.6 mile (1 km)

meteorology the scientific study of the atmosphere and its processes

model a mathematical description that includes data, defining equations, and assumptions from which predictions can be made, for example, weather and climate models

monsoon winds that change direction with the season, most commonly applied to the winter and summer monsoons that affect the Indian subcontinent

nesting in an atmospheric model, placing a finer grid pattern within a coarser one to identify weather processes in a smaller region

nomogram the graphical representation of an equation in three variables. When a straight line connecting known variables is drawn across the graph, it provides a solution to the equation

NWP numerical weather prediction—the creation of weather forecast maps by computer model

objective forecast a weather forecast made by solving equations

orographic pertaining to mountains

paleoclimate climatic conditions that occurred before the introduction of scientific meteorological instruments and may only be reconstructed with historical documents or climate proxies such as ice cores or tree rings

periodicities events, in this context weather events or conditions, that occur regularly in time or space

persistence forecast a forecast that is based on current weather conditions' staying the same

pilot balloon a small, typically red helium-filled balloon used to determine upper-level wind speed and direction

polar front the semipermanent, semicontinuous boundary between polar and tropical air masses

pressure also known as atmospheric pressure, the weight of the column of air above a given location on Earth's surface

pressure gradient the difference in air pressure between two locations at a given time. The larger the pressure gradient between two locations, the greater the wind speed

proxy a biological (fossil, pollen, tree rings) or geological (ice core, sediment core) structure of known age from which scientists may determine information about past climates. Historical documents (for example, harvest records) may also serve as a proxy for past climates

qualitative values for which there is no numerical description. For example, "warm" is a qualitative description of air temperature

quantitative values that are measurable, specifically by calibrated instruments

radar (*ra*dio *d*etection *a*nd *r*anging) an instrument that sends and receives microwaves to determine the location of objects. Meteorologists use radar to determine the locations and types of precipitation

Reamur a temperature scale for which water freezes at 0°R and water boils at 80°R

resonance a vibration of large amplitude caused by a small stimulus of the same (or near-same) period as the natural vibration of an electrical or mechanical system

rime opaque, grainy-looking ice that forms when supercooled water freezes rapidly

sink a reservoir by which a measurable quantity leaves a system. For example, when plants absorb carbon dioxide that process constitutes a carbon dioxide sink

smog naturally occurring fog contaminated by pollution. This term is also applied more generally to heavy air pollution that obscures visibility

source a location whereby a measurable quantity enters a system. For example, automobile exhaust is a carbon dioxide source

squall usually used as *squall line*—a line of intense thunderstorms that moves in advance of a fast-moving cold front. It may also refer to a wind that arises quickly, lasts for a few minutes, and then dies down just as quickly as it arose

stratosphere the atmospheric layer lying above the troposphere and beneath the mesosphere, approximately 33,000–56,000 feet to 164,000 feet (10–17 km to 50 km). The stratosphere is the location for ozone formation

subjective forecast a weather forecast based solely on a person's interpretation of weather data

sunspot a relatively large, dark mark on the Sun's surface that is cooler than its surroundings

supercooled water that exists in a liquid state below freezing

teleconnection a linkage between weather events that are occurring thousands of miles apart

theodolite an instrument much like a surveyor's transit that is used to track a pilot balloon. By looking through a scope, the observer notes the angle of elevation to the balloon (thus determining elevation) and the angle of arc between north and the balloon's path (thus determining direction)

topography the physical relief of Earth's surface, including mountains and valleys that influence weather patterns

trade winds the prevailing winds equatorward of 30° latitude, which blow from the northeast in the Northern Hemisphere and the southeast in the Southern Hemisphere

tropopause the isothermal layer of the atmosphere between the troposphere and the stratosphere

troposphere the lowest layer of the atmosphere, which is marked by decreasing temperature with increasing altitude. The troposphere is the site of most weather

unit a quantity adopted as a standard measure, for instance, of heat, length, or time

vorticity a vector measure of the local rotation in a fluid

weather the short-term (minute-to-minute) variations in the atmosphere

weather modification human-created changes to the atmosphere. The changes may be deliberate, as in cloud seeding to induce precipitation or disperse fog, or inadvertent, as in the effects of air pollution on weather processes

wet-bulb temperature the temperature taken when the bulb of the thermometer is covered with wet muslin. Since evaporation causes cooling, on a very dry day the wet-bulb temperature is lower than the ambient air temperature taken from a regular thermometer. On a foggy day, the wet-bulb temperature may be the same as that taken with a regular thermometer. The greater the difference between the two readings, the lower the moisture content (relative humidity) of the air

Further Resources

Books

Allaby, Michael. *Encyclopedia of Weather and Climate.* 2 vols. New York: Facts On File, 2002. Contains more than 3,000 cross-referenced entries on meteorology and climatology for young adults.

American Men and Women of Science. 22nd ed. 8 vols. Detroit: Thomson Gale, 2004. Contains approximately 120,000 biographical entries on living physical and biological scientists.

Fleming, James Rodger, ed. *Historical Essays on Meteorology, 1919–1995. The Diamond Anniversary History Volume of the American Meteorological Society.* Boston: American Meteorological Society, 1996. Twenty-one historical articles on developments in meteorology, climatology, and hydrology during the first 75 years of the AMS.

Gillispie, Charles Coulston, ed. *Dictionary of Scientific Biography.* 18 vols. New York: Scribner, 1981. Contains biographical entries on deceased scientists.

Glickman, Todd S., ed. *Glossary of Meteorology.* 2nd ed. Boston: American Meteorological Society, 2000. An alphabetically arranged list of the most important terms in meteorology and related sciences.

Good, Gregory A., ed., *Sciences of the Earth: An Encyclopedia of Events, People, and Phenomena.* 2 vols. New York and London: Garland, Inc., 1998. Contains historical background on a wide variety of Earth science disciplines and topics, arranged alphabetically.

Monmonier, Mark. *Air Apparent: How Meteorologists Learned to Map, Predict, and Dramatize Weather.* Chicago: University of Chicago Press, 2000. The geographer Monmonier tells how meteorologists developed weather maps and now use them for forecasting.

Moran, Joseph M., Michael D. Morgan, and Patricia M. Pauley. *Meteorology: The Atmosphere and the Science of Weather.* 5th ed. Upper Saddle River, N.J.: Prentice Hall, 1997. An entry-level textbook describing meteorological processes, climatological schemes, and current issues in weather and climate.

Reynolds, Ross. *Cambridge Guide to the Weather.* Cambridge and New York: Cambridge University Press, 2000. Includes climate data and statistics by country, information on severe weather, and discussions of El Niño and the greenhouse effect.

Schaefer, Vincent J., and John A. Day. *A Field Guide to the Atmosphere.* Boston: Houghton Mifflin Company, 1981. A guidebook to atmospheric phenomena with many photographs and line drawings.

Smith, Jacqueline. *The Facts On File Dictionary of Weather and Climate.* Rev. ed. New York: Facts On File, 2006. Contains more than 2,000 cross-referenced entries related to weather and climate.

Taba, Hessam. *The* Bulletin *Interviews.* Geneva: World Meteorological Organization, 1988. Thirty-two interviews with world-famous atmospheric scientists that first appeared in the *WMO Bulletin* between 1981 and 1988.

————. *The* Bulletin *Interviews.* Geneva: World Meteorological Organization, 1997. Thirty-three interviews with world-famous atmospheric scientists that first appeared in the *WMO Bulletin* between January 1989 and January 1997.

Internet Resources

"Atmospheric Chemistry." NASA Goddard Space Flight Center. Available online. URL: http://aura.gsfc/nasa.gov. Accessed March 16, 2006. Contains information on the *Aura* satellite, which provides data for the study of ozone, air quality, and climate.

"Earth and Environment Classroom Resources." National Science Foundation. Available online. URL: http://www.nsf.gov/news/classroom/earth-environ.jsp. Accessed March 16, 2006. Primarily for educators and students, this Web site contains links to resources related to a variety of earth science topics, including weather and climate.

"El Niño Theme Page." Pacific Marine Environmental Laboratory. Available online. URL: http://www.pmel.noaa.gov/tao/elnino/nino-home.html. Accessed March 16, 2006. Contains links to basic information about El Niño, as well as real-time data, products, and analyses related to this weather phenomenon.

"Global Climate Change: Research Explorer." The Exploratorium. Available online. URL: http://www.exploratorium.edu/climate/index.html. Accessed March 16, 2006. Terrific Web site containing links to information on the atmosphere, hydrosphere, cryosphere (ice), biosphere, and the global effects of climate change.

"Global Warming." The Pew Center on Global Climate Change. Available online. URL: http://www.pewclimate.org/. Accessed March 16, 2006. Contains basic and advanced information on global warming, and links to recent articles on climate change.

Intergovernmental Panel on Climate Change. Available online. URL: http://www.ipcc.ch/. Accessed March 16, 2006. Contains links to IPCC publications, the latest news on climate change, and a schedule of upcoming climate-related meetings.

"Life on Earth." NASA: The Environment. Available online. URL: http://www.nasa.gov/vision/earth/environment/index.html. Accessed March 16, 2006. Explore the links to articles and video clips on ozone, climate change, and weather forecasting.

"National Weather Service." National Oceanic and Atmospheric Administration. Available online. URL: http://www.nws.noaa.gov/. Accessed March 16, 2006. The home page of the National Weather Service, this Web site contains links to current weather data, including radar and satellite images, forecasts, and warnings.

"NOAA History: A Science Odyssey." National Oceanic and Atmospheric Administration. Available online. URL: http://www.history.noaa.gov/. Accessed March 16, 2006. Contains historical articles and more than 20,000 public-domain images dealing with meteorology, oceanography, and climatology.

"NOAA Paleoclimatology." NOAA Paleoclimatology Program—NCDC Paleoclimatology Branch. Available online. URL: http://www.ncdc.noaa.gov/paleo/paleo.htm. Accessed March 16, 2006. Contains links to information on paleoclimate proxies, for example, tree rings, coral, pollen, ice cores, and lake sediments.

Science Daily. Available online. URL: http://www.sciencedaily.com/. Accessed March 16, 2006. Contains the latest in scientific news on a variety of topics, including Earth and climate; updates breaking news every 15 minutes.

U.S. Global Change Research Program. Available online. URL: http://www.usgrcrp.gov/. Accessed March 16, 2006. Contains links to articles on the U.S. government's research plans connected to climate change, including climate variability, the global carbon and water cycles, and how humans contribute to climate change.

Periodicals

Bulletin of the American Meteorological Society

Published by the American Meteorological Society
45 Beacon Street Boston, MA 02108-3693
Telephone: (617) 227-2425
www.ametsoc.org
Monthly journal devoted to meteorology and related topics

Discover

114 Fifth Avenue
New York, NY 10011
Telephone: (212) 633-4400
www.discover.com

Popular monthly science magazine containing nontechnical articles on a variety of topics.

Nature

Published by the Nature Publishing Group
The Macmillan Building, 4 Crinan Street
London
N1 9XW
United Kingdom
Telephone: +44 (0) 20 7833 4000
www.nature.com/nature/index.html

Prestigious primary-source scientific weekly.

Science

Published by the American Association for the Advancement of Science
1200 New York Avenue NW
Washington, DC 20005
Telephone: (202) 326-6500
www.sciencemag.org

One of the most prestigious weekly scientific journals, publishing on all areas of scientific discovery.

Science News

Published by Science Service
1719 N St. NW
Washington, DC 20036
Telephone: (202) 785-2555
www.sciserv.org

Weekly science magazine providing short articles on news of scientific importance.

Scientific American

Published by Scientific American, Inc.
415 Madison Ave.
New York, NY 10017
Telephone: (212) 451-8200
www.sciam.com

Semipopular monthly science magazine publishing on a broad range of topics and current issues.

Weather

Published by the Royal Meteorological Society
104 Oxford Road
Reading

RG1 7LL United Kingdom
Telephone: +44 (0)118 956 8500
www.rmets.org/

Monthly journal written for meteorologists and the nonprofessional interested in meteorology.

Weatherwise

Published by Heldref Publications
Helen Dwight Reid Educational Foundation
1319 18th Street, NW
Washington, DC 20036-1802
Telephone: (202) 296-6267
http://www.weatherwise.org/

Popular bimonthly magazine containing articles on weather processes, phenomena, and people involved with the weather.

Societies and Organizations

American Association for the Advancement of Science

1200 New York Avenue NW
Washington, DC 20005
Telephone: (202) 326-6400
http://www.aaas.org

American Geophysical Union

2000 Florida Avenue NW
Washington, DC 20009-1277
Telephone: (202) 462-6900
http://www.agu.org

American Meteorological Society

45 Beacon Street
Boston, MA 02108
Telephone: (617) 227-2425
http://www.ametsoc.org

National Weather Association

1697 Capri Way
Charlottesville, VA 22911-3534
Telephone: (434) 296-9966
http://www.nwas.org

Index

Note: *Italic* page numbers refer to illustrations.

qualitative 10
quantitative 10–12
with rockets 125–126
standards for 10–12
of thunderstorms 99
timing of, coordination of
10–11
units for reporting 11, 12
upper air 12, 13. *See also*
balloons
during World War I 25–26
observation stations
for aviation forecasting 54–56
in hurricane research 96
in International Geophysical
Year 115–116
during World War I 27–31, *28*
during World War II 86–87
Observatoire de Météorologies
Dynamique de Trappes 5
occlusion process 80
ocean(s)
carbon dioxide in 119
circulation of
in ice ages 16–18
models of *198*, 198–199
core samples from 157, *158*,
175, 180
global warming and 181, 182,
196, 196–197
satellites for forecasting over
148–151
sea level of *196*, 196–197
in technological fixes 201
temperature of
Bjerknes (Jacob) on 59
in El Niño 138–139, *139*
and hurricanes 98
Oeschger, Hans *168*, *191*, 219
oil. *See also* fossil fuels
in energy policy 182
hurricane control with 98
oil industry, on global warming 195
Olsen, Paul E. 175
orbit, Earth's *36*, 36–37, 120
overgrazing 154
oxygen isotopes 175
ozone 158–162
dangers associated with 158–
159
definition of 158
international agreement on 180

in stratosphere 158–162, *159*
depletion of 159–162, *160*,
167, 178–180
hole in *161*, 178–180
temperature of 5–6
technological fixes for 201
in troposphere 158–159, *159*

Pacific Ocean
core samples from 175
El Niño in 59
hurricanes in 95, 133
Southern Oscillation in 138–
139
paleoclimate 37
in climate change research 175,
192
proxies for studying 157–158,
175
Palmén, Erik *85*, 112, 213
Panama Canal Zone 89
Pan American Airways 96
periodicities 4, 42–45
persistence forecast 2
persistence models 152
Petterssen, Sverre 88, 213
Phillips, Norman A. *107*, *109*, 113
photographs, satellite 126–130, *129*,
150–151
physics
of clouds 71–77
of cyclones 7–9, 17
in meteorology xix, 7–10
phytoplankton 201
pilot balloons 13
Pinatubo, Mount *168*, 193, *194*
Pisharoty, P. R. 216
planets 4, 45
plants
and carbon dioxide 118
in climate classification 35–37,
64–66
fossilized pollen from 157
global warming and 192
in technological fixes 201
Plass, Gilbert 122
plastic atmosphere 43
Platzman, George *109*
Pluvius, Project 80
Pockels, Friedrich 2
poison gas 24–25, *26*